Treating Victims of Torture and Violence

Treating Victims of Torture and Violence

Theoretical, Cross-Cultural, and Clinical Implications

Peter Elsass

Translated by John Andersen and Harald Fuglsang

NEW YORK UNIVERSITY PRESS

New York and London

NEW YORK UNIVERSITY PRESS
New York and London

Library of Congress Cataloging-in-Publication Data
Elsass, Peter.
[Torturoverleveren. English]
Treating victims of torture and violence: theoretical, cross-cultural, and clinical implications / Peter Elsass ; translated by John Andersen and Harald Fuglsang.
p. cm.
Includes bibliographical references (p.   ) and indexes.
ISBN 0-8147-2201-6 (acid-free paper)
1. Torture victims—Rehabilitation. 2. Torture victims—Mental health.   I. Title.
RC451.4.T67E3813 1997
616.85'210651-dc21   97-21088
                                    CIP

New York University Press books are printed on acid-free paper, and their binding materials are chosen for strength and durability.

Manufactured in the United States of America

10 9 8 7 6 5 4 3 2 1

*To the "fifth province"—
the psychotherapists at the
Rehabilitation Center for Torture
Survivors (RCT), Copenhagen*

Contents

Preface

Once people have decided to eliminate evil, they may discover that to some extent they also suffer from the very thing they are trying to combat in others. This realization is a great challenge to one's own professional intellectual makeup, and requires good colleagues.

I have interviewed several torture survivors and their therapists. An important part of the therapeutic process is for the evil to penetrate both of the individuals involved, for the therapist must also feel the torture, in a figurative sense, in order to be able to eliminate its effect. This is a great and often superhuman task, but I have seen myself how torture survivors, together with their therapists, have in the end found a new meaning in life, enabling the survivors to keep going.

I have taken part in this process as a supervisor. My most important functions were to create an environment for reflection and to establish a professional culture in which the therapists could protect their work. This required a special combination of comradeship and professionalism.

Together with the psychologist Rasmus Jordan and the psychotherapists at the Rehabilitation Center for Torture Survivors in Copenhagen (RCT), I took part in establishing a supervision room from 1988 to 1995. We called it the "fifth province" to indicate a group of people who met to create their own culture. The death of Rasmus Jordan in 1992 was a great loss; we had to continue on our own.

Supervision takes place in a closed room. One big problem is that such a room can feel too closed, can detach itself from the life of the institution as a whole; such isolated work can appear like a form of subversive activity. However, the psychotherapists at RCT were extremely generous in allowing me to interview their clients about the results of their treatment. It is rare for therapists to allow someone to intrude on their work. It was my task to accept this generosity and to return it by way of professional feedback, a contribution to their difficult work. This book is the result.

The book is written for professionals and may therefore at times be difficult to understand for those without a psychotherapeutic background. But with some effort and flexibility from the readers, I hope the book will stimulate their academic way of thinking, the precondition for making "psychotherapy of the traumatized refugee" a professional challenge.

I am grateful to the therapists and RCT for making this book possible. It has been an unbelievably rich learning experience for me.

I also thank RCT's other staff members, in particular the medical director, Inge Genefke; the head librarian, Svend Bitsch Christensen; and the scientific committee, from which I derived inspiration, especially from many discussions with Anders Foldspang.

Thanks to John Andersen and Harald Fuglsang—not only for this translation, but also for their corrections in the text. I also wish to express my gratitude to Leo Goldberger for his ardent scholarly stimulation and for his interest in seeing this book published.

I am also grateful to Espen Hougaard of the Institute of Psychology, and to my dear colleague Bent Rosenbaum, head of the department of clinical psychology and psychotherapy at the Psychiatric Hospital in Århus. I also thank my secretary, Kirsten Rode, and my other good colleagues at the department. In addition I am grateful to Klaus Kaasgaard and Peter Lauritsen, humanistic computer scientists, who have helped with the analyses, including the narrative material. The work has also received inspiration and support from the research groups attached to the projects "Health, Culture, and Man" and "Communication within the Health Services" of the Humanistic and Health Science Research Councils. RCT and the Humanistic Research Council have given financial support.

While I wrote this book, the Odin Theatre's performance of *Brecht's Ash* was going around endlessly in my head.

Finally, I thank the torture survivors for generously allowing me to interview them. They cooperated without safe guarantees against being included in indifferent scientific reports, which at worst could lead to more suppression and pathology. It has been more important for them to speak than to keep silent—to break the "conspiracy of silence," which otherwise so often obscures torture and its consequences.

Treating Victims of Torture and Violence

Introduction

Torture is among the most gruesome of human manifestations, particularly because it does not have its origin in animals, primitive man, or pre-culture. On the contrary, it is planned, and it stems from social order. It is a display of force, the aim of which is to break an individual's judgment. As a consequence, it breaks down parts of the victim's personality. The greatest challenge to the torture survivor is therefore to remain a human being under these inhumane conditions.

Torture gives an insight into some terrifying contradictions. For instance, torturers are not particularly perverse or sadistic: they are often "normal" people. Their crime is a consequence of a social order that often has mutual popular support. The victims themselves are dehumanized by the crime, inform against their friends and families, and admit to crimes they may never have committed. All these contradictions are so difficult to sustain that they cause the worst repressions of all—silence and indifference. Either we deny the problem and leave the torture survivors to their own self-healing, or we ascribe the torture trauma to ordinary psychological/pathological reactions, to be treated the same as in ordinary patients in crisis. It has become one of the orders of the day to talk about being in a crisis, and crisis intervention has become everyone's property.

It is disheartening to confront this silence or generalization. Even clinical psychology has been hit by this mental block, and the most gruesome subjects—violence and terror—escape our research interest and are surrounded by silence, though subtopics such as trauma syndromes and the treatment of post-traumatic stress are dealt with. Of late we have also seen some publications on torture survivors, and there are many ongoing treatment activities. But the topic of "torture survivors and their treatment" needs to be taken on by the academic world for a clarification of concepts and theories in relation to other research and development within psychotherapy and for cross-cultural understanding.

There are several reasons for the torture survivors' silence and mental block. In the transition of the welfare state we have become survival artists of sorts who have continuously to think of new ways of coping with the limited possibilities for growth and with the problems of the Third and Fourth Worlds. New ways of speaking are created in a transition period, and the risk of being led astray increases. Thus, the concept of trauma and crisis now covers almost every human suffering and changes parts of normal psychological development to something pathological that needs professional treatment. Consequently, some of those who are in crisis because of truly traumatic experiences are met with vague and unspecific attitudes toward treatment that could be applied to anyone.

Other signs of the times are the violent and destructive cultural confrontations that drive people to war and to flight. The encounter with the unfamiliar provokes our society's most indomitable trait: the desire for order and control. The result has been that we react with repression and simplifications and therefore cannot admit that our problem with foreigners is growing day by day. They appear to crowd into us, and we react with racism and terror. Though cultural scientists try to develop an understanding of what is happening, they nevertheless have worked very little with some of the horrible consequences such as hunger and terror.

Purpose

The purpose of this study is to uncover the repression of which torture survivors and their treatment have been easy targets. Based on a review of the literature, I will put forward some hypotheses and test them in a systematic, qualitative study of torture survivors and their therapists. The approach will be based on a psychodynamic and psychoanalytically oriented view, often combined with cognitive psychology. The focus will often be on theoretical and even metatheoretical considerations in order to give a perspective of the already existing prescriptive and practice-oriented descriptions.

When one's aim is to reveal some repressions, it is sometimes useful to abandon the controlled academic way of thinking. Every professional representation defines its subject, maintains its integrity by sticking to its specific definitions, and reproduces itself by repeating them. This is unfortunate, and therefore I have focused on creating lively associations of ideas by the juxtaposition of opposing views from different professional traditions such as psychology, psychiatry, and anthropology.

The individual psychotherapeutic forms of treatment are one of the necessary bases for an understanding of the wider and more important subject:

the psychological results of war and flight and their psychosocial consequences. This subject will be mentioned here only briefly; fortunately some clear-sighted researchers and clinicians have already begun to give it top priority (Agger 1995, Agger & Jensen 1996, Arcel 1994, Arcel et al. 1995, Brunvatne et al. 1995, Kalicanin et al. 1994, Stæhr et al. 1993, Somasundaram & Sivayokan 1994, Sveaass 1994, Teodorao & Sicam 1995, Mollica et al. 1987, Willingen 1993).

The practice of state-organized violence, including torture, constitutes a worldwide epidemic (Basoglu 1993). This book focuses on torture survivors, but it also has relevance for prisoners of war (POWs) and for those exposed to the multitraumatic situation of the consequences of wars, especially flight and emigration. Former prisoners of war and refugees number several million people in the United States and more than 20 million refugees worldwide. Health records of POWs imply that acute or subacute sequelae of torture are presented infrequently to clinicians in the United States. More common are the chronic medical, neurological, and psychiatric disorders that recur over a lifetime and manifest themselves in later life. Refugees and POWs from wars half a century ago may not relate their current health problems to trauma, malnutrition, and losses that occurred decades ago. Clinicians must compensate for such oversight (JAMA 1996).

Historical Background

A number of scientific papers have already been published about torture survivors and their treatment. A rehabilitation practice has been developed, and treatment centers have started to appear. By 1995, sixty-seven centers for the rehabilitation of torture survivors had been established in forty-three countries (Torture 1995). Some centers focus more on the medical aspects, others on the psychotherapeutic, and some take a psychosocial approach involving a cultural and social network.

Psychotherapy of torture survivors as an institutionalized practice originated in the Danish rehabilitation center for torture survivors (Rehabilitation Center for Torture Victims, or RCT), founded in 1982. It was established as a result of the experiences of treating survivors from the concentration camps of World War II. Another important basis for psychotherapeutic rehabilitation was found in the treatment in the United States of veterans of the Korean and Vietnam wars. Symptoms such as flashbacks and uncontrolled outbursts of anger stimulated treatment research and the development of therapy programs. One of the results was the establishment of a diagnostic criterion for Post-Traumatic Stress Disorder, PTSD (DSM-IV, ICD-10), which more broadly led to the recognition of the symptoms of severely traumatized cases. At the same time there has been a tradition of working with tortured people in countries that were using torture methods themselves. Such work was taken on mainly by human rights groups that often worked underground. This work is different from that in countries where the torture survivor is in protected exile, and where the therapist does not run any risk of reprisal.

The development of treatment was based on two different approaches. The center in Copenhagen was mainly medically oriented, with hospital patient care. By contrast, a group in Toronto (Canadian Center for Victims of Torture, or CCVT) worked with a decentralized program to make optimal use of existing treatment services instead of establishing new institutions (Landry 1989).

RCT was founded by a group of doctors associated with Amnesty International who worked partly to reveal the practice of torture in countries that were denying its existence (Danish Medical Bulletin 1987), and partly to document the medical consequences of torture (Rasmussen 1990). It became clear to this group that the information gathering and documentation work could not go on unless the torture survivors were offered some form of treatment; therefore, since 1982 the group has had facilities for the treatment of its clients, for instance in cooperation with the university hospital, the Rigshospitalet. Furthermore, an international section was created (the IRCT), which has helped in creating the large number of centers and in preparing aid programs in twenty-nine countries (Torture 1995).

The CCVT was also founded by a group of doctors associated with Amnesty International, but in their documentation work they focused more on revealing the social and psychological consequences of torture. Their treatment therefore focused on the psychosocial integration of the survivors. They were concerned that a medical approach, hospital-oriented and with the possibility of admission, might give the survivors the impression that they were psychiatric patients and might isolate them. They focused on the creation of a decentralized network of professionals who worked with several different sequelae of torture, and they served as mediators between therapeutic professional organizations and human rights, political, and volunteer organizations.

Looking at the activities of the two centers today, the above description should be taken as an unfair simplification, and therefore the two different approaches can no longer be used as models. Nevertheless, both have had a conceptual effect on the treatments that have been carried out elsewhere, although usually each new center has built on or adapted to the existing knowledge and limitations (see review in Cunningham & Silove 1993, Landry 1989, van Willigen 1992). In London, as in Toronto, a decentralized network was created, but it specialized in forensic medicine. In Paris an integrated medical, social, and legal system was created, which in the beginning focused less on psychological treatment. In Holland the treatment became part of the official national health system, and one could concentrate more on cultural and psychological rehabilitation since the survivors had been invited to the country and therefore did not have the problem of applying for asylum. In Belgium a group of therapists was formed that consisted of exiled psychologists and social workers united by political and cultural convictions. In Boston a group was established that had close contact to Harvard University and was therefore given status as a hospital unit, although the therapists were exiles and did not want to create the atmosphere of a medical institution.

The financing of these centers varies but is considered insufficient in all cases. Some are government financed, others rely on donations from volunteer organizations. Amnesty International, the International Rehabilitation Council for Torture Victims, and the United Nations Voluntary Fund for Torture Victims send representatives to meetings and evaluate treatment initiatives as projects. Although these organizations cannot finance the creation of treatment programs and centers, they make a contribution by giving international attention that may lead to financial donations. Some centers within the torture survivors' own domiciles survive without economic support of any kind and are even persecuted by the local governments.

It is difficult to give a fair account of the variety of treatment activities. To evaluate them comparatively is completely impossible, since they work under such varied conditions. Van Willigen has written a detailed review of treatment and rehabilitation activities, in which she divides the centers into three broad categories: those situated in the survivors' home countries in which torture is or has been practiced; those in Western countries; and those in countries of the same cultural region as the torture survivors' home countries (van Willigen 1992: 280).

Political repression is usually a very real threat for the centers working in the torture survivors' own country. Their similarities are therefore greater and are marked by strong political involvement and acts directed toward gaining the attention of the international world by way of demonstrations and other human rights activities.

Most centers have had to accept gradually one feature of decisive importance for treatment, that is, to look at torture in a wider context that continues to traumatize the survivor, even if in reality he or she escaped from the torture chamber long ago. The destructive consequences continue, for instance in the form of exile to a new country, where survivors and their families are stamped as foreigners and have to adjust to the terms of another culture. Therefore, the diagnosis of *post*-traumatic stress cannot be used, and treatment institutions must always take precautions to give the survivor a feeling of safety, meaning, and belonging. The treatment thereby is different than that used for patients and clients with somatic and psychological problems. The survivor's presence in another culture and the political and historic importance of the torture are important features in the treatment process. Institutions that do not formulate an objective treatment strategy to this end usually fail because they lack quality.

It is interesting to note that recent years have shown the need for a common culture for these centers, and that therapists meet at conferences despite their different approaches. These conferences are a mixture of scientific and practical exchanges, but they also become forums for declarations of intent and solidarity in calling the attention of the international community to torture and its sequelae.

Problems

Though there are a variety of professional services to help the torture survivor, the number of treatment centers, and their financial backing, is too small (Genefke 1992, 1993a, b, 1994). One of the reasons for this is probably that societies for years have had repression and denial mechanisms in place concerning the recognition of torture. It is such a commonplace phenomenon that it is painful for a democratizing process to admit that torture takes place in hidden rooms, sometimes in one's own backyard. Torture is practiced with the knowledge of the government in seventy of the world's 183 countries (Genefke 1992, 1993a, b, 1994). The fight to make torture a visible phenomenon is therefore to a large extent a fight for democracy (Genefke 1993a, b). This fight is so full of conflicts that the recognition of torture and the process of treatment for it become political issues. This is an uncontrollable activity that eludes academic reflection. Although this fight has been very extensive and is characterized by a lot of enthusiasm, several aspects remain to be clarified and problems to be solved.

Definition of Torture Trauma

It is necessary to distinguish torture trauma from other traumatic events. Many nontortured people can feel repressed and exposed to violence to the extent that they experience it as "pure torture." In some families, for instance, violence and incest may take place and be described as torture by the victims. Unfair intervention from the authorities, such as solitary confinement or wrong medical or psychological treatment, may also be perceived as torture. But it is lack of insight not to be able to distinguish these conditions from real torture. Research is therefore needed to determine whether there is a specific torture syndrome.

Treatment of Torture Survivors

There is a great need to spread and exchange treatment experiences. To this end, many prescriptive accounts have been published, and they have been of great value for the many new centers around the world. But there are all too few systematic studies of the various forms of treatment processes and their results. This is a problem for psychotherapy research in general, but systematic examinations are also necessary, particularly within a loaded subject such as torture. Furthermore, psychotherapy of torture survivors is surprisingly traditional. True enough, there are detailed descriptions, for instance, of the so-called testimony method, but apart from that the ordinary descriptions are often a stereotypical account of "the need to tell and live through the traumatic event, but without the provocation which otherwise may characterize crisis intervention." There are surprisingly few descriptions, for instance, of cognitive therapy and psycho-educative work with torture survivors, even though these therapies are fully developed within other groups of clients.

Importance of the Cultural Context

Making a diagnosis and dispensing psychotherapy are manifestations of the wealthy Western world in which they were developed. It is questionable whether it is meaningful to transfer these practices to the Third and Fourth worlds. Symptoms such as anxiety and depression signify something different in foreign cultures, and guilt and shame can have completely different effects in a therapeutic course than what is described in Western experiences. The interpreter's function in the treatment and the importance of cultural differences are decisive for the understanding of the treatment results. All in all, a cultural psychological understanding of foreign cultures is important when planning interventions to counteract the sequelae of torture. The reintegration of refugees into new social contexts in the country of exile works as an important antidote to the torture; of equal importance is a considerate approach and an understanding of the political influence of the treatment institution. There is a surprising lack of interest in research into the context in which therapy takes place—the so-called extra-therapeutic factors.

Reestablishing a Meaning

One of the big problems for torture survivors is to reestablish a meaning. Insight-giving psychotherapy works implicitly with the establishment of meaning, but in work with torture survivors one must give the creation of meaning an explicitly high priority. This cannot be done only by establishing a course of treatment in a political context of solidarity with the torture survivors in their fight against torture. It demands a more complex, respectful attitude for the torture survivors' construction of meaning, which must take place completely on their own conditions but in cooperation with the therapist. Modern research on the therapist's perspective of psychotherapy, and on the construction of the life story, the narratology, should be brought in as part of the treatment.

Establishing a *Science of Practice*

It would be stifling for a research initiative in a newly started treatment center to require controlled and systematic data collection of such magnitude that it can be used for statistical and descriptive purposes. The treatment centers are small and preoccupied with their own survival—getting financial support, obtaining a legal basis for their work, and creating a political platform in their society. The conditions for humanitarian aid work are often so difficult that it would be quite unreasonable to demand that treatment centers meet academic and university standards to compete in international research. Science should not become a burden but should have a liberating and knowledge-improving effect on practice. It is therefore important to try to find and develop a method that works for the torture survivors and their therapists—a science of practice that makes the survivor a coresearcher who gives the therapists knowledge they can use in their daily work.

This book discusses the topics described above. Its purpose is to bring the treatment of torture survivors into new contexts—not to break down an established treatment practice, but to challenge experiences.

Only by replacing old ways of speaking with new ones can we avoid being led astray. There are many features of seduction, denial, and illusion in the subject of the most repressive power drama of all; torture and its survivors.

1

Torture, Violence, and Aggression
Scientific Difficulties in Containing the "Absolute Evil"

Definition of Torture and the Fight for Democracy

"Torture" is relatively simple to define, and in practice there is seldom any doubt as to whether a person has been exposed to torture (Genefke 1993a, b, Montgomery & Foldspang 1994).

In the United Nation Convention of 10 December 1984, torture is described as follows: "Any act by which severe pain or suffering, whether physical or mental, is intentionally inflicted on a person for such purposes as obtaining from him or a third person information or a confession, punishing him for an act he or a third person has committed or is suspected of having committed, or intimidating or coercing him or a third person, or for any reason based on discrimination of any kind, when such pain or suffering is inflicted by or at the instigation of or with the consent or acquiescence of a public official or another person acting in an official capacity. It does not include pain or suffering arising only from, inherent in, or incidental to lawful sanctions."

There are some aspects that are not included in this definition, but which the treatment of torture victims has revealed. The aim of torture is not always to make the victim confess and give information. The primary aim is more to break down the identity of the victim. The pain consists in particular in this breaking down and in the destruction of the personality.

Cassel (1982) writes in an analysis of the nature of suffering that it reaches its maximum when it threatens to dissolve the person's integrity. Even if the suffering is caused by physical pain, it is the psychological component which is the actual core of the suffering and which culminates when the pain threatens to destroy the person's intactness and integrity (Cassel 1982: 640). In discussing a theory of violence Gilligan (1996: 96) wrote: "The death of the self is of far greater concern than the death of the body."

Today, torture is practiced according to scientific methods by which the psychological influences are usually experienced as being the worst. To be burned with cigarettes, to be beaten and kicked, to be suspended or exposed to electrical torture are not so hard as to witness the torture of others such as one's own child, spouse, or parent.

Torture is practiced in a systematic and conscious way. It is "a technique and should not be mistaken for lawless, unrestrained rage" (Foucault 1977: 34, ref. from Agger 1991: 141). Torture in a larger context is not something perverse that occurs rarely, but it is a form of display of force that has been known since the days of the old Egyptians (DuBois 1991, Suedfeld 1990). Torture is a political ritual that takes place in a third of the world's countries to an ever increasing extent (Agger 1991: 142). "It is part of 'the liturgy of punishment,' and shall meet two demands: to mark and disgrace its victim, and to have a terrorizing effect" (Foucault 1977: 35).

Today, torture takes place largely with the consent of governments. Important persons such as leaders of ethnic minorities, human rights activists, trade union leaders, politicians, and student leaders are the preferred victims of repressive regimes.

There is no reliable estimate of the prevalence of torture in the world (Basoglu 1993). Amnesty International and the American Watch Organizations report that government-supported torture is practiced in 70 countries and that systematic torture takes place in 110 of 161 countries (Amnesty International 1993, Basoglu 1993: 611). The United Nations Convention against Torture has been ratified in only 72 of the world's 183 countries (Genefke 1993a, b). The United Nations High Commissioner for Refugees (UNHCR) estimated in 1988 that there were about 12 million political refugees, of whom 4 million were in exile in Western countries. According to a Danish report (Kjersem 1987, ref. from Agger & Jensen 1993: 685), 20 percent of the refugees who ask for asylum were exposed to torture.

If one does not take up the fight against torture, one risks becoming part of the general weakening of self-esteem and identity that is presently occurring. Therefore, those who are aware of what is going on must speak out.

The torture survivor and his therapist have the greatest knowledge about torture and its sequelae. They know that the most important goal of torture is to break down the victim's sense of what is right and wrong. One of the torture survivor's problems is that this inhuman process makes him lose his humanity—he may become so weak that he will confess and inform against his family and friends. It is a mistake to question which of these two forms of human manifestation—these two faces of Janus—is the true one and which is the false. One face is no more "true" than the other. Both have all along been part of the victim's personality; they simply emerge at various times and under various conditions. The "good" face only appears normal because it, in contrast to the other, is favored by normal conditions (Bauman 1994: 23).

We find it provocative to get an understanding of the evil inside us, and to know that torture can be carried out by people who are not particularly perverse or sadistic. But even if the ability to perform torture is part of the common human potential, it can be repressed because it surfaces only under a special and unique meeting between ordinary circumstances. Such confrontation is largely due to the fact that the political state, with its monopoly on power and its bureaucracy, has evaded the control of society: it has succeeded in gradually breaking down the nonpolitical power resources and the institutions of social self-government. The use of torture is thus a special consequence of the state having won control over society. Torture is therefore incompatible with democracy, and the fight against torture is to a large extent a fight for democracy (Genefke 1992).

Concepts of Aggression and Violence

Such evil needs explanation and interpretation. The most pleasant explanations are that it is pre-cultural, a part of our animal heritage, built into our genes, and as such the subject is not open for discussion. The slightly less pleasant explanations are that man is split between good and evil, and that strangely we are unable to learn from common sense and experience. When we try to understand aggression and violence, the myth of the Fall of Man is turned upside down; one has not learned by bitter experience, but has suffered instead. Nevertheless, we carry on our sciences and humanity without suspicion.

There are numerous definitions of "aggression" and "violence." Van der Dennen (1980, ref. from Kuschel 1991: 16) collected and commented on no less than 106 definitions of "aggression" and 48 of "violence." A big problem is that many definitions try to interpret this social act as an isolated phenomenon, and, for instance, define aggression as any act that harms or threatens another person's existence. But when looking at violence and aggression purely as behavioral, one risks grouping various behavioral forms together, even when they have very different motives. To quote Kuschel: "It may lead to categorizing the following in one group: boxing somebody's ears, kicking a dog, self-defense, road fatality, contract killing, homicide, murder, dropping an atomic bomb, etc." (Kuschel 1991: 17). In order to understand an act of violence one needs to look at the conditions that start and maintain the action, and at the conditions that make its control difficult.

Similarly, it may also be difficult to make use of concepts about aggression and violence when describing the conditions to which severely traumatized patients have been exposed. It is therefore important for a definition of torture to be relatively simple and to be applicable in various cultural contexts. If imprecise definitions of violence and aggression are attached to its practice, one may well change their meaning so that an action, seen from various cultural perspectives, may be misinterpreted. For instance, "to beat one's wife" may be considered "wife battering" in one context, but in another context it may be a manifestation of a husband's interest in his wife. This was the case described by Chagnon among the Yanomami Indians, where "women expect that kind of treatment, and where many of them measure their husbands' interest for them in relation to the number of small strokes they get from them" (Chagnon 1977: 83, ref. from Kuschel 1991: 26).

To understand torture survivors and their therapies, we must be prepared to redefine some central concepts. What Western societies consider as torture does not necessarily have the same meaning in other societies. For instance, the Western world's great attention to torture and other violations in developing countries has been called an act of indulgence in order to obscure the fundamental problem of the economic inequality between rich and poor countries. When in June 1993 Amnesty International introduced the concept of torture at the Vienna Convention and applied for help to document it and to treat torture survivors, several developing countries reacted by claiming that the real problem was one of development. To end torture, they preferred development aid to equalize the economic differences rather than humanitarian aid.

The use of torture may thus be considered a symptom of a more serious underlying problem. While some forms of torture are considered harmless in some countries and not as violations of human rights, in other countries they would call for an unambiguous appeal for humanitarian and human rights intervention.

It is therefore important to be prepared to understand the cultural, social, and political context in which our concepts about torture and treatment were formed. As with the concept of torture, our psychological concepts of violence and aggression may be of no value for our understanding of, or as guidelines for, a theoretical development, because these concepts were developed in the West. Psychotherapy is to a large degree a Western phenomenon, generated from the more wealthy segment of society, and may therefore not be applicable to torture survivors from other cultures.

Categorization can be culture-bound, and one may be blind to the meanings of concepts in contexts other than one's own. In working with the concept of torture and its treatment, one must consider the aspects that are universal to all cultures as well as those that require a translation in which the problem of translation in itself can lead to blindness.

Aggression as Essentialism or Relativism

Within psychology, aggression has placed itself uneasily between two poles: the essentialistic concept, according to which aggression is considered a basic characteristic of human nature; and the relativistic concept, according to which aggression is considered part of the culture and should always be seen in relation to it.

Clinical psychologists have often seen aggression as an inherent part of human nature, as a kind of inborn potential that must be guided and controlled to maintain social human relations. Winnicott has stated that "the main idea behind this study of aggression is that if society is in danger, it is not because of man's aggressiveness but because of the repression of personal aggressiveness in individuals" (Winnicott 1975: 204). Even though aggression is seen as something within the individual, its control is determined by social, legal, ethical, and religious considerations. In this way, clinical psychologists have found a justification to supplement their individual-oriented approach with social involvement.

By contrast, social and cultural psychologists will often claim that one cannot assume that aggression a priori is a human instinct, but rather that it is a characteristic of Western culture within which we call certain forms of behavior "aggression." When they describe violent behavior in various cultures, they want to show that the relationship between various concepts and scientific theories about human nature tells more about the cultural context in which the research was carried out than about some common human qualities.

Therapists of torture survivors tend to oscillate between these two views. On the one hand, they can use the culture-relativistic view and look at violence as part of certain cultural contexts. On the other hand, they must also search for fundamental human traits common to several cultures, if only because it is within such universal human traits that we can find the basis for a common and global understanding that will lead to the prevention of torture.

For the clinical psychologist, aggression is not always synonymous with violence. For instance, aggression can be described as the intention to cause harm or to be in a superior position of power vis-à-vis others, but the intention does not necessarily lead to violence. By contrast, one cannot always consider violent behavior as an indication of an internal aggressive instinct. For instance, we cannot assume that aggressive feelings were present in the pilot who, from a great height, dropped the bomb over Hiroshima. Violence—or at any rate war—is a social and cultural phenomenon, not necessarily a psychological one. Another example is given in a study by Kull, who interviewed eighty leaders of the American defense ministry at the Pentagon and compared the findings with similar data from thirty leaders at the corresponding ministry in the former Soviet Union. The two groups were surprisingly similar; very few could give qualified explanations of why they were working with war and violence, and psychologically they were unformulated and naive and characterized by denial and idyllization (Kull 1988).

Most cultural psychologists are skeptical about whether it is possible to extract from some cross-cultural studies an "essence" of aggression, which, as a natural property, can be seen in different varieties in various cultural contexts. For instance, the concept of a fundamental harmful and destructive potential within human nature is said to be deeply anchored in the Judeo-Christian tradition and its ideas about guilt and shame, and that this concept is not found in many other cultures (Heelas 1982).

The word "aggression" was introduced in psychology as a relatively neutral concept, without undertones of guilt and shame. Fromm (1973: 189) describes how the etymological meaning came from Latin: when "ad" and "gradior" are put together they mean "a movement toward." Freud was one of the first to use the word as a scientific concept. For him aggression was a commonsensical concept that should liberate some subjects from moral and religious overtones. Freud said: "Man is not only a mild and friendly creature aiming at love, and only defending himself if he is attacked, but . . . a powerful target for man's instincts is also aggression which should be acknowledged as part of the instinctual outfit" (Freud 1930: 50).

But even if this type of statement began as a scientific contribution, it was quickly transposed to popular concepts which, unreflected, confirmed our prejudices. To the great enjoyment of many people, several popular science books appeared which maintained that man is an aggressive animal. For instance, in Lorenz (1966) and Eibl-Eibesfeldt (1979), man was an animal, steered by some aggressive biological potentials that could explain not only our evolution, but also some daily manifestations. Such publications have been easy to reject as metaphysical constructions masked as science. Behavior is never culturally neutral but is anchored in the meanings we share with one another. Howell and Willis take exception to the essentialistic idea that aggression is a general human biological potential by stressing that "we must take as our starting point the interpersonal, intersocietal behavioural forms in the discourse of ideologies and what is practised in the societies in question" (Howell & Willis 1989: 7).

It is of course always correct to begin from such a contextual starting point, but it can easily become too vague and intellectual. The question is whether it is possible to combine it with the idea of aggression as something that is universal to all mankind.

The Death Instinct: Thanatos

The essentialistic idea was developed from Freud's first formulations. He included culture in his psychoanalytic way of thinking and said, for instance, that "culture must create barriers against man's aggressive instincts and keep them at bay by means of psychological reaction formations" (Freud 1930: 51). Freud had a naive concept of "culture," and he saw aggressive instincts as dynamic needs that, in the fight with libidinous drives, might give way to dramatic expressions, including violence. Huxley said the same in a concise and condensed way: "Violence is the shortest distance between two instincts" (Huxley 1967).

Freud developed his concepts of aggression and *thanatos*, the death instinct, at a late stage (Freud 1920). His basic statement was that eros and thanatos had the same goal: avoidance of an inner tension, so intense that it is perceived as dangerous, unpleasant, and "indigestible." But the life and death instincts try to achieve this goal in different ways, and Freud gave the death instinct—the aggressive instinct—a position different from the libidinous instinct. Truly, thanatos was an unconscious, compelling force, but it was not represented in the unconscious. It was as if Freud, who very often thought of his own death, tried to persuade himself, at least in theory, that in his own inner ego, at any rate, there was an area that could not be tormented by the fear of death, that is, the unconscious (Igra 1990: 28). His argument was that death could not be represented in the unconscious, because something nonexisting, a negation, could not take shape as an unconscious formation. This was his way of saying that the death instinct had nothing to do with death.

This artifice has been difficult to understand. It has been only with the development of the British tradition within object relation theory that psychoanalysis has defined the clinical manifestations of thanatos. Aggression here is considered a defense mechanism to identify and neutralize threats against the individual. Thanatos can be at the service of life, death, and psychopathology. "Thanatos is combined with a longing to regain the peace, timelessness, and relative freedom from needs that we may assume is characteristic of life in the mother. The death instinct is not a child of womb-longing, but a state we associate with the environment of the womb" (Igra 1990: 25).

Behind this metaphorical formulation is the clinical observation that, when aggression gets out of control and becomes thanatos, therapy comes to a halt; after all, neither physical nor mental work is necessary in the "womb." The precondition of life is to move between the two poles of differentiation and integration. The instinct of life will try to connect different parts to larger and larger units. But the instinct of death will stick to one of the poles and seek peace and harmony by isolating psychological formations.

The essence of this psychoanalytical way of thinking is that, when aggression gets the better of psychological instincts, it does not necessarily lead to dynamic expressions that move and change. On the contrary, it leads to stagnation, a standstill, in which actions repeat and confirm themselves in their structures.

Whether or not one is a supporter of the psychoanalytical school, it is one of the very few areas in which violence and aggression are characterized by an adynamic standstill. It is exactly this static feature that is often overlooked in the prevention of torture and in the treatment of torture survivors. Even if torture and violence in public, for example in the press, are given an active and highly dramatic presentation, the structure of violence is at a standstill that is almost obsessive in its immobility.

This repetitive immobility characterizes the torture survivor's story and symptoms. Even if these seem dramatic, there are some structural dynamic features behind the surface that determine a status quo situation, an unpredictable standstill. Herman quotes one of his severely traumatized patients as saying: "The thing I hate most about it is that it's boring ... It was a terrible thing. I'm not saying it was boring that it happened, it's just that it's been years and I'm not interested in it any more. It's very interesting the first 50 times or the first 500 times when you have the same phobias and fears. Now I can't get so worked up any more" (Herman 1992: 195).

I stress this repetitive immobility here in the beginning to emphasize the danger of being led astray and perhaps of being attracted by the external drama that makes one react with anger and indignation. Engagement is important for scientific work, but one should not succumb to the indignation of the moment or one's culture but be able to penetrate the mobility and try to get to the underlying, predictable, and constant structures.

In the same way, in the real work with torture survivors, it is necessary to understand that treatment demands a lot of patience and perseverance from the therapist. Again and again the therapist must work with the personality structures that have been destroyed by torture and that continue to appear on the therapeutic scene with monotony and obsessive repetition.

Torture's Three Partners

When we hear about violence and torture, they are typically described in different ways, according to the person's position and role in relation to them. The words "violence" and "torture" are used only by those who are witnesses or by the victims themselves. Those who practice violence, on the other hand, use other forms of description and look at their deed as a necessary and justifiable action. For instance, a terrorist will argue that his actions are legitimate while a victim considers them illegitimate. Both refer to social norms and values, and each of them assert that justice is on their side. As the anthropologist Riches has said: "When the term 'violence' is being used, attention should crucially be focused on who is labelling a given act as such and most especially their social position. It follows that violence is a concept which can easily be manoeuvred into an ideological ambivalence, coming particularly to symbolize moral impropriety in a range of actions and policies" (Riches 1987: 4).

Torture has three partners: the torturer, the victim, and the witness. Each has his own language to describe the same external occurrence. It is typical that the different actors—the military and the torturer, the victim and the survivor, and the therapist and the human rights activist—emphasize different aspects of the torture scene.

Elsewhere I have analyzed how an attack was described by the different actors involved in it: the military, the guerrilla, the government, and the people (Elsass 1991). In 1985 members of a guerrilla movement in Colombia decided to occupy the Ministry of Justice to put pressure on the government. But the military was alerted and fought against the occupation. In order to win the battle, the guerrillas took hostages and the military responded with bloody killings. The guerrillas described the occupation and the killings as "necessary actions," often in neutral language, compared to the dramatic and emotional language of the victims and their relatives and by the government and the military. The government described its own killings as "justified countermeasures." In their descriptions of the attack, the different players emphasized different aspects. Those responsible for killings and exterminations did not mention the deaths. There was a tendency to prevent the channeling of information about one's own violent behavior to those who did not know about it.

Neutralization and Repression

This form of neutralization and repression is also found in the descriptions of torture and its treatment, a defense mechanism that may have been the reason why "torture survivors and their treatment" appears only now as a research subject.

The same repression also took place during the persecution of the Jews, when the Holocaust was possible only as long as it was not discussed. Words such as "homicide" and "extermination" did not appear in the topmost secret documents. Instead, the words were camouflaged as *Endlösung der Judenfrage*, *Sonderbehandlung*, and *Evakuierung* (Hilberg 1980: 23).

Participants at the scene of violence tend to use language to neutralize their own responsibility for the violence. The Argentine journalist Jacobo Timerman has given a similar description of how Argentina developed several euphemisms to conceal the government's own use of violence while it violently depicted the underground movements as the enemy. Timerman says that the purpose of this linguistic trick was "the demand for clarity and order in the world. Everything that is intangible, any incompatibility or complexity disturb, frighten, and become intolerable. Then an attempt is made to get rid of the unbearable by the only available means—violence. Political solutions, strategies, or gradual clarifications of conflicts become unrealistic possibilities. The monopoly of power is for disposal and is used with complete ruthlessness, led by the indomitable desire for simplification of the reality" (Timerman 1981: 103).

In general, this linguistic trick, with neutralizations, simplifications, and camouflages, covers the fact that the structure of the physical world is continuous while the mental landscapes are discontinuous. The outer reality is moving, the ideal inner world is displaced. There will always be an attempt to get connection and continuity between these two states, in which the essential quality of violence will try to bring balance and order between these two worlds (Corbin 1987: 29).

The Torturer and the Victim

The relationship between a torturer and his victim is one of the most intimate that can arise between strangers (Simpson 1993: 672). The structure of violence contains the paradox that some of the qualities one tries to fight in others become an essential characteristic of oneself.

To some extent one can say, with Timerman, that violence has its origin in our attempt to create predictability and coherence. But "if conditions become too unpredictable and chaotic, violence will come forward as a defense mechanism against fear. The inexplicable part of the world is called the enemy and is exterminated, but the paradox is that exactly that unpredictability one fights in others becomes a part of oneself" (Timerman 1981: 104).

The structures reproduce each other. The contrasts become each other's parts, the negations are abolished, and the similarity between friend and enemy is evident; all this to create order.

The approach assuming that partners are somehow able to change places is found in the torturer–victim relationship. Here one part symbolizes powerlessness and the other the control of power. But the asymmetry can suddenly change the center of gravity. Just as Jesus at the Crucifixion received a crown of thorns, the powerless victim can be ennobled and reach perfection in death. Thus the relationship between the torturer and the victim has a stage during which onlookers are ready to affirm the victim's sublime and ennobled status (Brandt 1980: 141). In the same way, Lacan has pointed out that surprising and unexpected feelings of tenderness and sympathy can arise between torturer and victim. The torturer causes the victim to suffer from wounds, pain, and mutilations in order to make him break down and confess. But the victim will confess not only what he knows, but preferably also more than that—he will break down and give even what he does not have. In a psychoanalytic, Lacanian sense, this attempt to give what one does not have is the same structural situation that characterizes the demand for love (Lacan 1981). The victim wants the torturer to stop; he beseeches the heavens for help or appeals to a political cause to get strength to support the suffering and the humiliation. The result is that the victim becomes, in a figurative sense, more closely attached to the torturer.

These speculations can be transferred to the treatment of torture survivors. If one does not have some clear concepts and sees phenomena in their social and cultural contexts, one risks repeating the torture vis-à-vis the client. As a matter of fact, the therapist may unwittingly harm the client by emphasizing that he should recount his traumatic story in order to relive and work through it. The torture survivor may experience that this more or less unspoken requirement—to live through his trauma story and its sufferings—is similar to the situation in which he was forced by the torturer to undergo the worst humiliation and devastation. Therapists may unwittingly repeat the same repression mechanism if they are unaware of its background and structure.

There are some very strong forces behind torture, and, compared with other types of therapy, work with torture survivors can bring out antitransferral tendencies in which the structure of torture is repeated. Because the relationship between the victim and the torturer has a mutual confirmatory and intensifying effect, torture tends to become an unshakable routine after it has been practiced once. In reality, it seems almost impossible to abolish torture throughout the world, even though there are clear conventions against torture as a violation of human rights.

Violencia *and Bureaucratic Target Displacement*

We are used to blaming the politically powerful for torture. But several "violentologists" have documented that, even if the political situation in some countries has changed, the structure of violence, the *violencia*, has remained unchanged. This has caused some Colombian sociologists to consider that it was not the political and economic repression in their country that created violence and criminal acts, but rather the bureaucracy. Regardless of changing governments in Colombia since "the thousand days war" in 1899, the bureaucracy has administered the country in the same way, year after year. The Colombian sociologist Fernando Alvarez has said that Colombia, despite going through one violent *revuelta* after another, and despite the most dramatic descriptions of *violencia* by the press, the overall political, social, and economic structures have not changed. He thinks that most internal violent episodes can be traced back to the civil servants' administration, which, in a very competent way, impedes change in order to avoid major upheavals. On the face of it, it may seem reactionary to have a large and paralyzing bureaucracy. But in a country with many political upheavals, where politicians change from year to year, it may serve a purpose for someone in the administration to form a stable, continuous component. The cost of this stability is the continuous presence of violence (Alvarez 1988).

The same observation has been noted in the description of the Holocaust during World War II. According to Bauman, the most shocking revelation about the Holocaust was that the physical exterminations were a product of routine bureaucratic procedures: calculation of means and measures, budget balance, and strong adherence to rules. The extermination of the Jews was a consequence of a serious attempt to find rational solutions to various "problems." The executions were conducted as a result of one of bureaucracy's major blunders: target displacement, a weakness of most bureaucracies (Bauman 1994: 35).

The bureaucratic machinery also leaves its mark on torture. Though torture has always existed, one of the big problems is that it is practiced far more effectively today than previously. A precondition for torture is the dehumanization of the bureaucratic actions by expressing the targets in purely technical and ethically neutral terms.

The "Freezing" of Violence: The Incarnation

Paradoxically, violence has often fascinated puritan circles, which are remarkably goodness-seeking. At the moment we are in the midst of an attempt to create a global "political correctness" based on puritan, Protestant Christian principles. We tend to use stereotypes in our narratives and concepts of society, such as the humanistic stereotype of the gruesome suppressor and the noble victim, or the fascist stereotype of the noble master race and the subhuman slave race.

If it is true that violence is more visible now, for example in art and literature, psychotherapy, and political activities, it may be because we have long attributed humans with such an overwhelming goodness that violence has become fascinating as an alternative picture. One may also agree with Brandt (1994) that we are in a long period of peace, and that it is difficult to keep peace for so long without the appearance of various local manifestations of violence—the price of a long peacetime.

Whether we have a puritan vision of humans or hold the more cold-blooded view that they are able to do both good and evil, we must still fight some problems whether or not we understand them immediately. The goal of science is to examine what is behind our immediate experience. Our choice is not between having a theory of violence and not having one, because we cannot avoid dealing with violence. Whatever assumptions we make about it constitutes at least an implicit or inchoate theory. Our goal must be to have a conscious theory that we can examine, question, criticize, and improve, instead of an unconscious theory that will remain forever untested, neither provable nor disprovable, and therefore unimprovable (Gilligan 1996: 91).

Based on analyses of our myths, the French religious historian André Girard claims that aggression and terror have always been present. But in order to give aggression a cause, society invents a victim to incarnate violence. Harmony can be reinstated only when this victim has been lynched and killed. As long as the victim is alive, he will be blamed as the cause of the disharmony, and only his death can give rise to peace and order in the society. To obtain peace and avoid the fighting partners' killing each other in war, the object is made taboo, which none of the partners can touch or acquire. The victim, who used to carry the guilt, now becomes sacrosanct. To eliminate the evil violence, one replaces it with the good violence: the sacrificial act, victimization, which creates order and harmony. Thus, Girard says that, since the real object is never conquered, our culture will continue to repeat the sacrificial ritual. Our society gets into a "mimesis crisis," in which we continue to take revenge on several old killings in a long chain reaction that cannot be stopped, and in which violence is masked and transcribed all the time (Girard 1977).

The statement that "the object is made taboo, which none of the fighting partners can touch or acquire" may give us a key to understanding why our sciences pay so extraordinarily little attention to analyses of concrete cases of violence. Thus, violentologists in Colombia have wondered why so few have worked with an analysis of *violencia*, and also why it has lasted so long (Antropologicas 1988). The same astonishment has been expressed in the preface to Riches's *The Anthropology of Violence* (1987).

The same forbearance is found within clinical psychology. For example, the results of the psychological study of the Nuremburg war criminals was published only twenty-nine to forty years after the trial (Borofsky & Brand 1980, Cotler 1993). One of the alleged reasons for the long delay was that the conclusions challenged our last defense mechanisms against our own destructiveness (Taussig 1987); it was provocative to realize that normal people could be violent as well. According to general clinical criteria, not more than 10 percent of German SS members were considered "abnormal" (Kren & Rappaport 1980). Obviously we were part of the world that had performed the criminal acts ourselves, so the psychological experts tried to remain silent as long as possible. It is therefore important to break the silence and begin to speak about torture and treatment of its survivors.

The Conspiracy of Silence

Some descriptions show that, working with torture survivors, both therapists and their institutions can approach the problem by repeating the violence, thus becoming hostages of the torture; thus, in a wider sense, they begin to suffer from what they are trying to combat in others.

"The conspiracy of silence" has become a term for postmodernist society's "final blow," characterized by indifference, avoidance, repression, and denial of, for instance, the Holocaust (Danieli 1980, Krystal 1971). Similarly, torture survivors can meet a negative social attitude in their local communities, being left deserted and betrayed. One of the consequences may be a strong feeling of isolation and alienation, which may lead to increasing mistrust of people in general.

This "conspiracy of silence" also characterizes the interaction between the survivor, the psychotherapist, and the researcher. When the professionals are confronted with torture, it often becomes difficult for them to listen, understand, and help, because they themselves become participants in the silence. These reactions stem to a large extent from the nature of torture, which is such a powerful means of suppression that its consequences of intimidating, terrorizing, and paralyzing penetrate far beyond the immediately involved partners. It is society's most repressive form of social confrontation, and it demonstrates and re-creates at the microsocial level the fundamental display of force between the person in power and the one suppressed. When one becomes involved in the fight against torture and in the treatment of its consequences, one may be contaminated by underlying mechanisms that can cause a crisis in the institution concerned and affect one's own feelings.

The survivor's pathological reactions are transferred to the therapist, who may project them onto his organization, so that several parallel situations arise within the institution. One of the characteristics of torture is for the torturers to put on an act in which one part submits to the other and comes out with the absolute truth. It is this truth which is used to justify the torturer's actions. Similarly, in many treatment institutions the most authoritarian forms of leadership may suddenly stop a spirited debate, staff members are dismissed to bring back order, and Machiavellian techniques are used to stop criticism by the rest of the staff. A paranoid attitude toward the administration or groups of staff members may result in the suspicion that they are in this for power and control even though their behavior appears to be friendly and forthcoming. Such mutual projections break down the work alliance and put staff members in regressive positions characterized by so-called unconscious basic assumptions—paralyzing dependency, pairing, or flight or fight tendencies (Bion 1958). Bustos (1990: 150) gives some examples of how conferences of therapists of torture survivors and some treatment institutions have become contaminated by the torture. Buus Jensen, who has also dealt with this secondary traumatization, concludes that "the dilemma is that at the same time one talks about torture as the most gruesome cruelty in the world without respecting the strength of the effects of power and evil ... the client's symptoms and reactions to violations contaminate the therapists as well as the psychology and staff policy of the institution" (Jensen 1989).

In psychotherapeutic work, the drama of the torture scene can be transferred by overpoliticizing the torture phenomenon, so that torture survivors are almost looked on as heroes. Lederer (1965: 466) reports that among survivors from concentration camps, a "dominant doctrine" (*Die herrschende Lehrmeinung*) arose. It was alleged in a categorical way that psychological traumas could not engender chronic psychological symptoms unless they had caused organic brain damage. Survivors had many possibilities to resist and overcome a traumatic situation, and any pathological development had finally to be ascribed to themselves and to their moral and political beliefs. Survivors who demanded insurance compensation were diagnosed as "compensation neurotics." Such thinking is also encountered when the torture phenomenon is overpoliticized and the survivors are given hero status. On the other hand, survivors who do not emerge as heroes feel guilty and weak because they broke down, confessed, and finally cooperated with the torturers by divulging information about fellow conspirators. Behind this compensatory way of thinking, alleging that every torture survivor has the chance to be strengthened by the torture, is a denial of the destructive and subversive forces of torture. When this moral and political overdimensioning is combined with the development of intense emotional transference, the result may be a masochistic attitude by the therapist, who, like a Florence Nightingale, takes on the survivor's guilt and consoles and cares without proper insight and understanding.

The opposite reaction may be the survivors' isolation and separation from their social and political context. The survivors are transformed into patients, and their symptoms are diagnosed as a "torture syndrome" that has spread like an epidemic (Agger 1991: 142, Suedfeld 1990: xv) with several medical consequences (Rasmussen 1990). In itself there is nothing wrong with channeling one's medical and diagnostic experiences into humanitarian work, but the problem arises if the therapist resorts to traditional clinical methods. In the affective transference reaction, this attitude may be expressed in some sadistic attitudes toward the survivor, who must be looked at as any other patient in crisis who has to live through feelings of loss in order to be cured. The effect of therapy may be measured by the intensity of the patients' show of feelings, the depth of their crying, and so forth, without putting them into a broader context.

One can be led astray by the nature of torture and thus not see the psychological sequelae as depending on the person's individual capacity to organize and integrate internal psychological processes with external traumatic events (Bustos 1990, Danieli 1980, McKegney 1993).

The therapeutic approach should include a specific understanding and respect for the dynamics of the survivor's quite individual psychological personality, combined with a social and political understanding of the nature of torture. These are great demands on therapists and their institution, making the treatment one of the most demanding in psychotherapy.

Summary and Clinical Applications

• Experienced clinicians are seldom in doubt about whether a person has been exposed to torture. Even if the suffering is caused by physical pain, it is the psychological component that is the actual core. The goal of torture is not always to make the victims confess and give information, but to break down their identity.

• Committing torture is part of the common human potential. It is a political ritual that takes place in one-third of the world's nations to an ever increasing extent. The use of torture is a special consequence of the state having won control over society, therefore the fight against torture is to a large extent a fight for democracy.

• Behavior is never culturally neutral but is anchored in the meanings we share with one another. Some forms of torture are considered harmless in some countries, not as violations of human rights, whereas in other countries they appeal unambiguously to humanitarian and human rights intervention.

• Psychotherapy is to a large degree a Western phenomenon, coming from the more wealthy part of society, and may therefore not be relevant for all torture survivors from other cultures.

• Torture survivors do not have a need for aggressive revenge. Aggression is not always synonymous with violence, and violent behavior is not necessarily an indication of an internal aggressive instinct.

• When aggression gets out of control, therapy comes to a halt. Freud gave the aggressive instinct, the death instinct, a status different from the libidinous instinct. Thanatos was an unconscious, compelling force, but it was not represented in the unconscious. The death instinct had very little to do with death. Thanatos is combined with a longing to regain peace, timelessness, and relative freedom. The instinct of life will try to connect various parts to larger and larger units. The precondition of life is to move between the two poles of differentiation and integration. The instinct of death will stick to one of the poles and seek peace and harmony by isolating psychological formations—an adynamic standstill. It is exactly this static feature that is often overlooked in the prevention of torture and in the treatment of torture survivors.

• In our media, violence is usually given an active and highly dramatic presentation, but in therapy the structure of violence is at a standstill that is almost obsessive in its immobility. The repetitive immobility characterizes the survivor's story and symptoms. But the young therapist may be led astray and perhaps attracted by the external drama and react with anger and indignation. The therapist should not succumb to the moment's and his or her culture's indignation, but instead be able to penetrate the immobility and try to get to the underlying, predictable, and constant structures.

• Torture survivors are subjects for a "conspiracy of silence," which also characterizes the interaction between the survivor, the psychotherapist, and the researcher. The reason is a tendency to prevent the channeling of information about one's own violent behavior from those who knew about it to those who did not. This form of neutralization and repression may have been the reason why "torture and violence" only now appear as a scientific subject. Symptoms of this "conspiracy of silence" appear when it becomes difficult for professionals to listen, understand, and help because they themselves become participants in the silence.

• The structure of violence contains the paradox that some of the qualities the therapist tries to fight in others become an essential characteristic of the therapy. For example, the therapist may unwittingly harm the client by emphasizing that he should recount his traumatic story in order to relive and work through it, similar to the situation in which the client was forced by the torturer to undergo the worst kind of humiliation and devastation.

• The treatment institution may to a large extent repeat the same repression mechanism if it does not clarify its own background and methodology, for example in supervision. The survivor's pathological reactions are transferred to the therapist, who may project them onto his organization, so that several parallel situations arise within the institution. A paranoid attitude among the staff and suspicions of seeking power and control, as well as authoritarian forms of leadership may suddenly stop a spirited debate. Machiavellian techniques are then used to stop criticism.

• Other ways of transferring the drama of the torture scene is by overpoliticizing it, so that the survivors are considered almost as heroes. The consequence is that those survivors who do not appear as heroes feel guilty and weak because they broke down and confessed. The opposite reaction may be an isolation and separation from the survivor's social and political milieu, and the survivor is transformed into a patient with a pathological syndrome and therefore the therapist resorts to traditional clinical methods.

2

The Torture Syndrome

A Diagnostic Description of the Trauma-Provoked Condition and a Psychodynamic Understanding of the "Unbearable Helplessness"

The number of scientific articles that have been written about the psychological and social sequelae of torture are increasing with great speed. For example, a "Medline, Psychinf" search by Somnier et al. (1992: 56) gave about 150 references in 1992. The same search in 1994 produced 221 references and in 1996, 303 references. Furthermore, from their work with torture survivors, psychotherapists have reported on their experiences in their own practices (see review in Bustos 1992: 334, McIvor & Turner 1995). Some of these reports have been given the status of textbooks, for example, Basoglu (1992), Danieli et al. (1996), Herman (1992), Hjern (1995), Kleber et al. (1995), and van der Veer (1992). Thus there is sufficient psychiatric and psychological literature to give a detailed description of torture's sequelae and their treatment. But there are few systematic research results. It is as though this very engaging and absorbing work has given researchers a moment of advocacy that has removed them from their academic attachment to other psychotherapeutic research.

Some therapists are ambivalent about undertaking a traditional course of treatment because they believe that torture is a political phenomenon and the victims should not be classified as psychiatric patients (Kordon et al. 1992: 451). This ambivalence reflects an important problem: research should not only describe, understand, and explain torture and its sequelae, but it should also provide effective strategies to fight it. The question is whether these two roles—the traditional scientific role and the political advocacy role—can be combined (Hastrup & Elsass 1990). Mollica (1992: 30) writes that "torture treatment advocates here failed to critique their own clinical services through well conducted evaluation research."

The following discussion is therefore not based on systematic research results, but is the product of a variety of publications that mainly reflect the unsystematic clinical experiences of highly involved therapists.

One of the main points of discussion in the therapy literature is the question as to whether torture results in such fundamental changes in personality that the client's condition is different from other trauma-provoked conditions. Does a "torture syndrome" exist as a specific diagnosis?

Diagnostic systems help to make categories that can make clinicians agree on the demarcation of a condition. In developing a psychodynamic understanding, it is important to base it on a detailed description of some conditions in order to know that one is talking about the same types of patient. Description and diagnosis together are the starting point for referral to a specific treatment, but they do not in themselves give a psychodynamic understanding.

In the clinical evaluation of a person with a trauma-provoked condition, one makes a decision about the degree and content of the external stress situation, and about the degree of the experienced distress. One evaluates how it interacts with the individual's preexisting personality, making a comparison with what is typical for a representative population.

Some conditions within psychopathology are caused by stress or traumatic situations. But the provoking situation is usually defined only vaguely, with a grading from "minimal" to "catastrophic."

Some researchers (e.g., Cullberg 1983), use the word "crisis" for almost all reactions to severe life changes. A crisis situation is when "the soul is shaken" so violently that the anxiety and the acute stress are so overwhelming that the person in crisis becomes disturbed in his or her thoughts and feelings. According to this definition, one can be struck by trauma without "going into a crisis" (Davidsen-Nielsen & Leick 1993: 56). However, "crisis" has, little by little, become such a vague marker of loss that it is difficult to use as a term.

Trauma-Provoked Conditions: A Diagnostic Description

According to DSM IV (American Psychiatric Association 1994) the diagnostic possibilities for people with pathological reactions to stressful life events are "post-traumatic stress disorder" (PTSD), "adjustment disorder," or "brief reactive psychosis."

Post-traumatic stress disorder (PTSD) was coined to give a more precise description of the conditions provoked by severe trauma. The descriptive terms "concentration camp syndrome," "post-Vietnam syndrome," and "rape trauma syndrome" were previously used, based on some experience that severe traumas were provoked by similar conditions. The stressor concept itself was amended from recognizable stressors that cause significant distress in almost everyone to stressors that are outside the range of usual human experience and that are markedly distressing to almost everyone.

PTSD has been well suited for research and is considered an independent nosological entity that can be distinguished from other conditions. It is more suitable than the crisis models, which are more characterized by a general description than a systematic collection of theory and practice (Elklit 1994). PTSD is a descriptive diagnosis that does not in itself explain psychological trauma and how to understand the psychological interpretation of the external event. Nor does it give any explanatory model to understand which persons will react with a post-traumatic reaction pattern and for how long the reaction will last (Korsgaard 1993: 14). The diagnosis of PTSD is made when the event is unusual and markedly distressing to almost everyone. Elklit, who argues that this criterion is problematic because it is normative, emphasizes that it is necessary to include a personal relevance criterion in connection with the event. The event criterion is necessary, but not sufficient, since some people with several serious traumas behind them do not react with PTSD (Elklit 1994: 231).

Even a concept of a torture syndrome is largely dismissed in favor of the relative importance of PTSD. But a diagnosis of PTSD does not go far enough in explaining the wide range of symptomatology seen in torture survivors (McIvor & Turner 1995). Especially in non-Western cultures it can be questioned whether PTSD is a meaningful diagnostic category (Marsella et al. 1996, Mollica & Caspi-Yavin 1992).

POST-TRAUMATIC STRESS DISORDER

(DSM-IV, American Psychiatric Association 1994)

A. The person has been exposed to a traumatic event in which both of the following were present:
1. The person experienced, witnessed, or was confronted with an event or events that involved actual or threatened death or serious injury, or a threat to the physical integrity of the self or others.
2. The person's response involved intense fear, helplessness, or horror. (*Note*: In children, this may be expressed instead by disorganized or agitated behavior.)

(continued)

B. The traumatic event is persistently reexperienced in one (or more) of the following ways:
1. Recurrent and intrusive distressing recollections of the event, including images, thoughts, or perceptions. (*Note*: In young children, repetitive play may occur in which themes or aspects of the trauma are expressed.)
2. Recurrent distressing dreams of the event. (*Note*: In children, there may be frightening dreams without recognizable content.)
3. Acting or feeling as if the traumatic event were recurring (includes a sense of reliving the experience, illusions, hallucinations, and dissociative flashback episodes, including those that occur on awakening or when intoxicated). (*Note*: In young children, trauma-specific reenactment may occur.)
4. Intense psychological distress at exposure to internal or external cues that symbolize or resemble an aspect of the traumatic event.
5. Physiological reactivity on exposure to internal or external cues that symbolize or resemble an aspect of the traumatic event.

C. Persistent avoidance of stimuli associated with the trauma and numbing of general responsiveness (not present before the trauma), as indicated by three (or more) of the following:
1. Efforts to avoid thoughts, feelings, or conversations associated with the trauma.
2. Efforts to avoid activities, places, or people that arouse recollections of the trauma.
3. Inability to recall an important aspect of the trauma.
4. Markedly diminished interest or participation in significant activities.
5. Feeling of detachment or estrangement from others.
6. Restricted range of affect (e.g., unable to have loving feelings).
7. Sense of a foreshortened future (e.g., does not expect to have a career, marriage, children, or a normal lifespan).

D. Persistent symptoms of increased arousal (not present before the trauma), as indicated by two (or more) of the following:
1. Difficulty falling or staying asleep.
2. Irritability or outbursts of anger.
3. Difficulty concentrating.

4. Hypervigilance.
5. Exaggerated startle response.

E. Duration of the disturbance (symptoms in criteria B, C and D) is more than one month.

F. The disturbances cause clinically significant distress or impairment in social, occupational, or other important areas of functioning.

Specify if:

Acute: if duration of symptoms is less than 3 months.
Chronic: if duration of symptoms is 3 months or more.

Specify if:

With Delayed Onset: if onset of symptoms is at least 6 months after the stressor.

Adjustment disorders are maladaptive reactions to identifiable psychosocial pressures, with the reactions emerging within three months after the onset of the stressor. The signs and symptoms are not as specifically defined as in the post-traumatic condition. The reactions include some disorders of interpersonal relationships and of job-related functions, as well as some more maladaptive extremes such as anxiety and depression. When these signs and symptoms meet the criteria for another axis of mental disorder, such as anxiety and depression, the diagnosis of adjustment should not be made. Compared with post-traumatic stress disorders, adjustment disorders belong to a more open category. Both are serious conditions with a high level of personal distress, and both are often associated with suicidal tendencies. However, the prognosis of both conditions is very good.

Brief reactive psychosis has a sudden onset immediately following exposure to a stressful event and may last from a few hours to no more than two weeks. The clinical picture should contain at least one definite psychotic feature, often of a paranoid character.

Another diagnostic system, ICD-10, has similarly created a series of diagnostic categories of stress-related conditions, very similar to DSM IV, e.g., "acute stress reaction," "traumatic stress reaction," and "adjustment reaction," as well as a series of dissociative conditions or disorders (WHO 1994). This system also mentions that a "post stress pressure reaction" can be triggered by torture (ICD-10: 155).

Stress as a Psychopathological-Provoking Factor

Most PTSD conditions are easy to treat, and professional involvement is often not necessary. But Horowitz showed that the prognosis is poor when there is a latent period of more than six months from the time of the trauma to the appearance of the most pronounced symptoms, just as when there has been no change in the symptoms for more than six months. Thus, delayed or chronic PTSD conditions are difficult to treat (Horowitz 1986: 244).

The many empirical studies do not give any clear guidance for predicting which psychodynamic personality structure may give rise to specific reactions. However, Horowitz (1986: 241) has found that some personality structures present special reactions to serious life events, but these results are not particularly conclusive. There are even examples of the same personality factors being predisposed to greater resilience in some cases and to greater vulnerability in others. It is remarkable that, in population studies, the larger the exposure to serious life events such as natural catastrophes, the more stress disorders there are. But these studies do not give a better understanding of the psychodynamic content of stress disorders (Horowitz 1986: 241).

Some empirical studies show the relationship between trauma and mental disease. It is known that in general about 60 percent of patients with a psychiatric disorder have experienced a stressful situation two weeks before the start of the disease. By comparison, 20 percent of the population without the mental disease have experienced a similar stressful event (Brown & Harris 1978). Paykel (1978) concluded that in the period after a traumatic event there is a sixfold increase in suicides, a twofold increase in depressive disorders, and a somewhat smaller risk of developing schizophrenia-like conditions. But it can be concluded in summary that most serious losses, injuries, and disasters do not lead to the development of psychiatric disorders.

The empirical studies of the relationship between stress and psychopathology cover victims of violence as well as survivors of natural disasters, concentration camps, and torture (Horowitz 1986: 245, Elklit 1993: 75). Horowitz appears to be the only one who gives empirical examples that preexisting functional deficits are able to explain a person's reaction to trauma, but he notes that it is not always in a predictable way. For instance, some people with anxiety and depression can sometimes be surprisingly resistant to traumatic events, perhaps because the post-traumatic condition is well known to them, much more so than to people without psychological problems. Furthermore, Horowitz's empirical work shows that neurotic impediments to processing stressful life events can cause great vulnerability. For instance, psychopathology can be more easily triggered when certain irrational obsessions already exist, such as "bad thoughts cause real harm," a conflict of values, the habitual use of pathological defense mechanisms such as extreme externalization, or an ego perception of being valueless and incompetent (Horowitz 1986: 246). But there are very few published reports of PTSD accompanied by psychotic symptoms in patients with no prior psychiatric history (Pinto & Gregory 1995).

"The Torture Syndrome"

So far no study has investigated the qualitative and quantitative differences between the psychological effects of torture and those of refugee trauma. But in the diagnostic discussion about the definition of trauma-triggered psychopathological reactions, some therapists, based on their clinical experiences, have felt able to identify a "torture syndrome" (Goldfeld et al. 1988, Hougen 1988, Kosteljanetz & Aalund 1983, Lunde 1982). However, others claim that similar reaction patterns and long-term sequelae can arise in relation to war, rape, kidnapping, concentration camp experiences, and incest (Horowitz 1986, van der Kolk et al. 1984, van der Kolk 1987). But torture is distinguished from other severe traumatic situations by representing an extreme form of violation of both mental and physical character, and by an explicit political aim in a specific sociopolitical context. Torture is thus different from the Holocaust because of its significance and meaning. Torture is targeted at individuals and groups with the specific intention of causing harm, forcing compliance, and destroying political will, frequently in the absence of war (Somnier & Genefke 1986). The purpose of the Holocaust was collective trauma—the impersonal extermination of a group—whereas torture is individual persecution and suppression in a political context.

Most will agree that PTSD gives an insufficient definition of the sequelae of torture (Reeler 1994, Turner & Gorst-Unsworth 1990, 1993). A diagnosis of PTSD, for instance, does not include the torture syndromes that produce lasting changes in personality, because it excludes changed identity and personality as criteria. Thus, Klerman (1987), Mollica (1992: 263), and Somnier et al. (1992: 58) state that certain features of PTSD are probably central to all torture responses, while other symptoms may be associated only with specific types of torture events. Parker et al. (1992) found that the prevalence of PTSD was high in torture survivors—e.g., 39 percent in a group of imprisoned Turks who had been tortured and absent in those who had not.

Beal (1995) has demonstrated that for many veterans who were taken prisoner of war, PTSD has lasted fifty years.

Herman (1992) and Lansen (1993, 1994) have extended the PTSD diagnosis with a "complex PTSD-syndrome" that can include extremely traumatized clients, such as torture survivors. Others have stressed that torture is only one of a series of traumas and therefore characterize the torture syndrome as an "ongoing traumatic stress disorder" (Straker 1987).

EXTREME PSYCHOTRAUMATIZATION

(Lansen 1994)

- Chronicity of symptoms (also called "complex PTSD).
- Parallel diagnoses such as depression.
- Clinically difficult to classify personal suffering, for which the diagnosis "depression" or "dysthymia" is not satisfactory, and for which sometimes the diagnosis "existential emotional syndrome" is used.
- Severe affect regression, with reduced affect tolerance, anhedonia, and alexithymia.
- Proneness to new traumatization by seemingly innocuous events or normal life events.
- The internal representional world may be permanently affected by elementary patterns of aggression and victimization. It concerns cognitive-affective schema's that appear to lie dormant but have a tendency to dominate in interpersonal interaction. This may especially harm the relationship in intimate interpersonal processes: with partners, children, and also therapists.

Based on their experiences with severely traumatized clients, Ramsay et al. (1993) and Turner & Gorst-Unsworth (1990) have suggested four themes they consider unique for torture survivors: (1) incomplete emotional processing, (2) depressive reactions, (3) somatoform reactions, and (4) existential dilemmas. Incomplete emotional processing includes many of the types of reactions of PTSD. The depressive reactions, however, are different, since PTSD as a concept is put in the same category as anxiety conditions, but because of torture's many losses, the depressive conditions will often overshadow the anxiety. The somatoform reactions are also known from many stress-related conditions, but torture survivors often complain of several physical symptoms that partly suggest real sequelae of torture. They also indicate, however, that a series of somatic functions and immune defense systems do not function properly, so that new diseases develop more easily. The last criterion, "existential dilemmas," reflects the survivors' cognitive development of meaning, their perception of themselves and their presence in the world. Meaninglessness, alienation, and shame are some of the all-important and very specific sequelae of torture. It is the so-called existential dilemma that causes some diagnostic difficulties with respect to the torture syndrome because the behavioral and medical criteria, on which diagnoses are otherwise based, are exceeded. The torture syndrome also implies some moral, ethical, and political criteria on which the professional has to take a stand.

There are thus empirical, logical, and moral reasons to distinguish the torture syndrome from other trauma-provoked conditions. So far such empirical knowledge has not been established, but clinical experience suggests that the torture syndrome is more than a logically and morally founded entity (Reeler 1994).

One way of reaching a definition is to construct a syndrome based on quantitative empirical studies; another is to generate hypotheses based on clinical descriptions. The latter is considered preferable within clinical psychology.

Destruction of the Personality and Avoidance of the Trauma

The use of diagnoses eliminates several phenomena to facilitate the identification of an unrecognized condition. The diagnosis facilitates clinical description and improves communication. But as long as the torture syndrome has not been identified as a diagnostic category, it is important to retain the broader clinical descriptions and to examine whether they can open the door to an understanding of the unique psychodynamics of the torture survivor.

One of the big problems in establishing a specific diagnostic category for torture survivors is the question of which structural personality changes are caused by torture. Some articles have described personality changes in torture survivors, such as the Latin American Collective of Psychosocial Work (COLAT) in Belgium (Barudy 1989). But, based on an analysis of the work of twelve rehabilitation centers in Europe and the United States, Reid and Strong (1987, 1988) conclude that torture never reaches its ultimate goal—the total destruction of the personality.

It is difficult to get a good understanding of what is meant by a "changed identity" from the above studies. In order to open a discussion on the existence of a specific torture syndrome, I will start by discussing some statements by therapists to the effect that torture survivors are distinguishable from PTSD patients by the way in which they avoid their trauma during treatment. With other crisis interventions, however, emphasis is put on identification of the trauma and on reliving the feelings attached to the loss, obviously with necessary therapeutic tact and respect for the patient's integrity. Thus, Davidsen-Nielsen and Leick (1993: 60) mention that crying reduces anxiety, and that sobbing in particular helps to heal the trauma's psychological wounds. But this "necessary" regression in the ego's service is usually mentioned with more hesitation within psychotherapeutic work with torture survivors. By contrast, resistance to talking about the emotionally stressful subjects is sometimes mentioned as a positive coping mechanism, which is necessary to counteract further disintegration of the ego (Müller 1990). Verbalization of the traumatic experiences does not always improve the symptoms or increase the autonomy, and there are reports that the drop-out rate may therefore be high, and that the treatment contract with the client has often to be revised to avoid drop out (Müller 1990: 516).

Most psychotherapists agree, however, that each patient's "trauma story" can be used as a centerpiece of treatment (Mollica 1988). Some authors, e.g., Basoglu (1992: 419), mention that treatment consists in "getting the survivor to talk about his/her traumatic experiences and encourage free emotional expression in a therapeutic context." Other therapists emphasize that this is not always the case. Thus, Werbert and Lindbom-Jakobson (1993) claim that the torture experience itself becomes less important in long-lasting treatment. Baker (1992: 91) state that the survivors consist of a "silent majority," because they are not ready to talk about their torture.

The literature on the treatment of torture survivors often mentions the importance of proceeding cautiously and accepting a tempo the client can tolerate and accept (Reid & Strong 1988: 343). No therapists believe that the client should be provoked to delve into the trauma story's feelings and to relive them. But, compared with other traumatized clients, there is a qualitative difference in mentioning the necessity and usefulness of the trauma story to the torture survivor.

This shows that torture victims have been exposed to more severe trauma than other clients, and that one therefore has to be more cautious in revealing repressed feelings because the victims require a larger ego capacity to have the trauma integrated with previous structures.

There may be many reasons for avoiding confrontation of the trauma: denial of the reality, fear of being labeled as different or sick, fear of repression, guilt feelings, or the rationalization that it is too painful for others to hear about. Kordon et al. (1986), in a study of torture survivors, reported that the majority of those interviewed said it was the first time they had talked about the torture to others. In their experience with therapeutic work, the torture had been such a personal affair for the survivors that they could not talk about it in their daily lives, and often they were not able to talk about it even with one another. Mollica and Caspi-Yavin (1992: 253) mention this phenomenon as a hindrance to the diagnostic work. Instead of using an unstructured interview with open questions, they think that a more structured form of story taking, using a check list with specific questions, would be more effective in making the patients bring out significant symptoms. According to Solkoff (1992: 143), most Holocaust survivors refused psychiatric treatment and did not want to talk about their traumatic experiences, in contrast to other PTSD patients, who often gather around crisis therapists to be "debriefed." Grauer (1969) suggests that the reason is that many survivors come from a cultural context in which psychotherapy is not a well-known and respected form of treatment. Krystal (1978: 143) has suggested that survivors wanted to avoid any reminder of the trauma experience because of the fear of being stigmatized and of being perceived as so different that no mutual or general human understanding would be possible. Finally, Lifton (1968) suggests that psychotherapists may also resist treating torture survivors because they threaten the therapists' own defense mechanisms against death (Lifton 1968, ref. from Solkoff 1992: 143). Because of these complex transference and counter-transference phenomena, Lifton believes it took a long time before psychotherapy became a recognized method of treatment of Holocaust survivors.

Psychodynamic Understanding

Avoidance of the trauma can be interpreted in various contexts. From a cognitive physiological approach, the torture situation may be said to induce a neurogenic shock, causing a change of consciousness, which in a wider sense influences memory retention. Paradoxically, some parts of the traumatic situation cannot be remembered while others impinge themselves repeatedly as threats in the form of nightmares, intrusive daytime memories, and flashbacks. This has led researchers such as Horowitz (1976) and Stuker et al. (1986: 91, 1991) to consider PTSD as a cognitive memory disorder.

From a psychoanalytically oriented approach, torture influences the fundamentals of a person's identity, which is the corporal self that puts the individual in an extremely defenseless situation. Torture causes a deep regression in which words can no longer cover the experience. Some of the physical violations can be so intimate that they remove themselves from the person's usual self-image and provoke other strong experiences that he tries to avoid more or less consciously. One of the defense mechanisms, for instance, can be dissociation, whereby the body image is projected outside the body. This was illustrated by a torture survivor's statement: "My body no longer belonged to me, it had become a vegetable" (Timerman 1981). Kordon et al. (1992: 449) described the reaction as a provocation of "the narcissistic disillusion" that lies at a more fundamental and previously established structural level than what the external behavioral responses suggest. Only the somatic aspect of the trauma makes it resemble to some extent the incest experiences that clients also find difficult to talk about (Mollica 1992: 253).

It is not a case of whether one should approach the traumatic experience directly and make the client relive the associated feelings, or whether one should instead follow and respect the client's avoidance of the trauma. This question is too simple and thus it too easily becomes a derivation of the old discussion about cognitive behavioral treatment versus psychoanalytic-oriented treatment, about efficiency versus insight. The two viewpoints can be combined but given a different emphasis. For example, Basoglu follows the behavioral therapeutic tradition and claims that psychoanalysis and psychodynamic methods have not given encouraging results for Holocaust survivors (Basoglu 1992: 402). He describes how some psychodynamic treatments can cause an "incomplete exposure," resulting in a worsening of symptoms, as can be observed when clients feel worse immediately after recounting their trauma story (Basoglu 1992: 421). Basoglu suggests that the approach to the trauma must take place according to the rules of the behavior therapy regarding exposure and reinforcement. Others have suggested that it must take place according to the testimony method, in which the traumatic experience is "reframed" (Figley 1988) or gets a new meaning (Lindy 1986).

Psychoanalytic-orientated therapy does not emphasize behavior therapy's goals with respect to efficient and marked improvement in symptoms, but it gives a higher priority to insight and the importance of meaning. Thus, Davidsen-Nielsen and Leick (1993) include the meaning of the trauma in existential psychotherapy, for instance as formulated by Yalom (1980). When psychodynamic therapy is combined with existential thinking, it produces formulations such as "the trauma wounds the ego because we, quite unexpectedly, are confronted with the existential basic conditions in such an overwhelming and unbalanced way that it is natural that our ordinary defense mechanisms break down" (Davidsen-Nielsen & Leick 1993: 55).

The trauma can provoke a crisis condition when this mental "shake-up" gets sufficiently violent. Rieker and Carmen (1986 ref. from Saporta & van der Kolk 1992: 152) state that confrontations with violence shake and challenge our most basic ideas about the self-image being "invulnerable and worthy and about the world as being orderly and just." These cognitive fractures must be reconstructed, but Davidsen-Nielsen and Leick (1987: 37) look at the process as a possibility of a maturing process for the personality because the patient can reestablish some relationships with other people, enabling him to exchange some very fundamental feelings which he did not have the opportunity to do before. Thus, crisis intervention can combine an existential viewpoint with an object-theoretical way of thinking (Eagle 1987: 190). Other researchers have shown that torture survivors often have great problems with establishing relationships with primary objects (Lindy 1987), a problem that is made worse by the survivors' exiled situation (Fischman & Ross 1990, Gonsalves 1990). As a pathological consequence of maintaining "attachment bonds," they sometimes develop an emotional link with their tormentors. Such "traumatic bonding" has been seen in kidnapped people—the so-called Stockholm syndrome—and in incest victims, who often cover up their secret within the family (Bettelheim 1943, Dutton & Painter 1981, Eitinger & Weisæth 1980, Kempe & Kempe 1978, Saporta & van der Kolk 1992: 154).

Many torture survivors react with a depression. Freud, in *Mourning and Melancholia* (1917), wrote that a depression is a reaction of a person who is unable to have a normal reaction to grief. This normal reaction would stem from an obvious external loss, whereas depression is the clinical and pathological reaction to an object-loss at an unconscious level. Depression is combined with a negative self-image, whereas in a normal grief reaction the self-image is rather expressed as if the outside world is negative and terrible (Schneider 1980). With grief, the outside world is out of order; with depression, it is the ego.

Abraham (1927) and Freud (1917) characterized normal grief as a painful gloom with loss of interest in important fields of life, combined with inhibition of the display of activities. By contrast, pathological grief has new reaction patterns, such as panic, hostility against the self, and regression to narcissistic forms of self-centeredness. With pathological grief, it could be said that the energy attached to the lost object is not directed toward a new object but is withdrawn into the ego. In this way the object-loss is consequently transformed to an ego-loss with unconscious, hateful impulses toward the ego. Empirical studies, however, have shown that this hostility toward the ego is a quite common feature of normal grief (Parkes 1972, Raphael 1983, Wortman & Silver 1991).

The pathological reaction arises when the ego is, so to speak, destroyed by internal pursuers, whereas the normal grief process is able to reinstall and reintegrate the internal objects by internalizing new ones. Thus, the difference between pathological and normal grief processes depends on the torture survivors' ability not only to orient themselves outward and to use the external reality, but also to be able to turn inward and neutralize the inner evil object.

Realization of the Psychotic Universe

To gain entry into the phenomenology behind a torture syndrome, the means by which psychoanalysis developed an understanding of severely traumatized clients will be discussed first.

Freud, in *Civilization and Its Discontents* (1930: 89), gave the first description of the extreme suffering to which certain traumas can give rise:

> No matter how much we may shrink with horror from certain situations— of a galley-slave in antiquity, of a peasant during the Thirty Years' War, of a victim of the Holy Inquisition, of a Jew awaiting a pogrom—it is nevertheless impossible for us to feel our way into such people—to divine the changes which original obtuseness of mind, a gradual stupefying process, the cessation of expectations, and cruder or more refined methods of narcotization have produced upon their receptivity to sensations of pleasure and unpleasure. Moreover, in the case of the most extreme possibility of suffering, special mental protective devices are brought into operation. It seems to me unprofitable to pursue this aspect of the problem any further.

In this way Freud laid the foundations for some of the descriptions that he and his colleagues would later be confronted with during the Nazi period. It is very common to find descriptions in the Holocaust literature that are close to what could be called "realization of the psychotic universe." Elie Wiesel wrote: "Those who have not lived through the experiences will never know; those who have will never tell; not really, not completely. . . . Auschwitz means death, total, absolute death—of man and of all people, of language and imagination of time and of the spirit" (Wiesel 1961, ref. from Grubrich-Simitis 1981: 416). Others, such as Bettelheim (1943, 1986) and Federn (1946), have written about their experiences in the camps from a psychoanalytical viewpoint. Friedman (1948, 1949: 417) was the first to describe the psychological sequelae in the survivors; he noticed that the continuous threat of death provoked a regression to infantile reaction patterns. Anna Freud and Sophie Dann, at an early stage, also published their observations on children who had escaped from Theresienstadt (Freud and Dann 1951: 418). It is noteworthy that it was as late as the beginning of the 1960s that mental disturbances in the survivors were described and taken seriously (Grubrich-Simitis 1981: 420). Later, conferences were arranged on mental disturbances of Holocaust survivors; the contributions have been published in supplements to psychotherapy journals (e.g., *International Journal of Psychoanalysis*, 1968, 48:298ff). Common to these presentations is the mention of the "realization of the psychotic universe."

Ego-Armoring

The Holocaust has some similarities to the torture situation. There are several descriptions of how torture has brought out repressed infantile wishes that produced regressive changes of the ego structure and consequently a breakdown of the defense structure, as in the concentration camps. During the Holocaust, denial took on a special character. The external unbearable reality was shut out, and, for example, the survivors lived in an idealized past or had fantasies of a future in a better alternative world, all to avoid becoming psychotic. Niederland (1968b: 423) called it "automatization of the ego," and Meerloo (1969) a "robotization"; both expressions refer to this global denial. These gradually developing automatized ego functions are also found in torture survivors as an armoring of the ego, which establishes itself as an adaptive survival mechanism to cope with the overwhelming anxiety.

Another defense mechanism against the psychotic survival method is narcissistic depletion, that is, the unlimited introversion that arose because of the external deprivation of the narcissistic supply. It could lead to superego changes, as in the form of "identification with the aggressor," or to dangerous introversion and resignation, the so-called Mussulman stage. Other destroyed ego functions are seen, including cognitive disturbances, in which one no longer has a feeling of time, because survival could last only from one moment to the next and could never relate to the future. Bettelheim, writing about his time in a concentration camp, described how the prisoners regressed and lived for the moment, without hope and solidarity with others; "friendships were created and dissolved from one moment to the next" (Bettelheim 1979: 79).

The psychotherapeutic treatment of torture survivors has reminiscences of these ensconced automatized ego functions. In order to survive, some of the internal objects with which torture survivors have armored themselves during the torture are reinforced. It can sometimes be seen as a repetition of the trauma after being freed, when the survivors put themselves in situations with masochistic features. It has been said that some concentration camp survivors retain the enemy-image and integrate it in their superego formation in such a way that it continues to steer their behavior after their liberation. As a consequence, some develop an antisocial personality structure even though they never had such tendencies before their imprisonment (Grubrich-Simitis 1981: 426).

Another consequence of this immobilization of lost objects is that the symptoms sometimes do not start until months, even years, after liberation. The survivor has perhaps built up a lost object in an unshakable wish that it is possible to find a beloved relative again, or that the outside world and the future are much better and more ideal. The symptoms start when this "post-disaster utopia" is replaced by reality (Wolfenstein 1957, ref. from Grubrich-Simitis 1981: 425). Emigration to a foreign country and the lack of rituals can alone lead to the condition of having no room to process grief so that the lost objects can be replaced by new ones.

Both in concentration camp and torture survivors, this ego-armoring leads to some ways of experiencing that are not found in other traumatized clients and that sometimes place the treatment in a qualitatively different position. The subjective experiences are closer to the psychotic perception in some torture survivors, thus making the treatment much more difficult than in other trauma clients.

There are many phenomenological descriptions of this changed ego-function that may qualify the psychodynamic understanding. Werbert and Lindbom-Jakobson (1993) describe this type of experience as "being a living death" and refer, among others, to Elie Wiesel (1961), who, after surviving a concentration camp, had difficulty in getting used to being alive: "I thought I was dead ... I thought I was a dead man who in his dream imagined that he was alive ... I was only the skin that the serpent left behind—which it never owned." There are similar descriptions from torture survivors who, for instance, talk about themselves as being a thing without a soul (Timerman 1981) or simply as being another person (Montgomery 1992). This experience of identity diffusion must be seen as one of the goals of torture—to break down the identity of the victim.

Regression to the Psychotic Core

The breaking down of one's identity can take the form of an experience of unreality in which the tortured cannot be free from seeing themselves as survivors at the end of the world. It is as if everything that used to be well known to them loses its importance and in some sense ceases to exist. But, compared with other trauma clients, these experiences are so difficult to integrate in the personality that the torture survivors rather look like borderline patients with irreversible mental changes.

Psychoanalytically oriented therapists describe this experience as a regression to a psychotic core of the personality, in which archaic relations to primary objects are reactivated (Frosch 1983). Torture is an enforced ego regression, in which consciousness is inundated by disaster experiences. It functions as a staged psychotic type of experience, created by means of physical violence. According to a paraphrase by Freud (1920), the aim of torture is to create a situation in which ego functions are replaced by unconscious anxiety-loaded formations; "where ego was, there id shall be." The relationship to the torturer establishes a transference in which dependence is created based on some early developmental stages, and in which the torture takes the place of the primary objects, but now as an exclusively evil-pursuing object. Aggressive bondings, cathexis, are mixed with a twisted libidinal bonding with extensive consequences for the victim's ego-ideal and superego (Werbert & Lindbom-Jakobson 1993: 167). The torture situation becomes a stage on which the victim is forced to live through his archaic inner conflicts, but with a consistent and persistent destruction of "basic trust."

This psychoanalytical viewpoint gives some understanding of why many torture survivors, during their therapy, need to work with some basic object relations rather than to tell and relive their trauma story.

Another situation that supports this psychoanalytical viewpoint is that several of the survivors express in various ways that the torture situation has the features of a trap in which they are caught in a relationship with the torturer that looks like a pre-oedipal inner relationship with an evil, persecuting mother. The consequence may be a symbiotic longing for and fusion with the torturer. Brandt describes how, in a paradoxical way, a feeling of tenderness for the torturer can develop in the tortured—a feeling of sympathy that can unite the partners (Brandt 1980: 141, Lacan 1981).

This is reflected during therapy as compulsive repetition and maintenance of the same destructive and aggressive relationships with the therapist as in the torturer-victim relationship. Several therapists, for example Herman (1992: 82) mentions that only by working with the reestablishment of the "basic trust" can this resistance against the therapeutic process be avoided. Thus, the establishment of "basic trust" is something very essential in the psychotherapy of torture survivors; it is shown in the fact that many torture survivors demand a high degree of safety and security from the institution in which the therapy takes place.

The Difference between the Torture Survivor and the Psychotic Patient: A Psychoanalytic Description

The torture survivors' experiences may thus resemble those of the psychotic patient, but there are also marked differences. Unlike the psychiatric patient, some of the survivor's symptoms have the features of resourcefulness and appropriate coping mechanisms, though they may immediately look like deficit and pathological defense mechanisms. The psychosis of the schizophrenic patient, for instance, is a regressive condition, usually generated from within, whereas in the torture survivor, it is created by severe external trauma. The psychotic psychiatric patient may be immersed for long periods of time, and be totally dominated by, an inner world populated by evil, unreliable objects, whereas in torture survivors, it is rather a question of islands with archaic structures, in which the present trauma is combined with previous traumas and unsolved conflicts. For the torture survivors, there is a fundamental experience of the torture situation's nonintegration with their previous understanding of the world. In the psychotic patients, the psychosis becomes rather the patients' own attacks on the outer world and its meaning (Werbert & Lindbom-Jakobson 1993: 168). Both tend to isolate themselves, the torture survivors in more limited areas. The latter avoid getting caught up in the network of sadomasochistic relationships into which they were forced vis-à-vis the torturer, and of which they are ashamed when such relationships are repeated in front of their near relatives. This is reflected in the torture survivors by the fact that, almost compulsively, they say that they can do no harm to anyone; they can become anesthetically denying when they are exposed to situations provoking anger and physical aggression. Some of the survivors complain of not having the warmth and empathy of their children and spouses as before, and they are embarrassed by being carried away by their feelings and their feeling of shame. The psychotic psychiatric patient, however, has a more fundamental autism, to which the therapist is almost always exposed in a more direct and unreflected way.

With the psychotic patient, it is a question of a deficit in early development, the "primary libidinal cathexis," so that, for instance, destructive and aggressive aspects dominate the relationship with the primary objects. With torture survivors, it is rather a question of a secondary libidinization of an aggressively bound, cathectic, dependence in the service of the Universal Evil (Werbert & Lindbom-Jakobson 1993: 168). Though the symptoms, such as social isolation, may be the same in both partners, they have their origin at different places. In the torture survivors, they are a defense against restarting a sadomasochistic relationship in the therapeutic relationship, while in the schizophrenic patient it is rather a deficiency in the structure of relationships, which may lead to a deficit vis-à-vis the therapist.

This difference between primary and secondary libidinization has its origin in the nature of the trauma. In the torture survivors, it is a question of an external trauma; in the psychotic patient, it is a question of an internal trauma in which the psychotic breakdown can function as a new trauma.

The Concept of Trauma in Psychoanalysis

A preliminary definition of trauma is that it is a reaction to a situation that penetrates a psychologically protective shield and makes a wound or a hole. Freud (1895, 1917) referred to the qualities of trauma as being able to penetrate "the protective shield." A precondition for this concept is that the ego has developed a structure, that is, there must be something that in some sense can be penetrated. The very early traumas, however, completely escape the ego, whereas later traumas penetrate an already developed ego-structure and may break down parts of it. Anzieu (1985) regards this protective shield as the "skin ego"; with a psychosis it is penetrated from within, with torture from without. However, it is remarkable that many torture survivors attach importance to physiotherapy's potential ability to repair "the protective shield."

Freud founded the concept of trauma when he learned from Charcot that some hysterical fits might be the sequelae of unprocessed experiences from an earlier period (Freud 1956, cited in Krystal 1978: 82). One of the great contributions of Freud was his emphasis on the importance of the "psychological reality" rather than what had actually taken place. By emphasizing the subjective experience and its unconscious aspects, he called attention to the importance of the emotions involved in the traumatic event.

Psychotherapeutic processing of the trauma deals with a distinction between what actually took place and the client's memory of what happened.

Gammelgaard mentions Freud's concept of *Nachträglichkeit*, which refers to the fact that we give additional significance in our memory to experiences, an importance or meaning they did not have at the time they were being experienced. "In our memory we do not repeat the traumas of the past with their involved passions. We create them. It is in the gap between the ego which was and which can never be recaptured, and the ego which looks back in the memory, that the conquering of the past becomes a living story" (Gammelgaard 1993: 13).

In Breuer and Freud's *Studies on Hysteria* (1895: 5), the following introduction was given to this concept: "In traumatic neuroses the operative cause of illness is not the trifling psychological injury, but the effect of fright—the psychical trauma. In an analogous manner, our investigations reveal, for many, if not for most, hysterical symptoms, precipitating causes. . . . Any experience which calls up distressing affects—such as those of fright, anxiety, shame or physical pain—may operate as a trauma of this kind." Thus, Breuer and Freud emphasize that the central feature of the mental trauma is that the individual is confronted with overwhelming emotions, that is, his affective reaction produces an unbearable mental condition that threatens to disorganize and even destroy all mental functions.

Exactly this description of the ego being "overwhelmed" thus appears very early in Freud's writings. Affect, trauma, and hysterical symptoms are put into context. As the emotions are unbearable, the repression starts, and since the memory retains the emotions, the hysterical patient is created, as someone suffering from incompletely abreacted psychical trauma (Freud 1893: 37, ref. from Krystal 1978: 83). "Abreaction" thus becomes attached to trauma at an early stage, and becomes for many, even today, the preferred treatment with cathartic methods in which the feelings attached to the loss should be identified and relived.

The Core of the Trauma: The Unbearable Helplessness

Freud's main thesis was that, when an emotion becomes unbearable, repression takes place and the memory absorbs the affect in such a way that hysterical patients suffer from "incompletely abreacted psychical traumas." The unbearable affects that are developed in the traumatic situation result in one of the consequences of stopping this unbearable state; the perceptions and associatively induced ideas that are repressed become unconscious and withhold their affective discharge. The outlet is "strangulated" because of the repression, not only because of the lack of "abreaction," but also because the cognitive process becomes distorted.

The phenomenology of the trauma is a paralyzed, overwhelmed state with immobilization, withdrawal, and with a probability of depersonalization and disorganization. The trauma challenges the person's evaluation of his own strength and questions how close he is to helplessness. Freud emphasized that it was the subjective experience of helplessness that decided whether a situation would become traumatic, compared with another dangerous situation. In this connection, the helplessness includes surrender and giving in (Krystal 1988: 143).

Many torture survivors describe how the most traumatic event was that at a certain point they surrendered; from active resistance they gave in and confessed. In the same way, there are also Holocaust descriptions of how the European Jews obeyed orders in an automatic way, took off their clothes, and, together with their children, lay down on top of the corpses of the mass graves and waited to be shot. In a wider sense, it is just this passive surrender that marks many of the survivors many years later, when suddenly they also collapse physically and have no resistance against insignificant infections.

The Stimulus Barrier

The concept of "the stimulus barrier" can further qualify the nature of the psychological trauma in torture survivors. Originally, the concept referred to the perception and threshold for the outlet. Anna Freud's viewpoint was that the organization of the defense mechanisms of the ego created a protective shield, and that any event in which the defense mechanism did not present sufficient competence could be potentially traumatic (A. Freud 1942, 1967).

But it is not necessarily the intensity of stimuli that decides whether a situation becomes traumatic for the individual. Even though many studies have shown the severity of the traumatic stressor as a significant predictor of post-traumatic stress disorder, few investigations have studied the stressor dose-response relationship in torture survivors (Basoglu 1995). A unique study has shown that despite the severity of a trauma, the number of exposures to torture did not predict post-torture psychological problems, whereas ratings of perceived distress did (Basoglu 1995). One reason is that the challenge to the integrity of the ego comes rather from the meaning and the resulting affective reactions that the situation presents.

We should not be seduced by the fact that Freud was originally inspired by

Newtonian physics when he founded his psychodynamic theory, but we must always remember that it is the subjective meaning of an external situation that is decisive for the understanding of the kind of situation that becomes traumatic for the individual. Thus Krystal refers to a study on psychic trauma in children by Terr (1979, ref. from Krystal 1988: 217), in which a group of children were kept hostage in a school bus for 27 hours. Even if they were exposed in this way to a seemingly traumatic situation, several of them did not experience the situation as traumatic and did not react with PTSD symptoms.

The severely traumatizing situation is characterized by the helpless surrender to what the person sees as an unavoidable danger. From this viewpoint the reactions can be expressed in "the psychogenic death" or be stopped at an early stage and manifest itself as an automatization or robotization of the person's functions. The person who remains in this state for a long period of time can have continuous and specific symptoms of psychopathology, the so-called torture syndrome. From this viewpoint the symptoms will not have a purely traumatic origin but be a result of the mental changes and adaptations to the trauma. The defense mechanisms will be efficient in repressing the trauma, but in the long term they can give some permanent changes of the defense structure, resulting in psychopathology. These changes should prevent new traumas from breaking down the personality and can be looked at as an immunological reaction to prevent further traumatic experiences.

It is typical that the torture survivor asks for treatment because of the symptoms caused by a deficient defense system such as poor concentration, nightmares, and experiences of depersonalization and derealization. These reactions have "defense features" when seen retrospectively, and they should prevent experiences that are even worse than the unpleasantness of the altered ego structure. The stimulus barrier protects the person against reexperiencing the previous psychological trauma by blocking some functions, such as the imagination and the ideational representation. In the same way, the person's capacity for pleasure, happiness, and satisfaction can be inhibited and result in anhedonism. These costs are thus the price for being able to block the intense and extreme pain. But it is just this same stimulus barrier that can block psychotherapeutic work.

Two Trauma Models: "Strain Trauma" and "Shock Trauma"

Freud emphasized that there was a difference between traumas of adult life and of childhood, and he worked with two separate models; one was "the unbearable situation" model, which stressed the affective state and which, among others, was developed from the study of war neuroses. The other was "the dynamic pathogenesis" model, which emphasized the constitutional conditions. The first model operated with one traumatic effect, whereas the other involved cumulative traumas that were stored during childhood. In both cases the subjective feeling was above all "the unbearable," "the overwhelming," and "the unacceptable," and in both Freud, as mentioned, defined the trauma as a penetration of the stimulus barrier. In the situation model, it is the structure of the ego that should have been able to prevent the trauma, and in the pathogenesis model the mother should have functioned as a temporary stimulus barrier for her child. In the first case, the trauma is caused by an obvious external event that can be identified in time and place. In the other case, the trauma is discovered retrospectively and the pathogenic effect of the trauma is considered to be the result of a wrong development, often with stage-specific features.

One of the reasons for confounding these two models is that often a retrospective conclusion, so to speak, is made, that is, any event that causes psychopathology in adults is defined as a trauma. On this basis, the two concepts of trauma are confused, and the term becomes meaningless. There is of course a connection between the two trauma models, and some persons have traumatic experiences more readily because their personality development disposes them to a particular sensitivity and vulnerability to certain experiences. In the therapeutic course, therefore, the processing of the trauma has a more psychodynamic approach to the personality as a whole and to its previously established development disorders. Freud therefore tried to unite these two concepts of trauma in one theory, an effort which, for instance, is reflected in his alterations of terms such as "affects," which was replaced by "excitations" and finally by "stimuli" (Krystal 1978: 87). Roughly speaking, he meant to describe how the summation of several partial traumas culminated little by little in an "unbearable" situation that produced the final trauma. The mental traumas of a person's past are predisposed to react in a maladaptive and excessive way with extreme and intense feelings.

Solnit and Kris (1967: 205) distinguished between strain trauma and shock trauma, writing: "Strain trauma not only promotes the development of rigid ego defenses, but such trauma also renders the individual more vulnerable to shock trauma. Thus an acute trauma is magnified because the individual does not have a repertoire of ego defenses necessary for a flexible adaptation to challenges from the environment or from the inner instinctual demands."

With this differentiation between strain trauma and shock trauma, it becomes more meaningful to look at the so-called inundation of feelings that produce the trauma, and in which the question is: Under which conditions do affects become a challenge to the ego and become potentially traumatic? Fundamental is the subjective experience of helplessness that is distinguishable from other experiences of painfulness and fear. The traumatic situation implies giving up, a feeling of powerlessness, surrender. This surrender has been described rather similarly in the literature, though with different names such as "helplessness," "freezing," the "catatonic reaction," the "primal depression," "aphanesis," etc.; all are characterized by the same helpless giving up, with anesthetized feelings (see review in Krystal 1978: 93). Allerton wrote, for instance, that "almost all available studies indicate that a stunned and bewildered response is a far more likely group reaction than is panic" (Allerton 1964: 206).

If one penetrates further into the phenomenology of traumatized patients, the emotional reaction often shows a vagueness and lack of specificity. The clients cannot give a varied description of their feelings during the traumatic event, though they can describe the particular external situation in detail, a phenomenon often seen in torture survivors who may have great problems in describing their emotional reactions.

By analogy with the early mother-child relationship, one of the most essential dimensions of the mother role is to allow the child gradually to learn to hold more and more intense feelings, while the mother must be able to step in and protect the child before the feelings become too overwhelming. If this does not happen, the child will be inundated by undifferentiated, somatic, preverbal, and timeless archaic affects. It is just this timeless horror that is the core of the trauma experience. It is not the fear of death, but the deathly fear that is traumatic.

The infantile trauma is distinguished from the adult traumatic state, the adult having developed cognitive capacity and an ego-function by which she can partly block emotions and partly construct a cognitive adaptive structure. In the adult traumatic state the observing ego has been maintained and the self-observing functions can develop a sensitivity for trauma signals in such a way that the individual's defenses can be activated when the traumatic situation occurs.

This developmental difference in the cognitive structure of the ego between child and adult is the reason why a childhood trauma consists of feelings in their archaic form. In the adult, however, it is not the feelings in themselves that constitute the trauma; it is the overwhelmed ego, the surrender to the total helplessness and hopelessness that makes the situation traumatic.

This special feature of the adult's trauma state, the psychological "closing off" or the affective anesthesia, can be felt paradoxically as a liberation to which one surrenders instead of to the very painful traumatic affects of the earlier developmental stages. Torture's pathological consequences for the ego structure are described as just such a progressive blocking of the mental functions in memory, imagination, and problem solving.

Krystal (1978: 104), with reference to Schneidman (1976), claims that adult traumatic phenomenology has many similarities with that of the suicidal patient. Mental trauma can develop to psychological death when the suicide attempt or another self-destructive action can promote a paradoxical manifestation of life, because the attempt indicates the individual's efforts to interrupt or disrupt his state of helplessness and surrender.

In summary, the trauma of torture survivors is something that is connected with an acute situation in which the normal ego functions are overwhelmed because of an external unavoidable danger. The unavoidable danger and the individual's surrender initiate the traumatic state that leads to a process which at worst can develop to psychological death. The infantile type should be distinguished from the adult type; in the child it has a more undifferentiated archaic form, because the ego has not developed the structures that can initiate a numbing of self-reflective functions; it may be followed by paralysis of all cognitive and self-containing mental functions. Paralysis and deterioration of the cognitive function in the adult can cause changes but not in the same regressive way as in the infantile traumas, in which the constitutional development is involved to the extent that it can result in actual development problems, and even in psychosis.

Cognitive Information Processing

Traumas in adults are distinguished from childhood traumas by their higher degree of certain cognitive disorders. Horowitz has collected the results from several empirical studies in a "theory of information processing," emphasizing the cognitive aspect, but on a psychodynamic basis (Horowitz 1986). He discussed the response to traumatic events in terms of processing new information that is incongruent with preexisting inner schematizations or mental models, and describes serious life events as those that will eventually change cognitive maps. The mind continues to process the new information until reality and inner models are brought into accord in what can be called a "completion tendency" (Horowitz 1986: 246). Until such memory traces of traumatic life conditions can be integrated in a mental schematization, they are stored in a specially active form for coding. Each repeated representation once again sets in motion information processing that may eventually revise cognitive schematizations. Only when a new schematization has been established can it become the subject of normal forgetfulness.

An important part of this process is described as an oscillation between "denial" and "intrusion." Horowitz (1986: 242) says that "a high level of control leads to the denial and numbing phase. Failures of control lead either to a continuation of outcry, as in prolonged panic-stricken states, or to an intrusive state." Just the oscillations between these two states, the denial and the intrusion phase, can constitute the healing process. The compulsive repetition can become a reliving of the event or a symbolic mastery, because the ego is now the active part, contrasting with the traumatic situation, in which the ego is passive. The intrusive state corresponds to the therapeutic situation, in which the therapist makes the framework for a regressive reliving of the trauma, but this time at the service of the ego. With crisis intervention it has been described as "an identification and reliving of the feelings of the loss," but carried out inside the protective room of the therapy (Cullberg 1983). But the denial phase may also have its healing potentials, because it is here possible to invest one's attention in exaggerated hobby activities or working achievements, which may give the individual a feeling that his psychological functions are not being completely inhibited by the traumatic event. In grief counseling and crisis intervention, this process has been described by Cullberg (1983) as "the reinvestment phase" and by Davidsen-Nielsen and Leick (1987) as "the acquisition and reinvestment of new skills."

However, in some of the most severely traumatized torture survivors, the oscillation between denial and intrusion does not cause this healing process in which the traumatic memory traces are wiped out from the short time memory and become the object of the normal oblivion. Instead, the trauma is repeated, for instance in the form of continuous nightmares (intrusion) and inhibition of daily functions, combined with isolation tendencies and paranoid symptoms (denial).

Juxtaposition of the Psychoanalytic and Cognitive Trauma Models

With this introduction, partly of the psychoanalytic and partly of the cognitive perception of traumatic states, it is possible to sum up the trauma concept and make a more differentiated picture of torture survivors.

Freud's model, as mentioned, is two-faceted, as others, for example Horowitz, continued to work with it. For Freud, a trauma starts when the ego becomes overwhelmed as a consequence of an extensive breach being made in "the protective shield" against stimuli (Brett & Ostroff 1985: 418). The ordinary adaptive capacity of the individual, however, is put out of function, and the individual returns to a previous and more primitive form of defense, "the repetition compulsion": the disturbing event is repeated again and again. By re-creating an event instead of experiencing the original situation and being satisfied with it, the individual is able gradually to master the situation. The fixation to the trauma is an attempt to remember it, and the aim of the defensive mechanisms that are then set in motion is for the trauma not to be remembered or repeated (Brett & Ostroff 1985: 418).

Kardiner and Spiegel (1947) worked with war traumas in soldiers from the First and Second World Wars. They noticed that nightmares are a cardinal feature of the traumatic sequelae, and that they impinge themselves, even if the clients have partial or total amnesia for the traumatic event. They looked at the trauma as consisting of a first component, which has a biological dimension and which shows as a disorder of the autonomic nervous system, the so-called physioneurosis. The other component consists of a restitutive phase, in which the client's adaptive functions slowly come into force, and in which the personality reorganizes itself in an attempt to compensate for its deficiencies.

By contrast, Horowitz regards the amnesia and other cognitive disorders as an attempt to defend oneself against the obtrusive and overwhelming affect after the trauma. Here the disorders are secondary rather than primary.

Others, such as Lifton and Olson (1976), consider that trauma is a destruction of "the ongoing symbolization of life." Trauma destroys the primary existential basic conditions: death, loneliness, meaninglessness, and liberty. Based on his observations on survivors from Hiroshima, he describes these disorders as loss of the capacity to feel and to be engaged in the outside world, and as various expressions of "the death imprint," "the guilt over survival," and "psychic numbing."

It is important to distinguish between childhood and adult traumas. Childhood trauma is, as mentioned by Krystal (1978), characterized by the child's being inundated by unbearable affects after or in connection with a disturbing experience. But in adults there is not the same gradual increase in the affects to a point at which they become unbearable. The adult surrenders to the helplessness with what Krystal (1978) calls "cataleptic passivity," in which the experience of the affects and its somatic components is blocked. This progressive limitation can lead, in the most extreme situations, to psychological death. Adult trauma thus contains two functional defects: a dedifferentiation, resomatization, and deverbalization of the affective experience, which can lead to a sort of alexithymia in which the person is unable to articulate his or her feelings; and a defect that is within the cognitive function of the higher mental functions, which may take the form of a narrowing and constriction.

Horowitz (1976, 1986) regards a trauma as an overloading of the individual's information processing system. He uses concepts such as cognitive schematization and control functions to regulate the information processing. The traumatic experience consists of new information, which the individual must integrate in his previous perception of himself, of others, and of the outside world. The reactions to a trauma go through the following phases: "outcry," "denial," "intrusion," and "working through and completion." Denial and intrusion are regarded as two main processes to work through the trauma. Denial is characterized by inattention, amnesia, constriction of the thinking process, and numbing; intrusion by intrusive-repetitive thoughts and imaginative images, sleep disturbances and nightmares, hypervigilance, and "pangs" of strong emotions.

These models about trauma are derived from many various contexts, both theoretical and empirical, but nevertheless it is possible to make a juxtaposition of the two different concepts.

One viewpoint is that the defensive maneuvers are a direct continuation of the individual's reaction to the traumatic instance. This model is thus common to Freud and Horowitz. With Freud, the perceptions and the immediately stalled memory traces lead to painful affects, which then start the defense. With Horowitz, it is the new information that does not fit into a previously established schematization, which leads to painful experiences and consequently to control and defense.

By contrast, the other viewpoint considers that the trauma's most essential quality is to produce a massive adaptive deficiency mechanism. Kardiner and Spiegel (1947), and also to some extent Krystal (1978), consider the amnesia and the psychic numbing as consequences of primary defensive deficits and not as the result of an oscillation between the repetitive recollections of the trauma.

This model of a primary adaptive failure, however, does not lead to the varied description of the trauma reaction with its differentiation of, for example, denial and intrusion. It has been developed by researchers who had studied clients exposed to considerably more massive traumas than those of Freud and Horowitz. Holocaust and torture survivors have been in situations of quite another kind than the clients who were assaulted or had been exposed to natural disasters.

The symptoms of the torture survivor may be regarded rather as adaptation mechanisms, aiming at preserving his concepts of himself, than as pathological deficit. But the organized violence created by man, with the purpose of physical extermination, can carry out a direct destruction of the ego's function that resembles rather the psychotic destruction than the more limited personality disorders seen by Freud and Horowitz. But on the other hand, their model of denial and intrusion gives a clinical understanding of why the torture survivor may sometimes be silent and undifferentiated in his description of his feelings at the same time as he is complaining of "flashbacks" and violently obtrusive post-traumatic images. This oscillation between intrusion and denial can also explain the frequent occurrence of underdiagnosing the torture syndrome, which has started to be recognized.

Summary and Clinical Applications

• Therapists working with torture treatment have failed to critique their own clinical services through well-conducted evaluation research. "Treating victims of torture and violence" is a phenomena that stimulates an advocacy role which is difficult to combine with the traditional scientific role.

• Some therapists, based on their clinical experiences, have felt able to identify a "torture syndrome." But it is not proven by systematic research that torture makes such fundamental changes of the personality that the condition is different from other trauma-provoked conditions.

• Both in DSM IV and ICD-10, torture is included as a special post-traumatic stress disorder, different from adjustment disorders or brief reactive psychosis. But PTSD does not include the torture syndromes that give lasting changes of the personality, because it has excluded changed identity and personality as criteria. Some have extended the PTSD diagnosis with a "complex PTSD-syndrome" or an "ongoing traumatic stress disorder," because torture is only one of a series of traumas.

• Even though the concept of a torture syndrome is largely discredited in favor of the relative importance of PTSD, a diagnosis of PTSD does not go far enough in explaining the wide range of symptomatology seen in torture survivors. Four common elements are often emphasized, including incomplete emotional processing, depressive reactions secondary to loss and adverse life events, somatoform symptoms, and, probably most significant of all, the effect on personal meanings and value systems.

• Survivors of torture and of the Holocaust are both characterized by a "changed identity" but seldom of a total destruction of the personality and a psychiatric disorder. Torture is different from the Holocaust. The purpose of the Holocaust was collective trauma, the impersonal extermination of a group, whereas torture is individual persecution and suppression in a political context.

• In therapeutic descriptions there is a qualitative difference in the necessity and usefulness of the trauma story to the torture survivor, compared with other traumatized clients. Resistance to talking about the emotionally stressful subjects is sometimes mentioned as a positive coping mechanism, which is necessary to counteract further disintegration of the ego. Verbalization of the traumatic experience does not always improve the symptoms. The client's "trauma story" can be used as a centerpiece of treatment, but the torture experience itself becomes less important in long-lasting treatment.

• Torture and the Holocaust bring out repressed infantile wishes and produce regressive changes of the ego structure and consequently a breakdown of the defense structure. The external unbearable reality is shut out to avoid becoming psychotic. An "automatization of the ego," "the Mussulman stage," and a "robotization" are expressions of this global denial.

• The aim of torture is to create a situation in which ego functions are replaced by unconscious anxiety-loaded formations. The tortured person is forced to live through his or her archaic inner conflicts with a consistent and persistent destruction of "basic trust." That is why many survivors need to work with some basic object relations during therapy rather than to tell and relive their trauma story. For example, the torture situation has the features of a trap in which the persons are caught in a relationship with the torturer that looks like a pre-oedipal inner relationship with an evil, persecuting mother. The consequence may be a symbiotic longing for and fusion with the torturer. The therapy might turn into a compulsive repetition and maintenance of the same destructive and aggressive relationships with the therapist as in the torturer-victim relationship. By working with the establishment of a "basic trust," this resistance against the therapeutic process can be avoided.

• Basic trust is something very essential in the psychodynamic psychotherapy of torture survivors. But from a behavioral therapeutic position it can be claimed that psychoanalysis and the psychodynamic methods have not given encouraging results because there is the possibility of an "incomplete exposure" resulting in a worsening of symptoms. Psychodynamic therapy emphasizes "basic trust" as the most important platform to shore up the disintegrated ego.

• Trauma challenges people's evaluation of their own strength and questions how close they are to helplessness. It is the subjective experience of helplessness that decides whether a situation becomes traumatic, not the situation itself.

• Torture survivors describe that at a certain point they surrendered; after active resistance they gave in and confessed. This surrender and giving in are central in a possible torture syndrome and are described as "helplessness," "freezing," "catatonic reaction," "primal depression," and so forth. This helpless giving up with anesthetized feelings leads to a process which at worst can develop into psychological death.

• The higher degree of certain cognitive disorders in adult traumas distinguishes it from childhood trauma, which contains two functional defects: a dedifferentiation, resomatization, and deverbalization of the affective experience, which can lead to a sort of alexithymia in which the person is unable to articulate his or her feelings; and a narrowing and constriction of the higher mental functions, with a repetitive compulsion between denial and intrusion.

• The defective egostructure, combined with a repetitive compulsion between denial and intrusion, gives the specific "torture syndrome": denial, characterized by inattention, amnesia, constriction of the thinking process and numbing; intrusion by intrusive-repetitive thoughts and imaginative images; sleep disturbances and nightmares; hypervigilance and "flashbacks." This oscillation gives a specific syndrome, where survivors are sometimes silent and undifferentiated in their description of their feeling while also complaining of violent obtrusive post-traumatic images.

3

Psychotherapeutic Treatment

The Supportive Attitude and the Combination of Psychoanalytic and Cognitive Ways of Thinking

The psychotherapy of torture survivors can take various forms. In the literature, different working methods have been described, ranging from cognitive, behavioral techniques (Basoglu 1992) and the testimony method (Cienfuegos & Monelli 1983), to psychodynamic, psychoanalytic methods with different emphasis on supportive and explorative techniques (Herman 1992). In practice, the various treatment centers have developed combination therapies of cognitive and psychodynamic working methods, especially adapted to the survivors. Many take their inspiration from therapeutic methods developed to treat various forms of post-traumatic stress conditions such as assaults and natural disasters (Horowitz 1988, McCann & Pearlman 1990).

Working with the Symptoms: Cognitive Restriction and Affective Anesthesia

The wide range of psychotherapeutic treatment methods of torture survivors is difficult to summarize, but since the psychoanalytic *theory* is still one of the most extensive and well articulated, it will be the basis for the following discussion. It does not mean implicitly that the psychoanalytic-oriented treatment *practice* should always be preferred in the treatment of torture survivors.

The previous chapter gave a psychodynamic description of torture survivors. The fundamental paradigm was that psychological trauma consists of exposure to overwhelming affects in such a way that affective response produces an unbearable mental state that threatens to disorganize and destroy other mental functions.

Unlike with other dangerous situations, it is the subjective experience of helplessness which decides whether a situation becomes traumatic. For the torture survivor, it is an essential experience in the traumatic situation that he surrenders at a certain stage, and from an active resistance gives in and confesses. In this connection, helplessness consists of surrender and giving up (Krystal 1988: 143).

The torture survivor resembles the Holocaust survivor, and the following will refer to experiences from the Second World War. But, as mentioned before, torture is qualitatively different from the Holocaust experience by being an individual traumatic state leading to destruction of the personality; the Holocaust was a collective trauma with the purpose of physical extermination (see page 35). Simply this difference between individual and collective destruction can make the torture survivor more isolated in therapeutic contexts than the Holocaust survivor. Therapy can therefore be the torture survivor's first communal experience with respect to the unbearable trauma.

One sees in a therapeutic context how both types of survivor try to suppress and block the overwhelming traumatic affects by means of psychological "closing off," "affective anesthesia," "psychic numbing," "immobilization," and "psychic death." As with alexithymia patients, who are unable to experience and tell about components of feelings, the survivors are unable to describe the affective content and rather relate how they survived by concentrating on small, limited parts of the daily routine. Thus, there are descriptions from the Lodz ghetto of many who tried to pretend that daily life was normal, even if they had perhaps lost some of their closest relatives: "After losing those nearest to them, people talk constantly about rations, potatoes, soup, etc.! It is beyond comprehension! Why this lack of warmth towards those they loved? Naturally here and there are some mothers weeping in a corner for a child or children shipped from the ghetto, but, as a whole, the mood of the ghetto does not reflect last week's terrible ordeal. Sad but true!" (Dobroszycki 1984, ref. from Krystal 1988: 151).

Torture survivors are often characterized by the same limitations of mental functions, including blocking and dissociation from the past. Many torture and Holocaust survivors react with suicide attempts and self-mutilation to get away from this stressful depersonalization and paralysis.

It is just this cognitive restriction and affective anesthesia that can make the treatment of torture survivors difficult. Chodoff (1980), Krystal (1988), and Drozdek (1996) find that psychotherapy of Holocaust survivors only gives limited results, primarily because of the destruction of their "basic trust" and their lack of ability to relive and describe their traumatic situation. Other therapeutic difficulties are due to the survivors' retroactive idealization of their childhood, their feelings of guilt at having survived, and their continuous aggressions, which are often managed by a rigid, religiously oriented superego. Chodoff (1980) simply characterizes the torture survivor as "intractable to psychotherapy." Krystal describes his experiences with Holocaust survivors in a similar way and relates how, despite prolonged psychotherapy, they nevertheless continue to have chronic depression and anxiety, a masochistic life pattern, and psychosomatic diseases. Especially when the survivors have lifestyle changes in their old age, it is often accompanied by anhedonism, rendering them particularly difficult to work with (Krystal 1971).

There are some parallels between psychoanalytic treatment and the aging process in persons whose past is unfolding in front of them, posing questions about how to confront it. Roughly speaking, the choice is either to accept the past or to continue to fight the ghosts. Parts of one's past will continue to generate painful experiences; the survivors continue to react against the painful, and continue with the affective process and the anhedonic perceptions.

With severely traumatizing events, the individual is broken down when his capacity to bear and contain distress is exceeded, due to his own affective reactions to the situation. If he rates the situation as unbearable and unchangeable, it will lead to deterioration. Recognition and acceptance of his helplessness dissolve his identity and dependence on others.

The ordinary crisis intervention of PTSD clients works with identification of a loss. The severely traumatized survivors have also been exposed to loss experiences, but in them the problems are created by loss of some ego functions, which could have established security and the possibility of an effective repression, rather than by the obvious external loss.

In the ordinary PTSD conditions, the individual's cognitive mastering of the traumatic event will take the course of a spiral, in which denial and painful recognition alter in such a way that the individual gradually integrates the painful truth. Horowitz's sequence of "denial-intrusiveness-reworking-mastery" is a description of such a crisis reaction to a loss (Horowitz 1976). But in torture survivors there is no automatic adaptation in which the individual will gradually be hardened and more capable of coping with more demanding stress. It is as if they continue to live in constant readiness and expectation of the return of the traumatic situation.

Working with the Transference: Traumatic Bonding

Kardiner was one of the first psychoanalytic-oriented therapists who, in the years after the First World War, tried to treat the severely traumatized patients from the war suffering from so-called war neuroses. Based on his descriptions, it is possible to obtain an understanding of the special therapeutic attitude that is required in working with torture survivors.

He became disillusioned by the poor treatment results, and it was only after a digression into anthropology that he again tried to treat war neuroses, this time after the Second World War. Together with Spiegel he argued "that the strongest protection against overwhelming terror was the degree of relatedness between the soldier, his immediate fighting unit and their leaders" (Kardiner & Spiegel 1947). Similar results have also been reported in studies from Vietnam, where soldiers in extreme stress situations became very dependent on their comrades and group leaders (Grinker & Spiegel 1975). It is true that torture survivors have been isolated and exposed individually to trauma, but nonetheless group solidarity with others in the same situation is of great importance and probably has a curative effect as well (Barudy 1989, Blackwell 1993). This confirms that the work with the relationship and attachment bonds between client and therapist is of the greatest therapeutic importance, rather than the content between the parties, the interpretations, and the clarifications.

In his first descriptions of war neuroses, Kardiner compared them with the hysterical patients once described by Janet (1889, ref. from Herman 1992: 11). He noted their capacity to go into trances of a dissociated form. The same mechanism has been described in torture survivors who dissociate themselves at times from the helplessness, and, at the perceptual level, have a feeling of indifference, emotional detachment, and basic passivity. Herman quotes a war veteran from the Second World War: "Like most of the 4th, I was numb, in a state of virtual disassociation. There is a condition ... which we called the two-thousand-year-stare. This was the anesthetized look, the wide, hollow eyes of a man who no longer cares. I wasn't in that state yet, but the numbness was total. I felt almost as if I hadn't actually been in a battle" (Herman 1992: 43). The same kinds of statement may be made by torture survivors, but in the context of treatment, it is characteristic that today there are similar descriptions of double-consciousness and trance-possibilities in borderline patients (Herman 1992: 87, 86) and psychotic patients (Parnas 1994: 52).

Gilligan has explained a dimension of violence that goes to the destruction of the eyes and tongue in response to being shamed. Anthropologists have found throughout the world that envy is at the root of popular belief in the evil eye. For example, the purported power of the Jew was so feared that the German word for evil eye remains to this day *Judenblick* (Jew's glance). And the word "envy" is also linked to the evil eye. The Latin word for envy, *invidia*, from which our word envy derives, consists of the verb *videre*, "to see," and the prefix *in*, meaning "against" (Schoeck 1981, ref. from Gilligan 1996: 68). It is in this perspective that the contact between the therapist and the survivor is contaminated by violent memories of an "anesthetized look" and "numbness." Gilligan (1996: 35, 277) describes the state of being "the living dead" as having the symptoms of defeat and punishment, and thus increased feelings of inferiority, loss of status, and shame.

Torture survivors change from this anesthetic state to feelings of intrusion and overwhelming sensual experiences that dominate the consciousness as if the stimulus barrier has broken down. The torture survivor is caught between extreme amnesia and a reliving of the trauma, between overwhelming feelings and no feelings at all—a dialectic bonding that in itself re-creates and retains the trauma in the same way as in borderline psychotic patients whose deficit is maintained by their fluctuating and unpredictable interaction. It is precisely this involuntary alternation which deprives torture survivors of an experience of autonomy and self-determination. Survivors can thus partly identify themselves with their torturers in a traumatic bonding in order to reestablish a fixed point in their destroyed identity, despite the fact that they are forced consequently into a dependence that undermines their own moral principles and betrays their basic concepts of interhuman relations (see page 20). Hoppe wrote that aggressive instincts are managed as a "reactive aggression" or a "hate dependence" in such a way that the tortured can protect himself from total identification with his torturer (Hoppe 1971, ref. from Krystal 1988: 231). But the anger causes new experiences of guilt and hatred that make the torture survivor distance himself even more from dependence on others and from retaliation and revenge. In the same way, borderline psychotic patients can create a split between an unrealistic idealization and a devaluation of people in their surroundings.

It is exactly such signs that should warn the therapist to be prepared for the development, when therapy is well under way, of very strong emotional bonding, full of conflict. It is only possible to protect oneself by being precise and strong, by defining borders and showing tact, both when rejecting the client's idealizations and when receiving hateful devaluations.

This imbalance and lack of ecological restfulness also takes place at the physiological level at which the severely traumatized client no longer has a baseline where he can find rest and comfort. On the contrary, he finds himself in a hypervigilant state in which even small stimuli can provoke "startle responses" and provoke a reliving of the trauma. This increased state of arousal in the torture survivor shows itself by marked physiological manifestations in the form of increased somatic illness such as high blood pressure (van der Kolk et al. 1984). Psychosomatic complaints are part of Niederland's "survivor triad," consisting of sleeplessness, nightmares, and psychosomatic complaints (Niederland 1968a, b, ref. from Herman 1992: 94). These symptoms give associations with the psychosomatic conditions in which the therapist, as an external regulating factor, must replace and re-create the destroyed homeostasis in the client.

The Visitation

As in all other psychotherapeutic work, the visitation is very important. The task with the torture survivor is the same as with other psychotherapy candidates—that is, to get an impression of the quality of mental functioning, in particular with respect to the strength of the ego. In this way the therapist may get an understanding of the extent to which he should emphasize supportive or explorative working methods.

By tradition, the ego function includes reality testing, intelligence, verbal skills, evidence of object relations, a good work or school history, and being psychologically minded. Suitable candidates for psychotherapy should therefore be attentive to their feelings, be able to verbalize them and to tolerate them even if they are painful, and furthermore they should have enough "basic trust" in order to be able to enter into a therapeutic relationship. Werman (1981, 1992) emphasizes the importance of a high degree of motivation in clients, an autoplastic conviction in the sense that their psychological liberation primarily depends on changes that will occur in them and will come about only if they strenuously try to effect those changes.

It is evident that many torture survivors cannot at all live up to these requirements. If they could, they would probably not be in need of psychotherapy.

However, it is not the primary aim of the visitation to separate the unsuitable from the suitable. It is rather to obtain a psychodynamic understanding of the torture survivor that may form the basis of later therapeutic work. Ideally, therapy should take the shape of an examination in which the therapist lets herself be guided by hypotheses, with some of them already formulated during the visitation. An important hypothesis in the work with torture survivors is the question of the fragility of their ego structure, and the extent to which torture has made them approach the borderline psychotic state.

As mentioned before, torture survivors distinguish themselves from the borderline psychotic state primarily because they are not suffering from a developmental deficit belonging to earlier undifferentiated stages of development (see page 46). But even when the torture trauma takes place in adulthood, it may cause the same disorders of the ego that can be seen in early developmental pathologies: lack of object-constancy, identity diffusion, tendency to splitting, and lack of a capacity for emotional bonding (Kernberg 1975). But in torture survivors, the disorders are placed on defined islands because they do not have the fundamental developmental basis. Thus, the concept of deficit should be seen in a context that comprises more than a theory about structural development.

In practice, the therapist must use the visitation to evaluate how the survivor's premorbid psyche was formed, and how his developmental potentials have been able to resist the destructive sequelae of the trauma. Cathartic crisis intervention might be possible without this thorough visitation and without an evaluation of the interplay between development and crisis. But if the purpose is to carry out more thorough and longer-lasting therapeutic work that makes an attempt to reconstruct the destroyed ego structures, it is necessary to try to reach an understanding of the unique structure of the individual client.

Development and Trauma: Conflict or Deficit Pathology

Development and trauma, maturation and crisis are parts of a larger entity, a never-ending process. They have each their special way of marking the course of time, one by means of smoothly gliding periods, the other by momentary cross sections, but even if they are mutually incompatible, together they make out the paradox that reflects our concept of the course of time (Elsass 1993a: 236).

Killingmo's distinction between conflict pathology and deficit pathology may help in gaining an understanding of the special relationship between development and trauma that creates the destroyed structures in the torture survivor, described in the previous chapter as "stress trauma" and "shock trauma" (Killingmo 1989) (see page 50). "Deficit," according to Killingmo, refers to a pathological condition in which the primary intentionality is lacking, that is, the self-representations have not been constituted as a center for the child's impulses, feelings, and actions. The child is not able to look at itself as the acting agent in its own life and cannot relate to the causes of feelings and actions. In conflict pathology, it is rather a question of the ego repressing the causes in the shape of concealed meanings. In deficit pathology, the lacking ego-differentiation will create disorder, confusion, and amorphous feelings of shame and guilt. "Thus, in pathology based on deficit, it is not a matter of defending oneself against anxiety connected with bad intentions, e.g., forbidden object-directed needs, fantasies and feelings, as in the case of conflict. What is defended against is primarily anxiety of fragmentation, i.e. losing one's own feeling of identity" (Killingmo 1989: 67).

Therapeutic work with the torture survivor with ego-deficit is not characterized by the fact that the archaic impulses should be brought out in the consciousness, and that they should have a new representation by means of the transference to the therapist. It is not the therapeutic working alliance in which one finds and gives priority to "the concealed meanings," but rather a relationship in which the therapist shall "assist the ego in experiencing meaning in itself. It is not a matter of finding something else, but to feel that something has the quality of being" (Killingmo 1989: 67).

This description corresponds with the statements of several torture survivor therapists—that is, the treatment is not a question of revealing a meaning, but rather about establishing a new one. The therapists therefore admit that they do not remain as silent and neutral as in explorative therapy. It is more a question of an active working alliance in which the client needs another person to represent a clear and well-defined object relation that opens possibilities for correction of his twisted object representations.

Killingmo's description of deficit includes "a quality of intentionality" as something very fundamental. He describes how the child who has been exposed to a trauma in which it did not intend to take part will later supplement by giving the confusing or terrifying experience a twisted meaning. But, in order to make the world more tolerable and to protect itself against the unlimited hatred that might have arisen, shame and guilt feelings are constructed without any reality. In the same way, torture survivors often construct feelings of shame and guilt in order to eliminate the terror and confusion. These feelings may resemble the neurotic conflict-constitution, but the primary thing is that a new meaning is created which, because of its twisted and unrealistic shape, can in itself create new conflicts of a more neurotic character.

Thus, torture survivors are not borderline patients of deficit, but parts of their psychological makeup are characterized by deficit and may be responsible for some other conflict situations. These conflicts will be of a secondary character, and if the therapy takes the traditional approach and works with neutrality and transference-interpretations, it will not be possible to carry out the reconstruction work of ego structures that will bring about a lasting change. Instead, the result may be that the underlying deficits can generate new conflicts.

The therapeutic approach should therefore rather be a provider of something that the client lacks. This approach does not involve being warmer and in closer contact, being more empathic than therapeutic neutrality otherwise requires. The torture survivor should of course have a very empathic response to understand that he is not alone, but the therapist should rather point out his aloneness and confirm his needs, not necessarily satisfy them. The traditional analytic approach, characterized by objectivity, patience, stability, and tolerance, should be supplemented by an attitude that focuses on establishing, together with the client, a meaning, on finding out (Killingmo 1989: 76). Work with the torture survivor therefore requires a very complex therapeutic attitude of both cognitive and emotional dimensions, in which meaning-creating and explorative aspects are essential.

Explorative or Supportive Psychotherapy

In his relationship with torture survivors, the therapist has to adopt a special empathic approach with which it is possible, to a large extent, to protect and mature those ego structures that were destroyed by the torture. In this approach, the therapist must be direct and clear with respect to his techniques, while at the same time being tactful. In the torture survivor's tumultuous situation, it may be necessary for him to support and attach himself to an external reality by means of appreciation and reassurance. This type of validation may not come from interpretations and clarifications and may not form an integrated part of some of his ego functions, but nevertheless it is a tactful empathic understanding of his situation.

The following presents some considerations of the technical aspects of psychoanalytic-oriented psychotherapy. The aim is not to make the torture survivor a psychiatric case, but to supplement and qualify therapy that has many similarities with the supportive therapy of psychiatric patients.

Work with the torture survivor requires a special combination of explorative and supportive techniques. Wallerstein (1986), referring to the Menninger study, states that many of the psychoanalytic explorative therapies contain more supportive elements than were previously presumed, and that as a rule these were the elements that had led to changes. These positive results of the supportive elements of psychotherapy have been backed up by other studies. Furthermore, it is increasingly recognized that neither psychoanalysis nor explorative psychotherapy is suited to a long list of clients, but since the competitors to the psychoanalytical theory are still few, there is increased interest to include the supportive elements in it (Rockland 1992, 1994, Rosenberg 1987).

Supportive therapy has as its most important ingredient the use of directive techniques such as manipulation. According to Bibring (1954) and Rockland (1992), the directive aspects can be differentiated in two types of technique. One uses emotional systems of a more primitive type, embedded in positive transference, and has as its goal the bringing about of symptomatic change, "a transference cure," or "a parasitic change," as Bibring calls it (1954: 760). By contrast, the other technique uses manipulative forces outside and independent of the transference, for example by appealing to the client's ethical principles. The last-mentioned manipulative techniques will often be used when work with torture survivors does not primarily include transference, as in the psychoanalytic-oriented therapies. But since all therapies always have a feature of transference, it is difficult in practice to maintain a sharp distinction, and the various types of technique are intermingled.

The mechanisms of therapeutic effect include both technical and curative factors. The technical factors refer to any purposeful verbal or nonverbal behavior of the therapist with the purpose of influencing the client toward the therapeutic goal. The curative factors refer to the effect mechanisms that are responsible for the changes. The curative mechanisms involve the psychological forces that are activated by the therapeutic techniques. In other words, within psychotherapy, techniques and psychodynamic constellations relate closely together. The choice of technique implies acceptance of the psychodynamic constellation and the curative factors.

SUPPORTIVE TECHNIQUES

Suggestion is an induction of ideas, impulses, feelings, and actions. The therapist takes on an authoritative position while disregarding the client's rational and critical thoughts for a time. In its most extreme form, this technique is known from hypnosis, but it can also be used as technical advice about how the client should carry out a special action. In certain cases, when the clients regress, it may be necessary to demonstrate and to demand that they do something to stop their

(continued)

regression, to prevent them from harming themselves. But in other cases, it may be necessary to recommend and encourage the clients to find new ways of solving their problems. Suggestion is often considered controversial in therapeutic contexts because it may involve an intrusion into the client's autonomy. The therapist uses her position to induce ideas and actions, which perhaps would never have been among the client's free conscious choices. Advice and directive reality correction are examples of suggestion used within supportive psychotherapy. In some cases it may be necessary to use suggestion with some torture survivors, for example to prevent a self-destructive action.

Abreaction, or emotional outlet, plays an important role in the various catharsis methods, used for instance by Breuer and early by Freud. The technique consists in letting out the dammed-up tension that has had an "abnormal discharge" of, for example, symptoms. This technique is also controversial, and many think that it has only an apparent curative effect that quickly disappears. Abreaction was originally considered to have a curative effect in itself, but today it is considered mainly a technical principle that may lead to insight if the regressive acting-out is followed up. It may be used in torture survivors, for instance to provoke a "flashback" in order to elicit the trauma material from repression. The method is often used in acute traumatic PTSD conditions with amnesia or other repressive symptoms, as in the so-called crisis interventions to stimulate a "re-living of the feelings of loss." The background for this healing effect of abreaction is the fact that, apart from giving immediate relief from tension, it also demonstrates to the client that the therapeutic situation allowed him to meet another person who, by her empathy, shows that the trauma's feelings are accepted, understood, and contained. Thus, it is not the abreaction that in itself constitutes the therapy, but its combination with other therapeutic techniques, such as manipulation and clarification, that lead to a reestablishment and possible repair of "basic trust," in such a way that the individual, paradoxically, can come out of the trauma situation more mature than when he entered it.

Manipulation is a therapeutic technique that can be practiced in a positive or negative form—either to produce favorable attitudes toward the treatment situation or to remove obstructive trends. Based on standard psychoanalytic practice, one refrains from giving manipulative advice, making demands of the client, and encouraging him to do something unusual. But in the treatment of torture survivors it may sometimes be necessary to use manipulative techniques to protect clients from their traumatic experiences, which impinge themselves and may cause pathological reactions. In a more neutral sense, all therapy might be said to be manipulation, because it is an artificial situation in its structure; but it is often one of the therapeutic goals just to become aware of the kind of manipulation that may take place between the therapist and the client. (Modified from Bibring 1954, Rockland 1992, 1994.)

Interplay between Supportive and Explorative Therapy

In general, supportive techniques aim to reorganize the dynamic forces through experiences rather than through insight and in this way establish a new dynamic equilibrium. They can open the way for insight-giving techniques, which aim more directly at enforcing the ego functions through a differentiated "self-awareness" and subsequently at better control through more realistic "knowledge" of oneself and the environment. This enforcement and increased awareness of the ego function is often the most important curative goal for torture survivors. For other, more psychoanalytic-oriented therapies, the next step is to create some functional systems within the individual to allow the lifting up of unconscious conflicts into the conscious ego structure. For torture survivors, this is usually a secondary goal.

But here also the border between supportive and explorative psychotherapy should be softened. It is a misunderstanding and simplification to insist that, in the ego-weak person, the ego-defense should be left untouched and only supported and strengthened by supportive therapy. A bringing out of unconscious material and related interpretations will not always lead to further regression. But the traditional attitude is that the weaker the ego, the more the defense should be strengthened by avoiding bringing out unconscious material. The client should not be provoked by, for example, arranging frequent therapy sessions. However, Kernberg (1984: 154) writes about another experience, partly from his clinical practice, partly from his studies of borderline conditions at the Menninger Foundation, namely that the use of primitive defensive operations are themselves ego weakening, but that the interpretation of these primitive defenses has ego-strengthening effects. He recommends that expressive and explorative psychotherapy be used together with the supportive working method. In the same way, one can work with explorative techniques in the treatment of torture survivors, but here the interpretations do not have the same weight as in other therapies in which the damaged ego structure is brought into the therapeutic interaction.

In practice, supportive techniques may resemble therapeutic techniques that are not particularly refined. Just interviewing the client implies that something can be done and that the therapist accepts the client as he is. The role of the therapist may be to examine the realities of the situation together with the client. "He nurtures, suggests, guides, and helps distinguish reality from fantasy. In short, he acts as an accepting, benevolent, level-headed parent" (Werman 1981: 154).

Some torture survivors are in a paradoxical situation because they can often obtain considerable and lasting help from a short course using abreaction and manipulative techniques. These techniques can give immediate relief of symptoms, after which the survivor's otherwise healthy personality will be able to take over and continue the remaining work: by letting out the worst tensions, some well-functioning parts of the personality will be liberated to continue the healing, confirming the popular saying that the therapist can appeal to the individual's own healing resources. By contrast, clinical experience also shows that some of the severely traumatized torture survivors have had such fundamental parts of their personality destroyed that psychotherapy may last a very long time and perhaps result only in modest improvement of function.

A big problem is therefore to aim at realistic goals. Just the traumatic situation itself can mislead the inexperienced therapist to assume an omnipotent position, from which she gives too much optimism with respect to the effects of treatment. This may have a positive supportive effect in the first part of therapy, but it will quickly be replaced by despair in the survivor, which may make him stop the treatment. Instead of both client and therapist aiming at crucial, significant changes, the therapy may sometimes be surrounded by a more positive atmosphere if it is compared with therapy of the chronic somatic diseases; these cannot be cured by a doctor, who, however, can minimize their effects by consultations. For some of the severely traumatized survivors it may be necessary for the therapist to emphasize that treatment goals are different from life goals, and that both parties should modify their expectations.

Pitfalls in Using Supportive Therapy

With respect to supportive psychotherapy, three conditions should be emphasized as big challenges and pitfalls.

First, the method demands great therapeutic experience. One of the basic mistakes is that this therapy is left to less experienced therapists because of its manipulative and suggestive techniques. It is wrong to assume that it can be left to a younger therapist, since there may not be room for refined psychoanalytic interpretations and clarifications.

Two other problems are the establishment of treatment goals and termination, two closely linked conditions. Especially when there is a cultural difference between therapist and client, it may be difficult for the therapist to accept that psychotherapy is an exclusively Western phenomenon that includes a clear demarcation of the difference between a friendly and a professional relationship. The precondition of the treatment is that both parties find at least some common treatment goals to work with. Different goals will lead to delay while the parties' unexpressed expectations are left in the air, sometimes in an atmosphere of "killing with kindness," which may be broken by confrontation and perhaps by a traumatic end to the therapy. Therefore, supportive therapy requires an explicit and direct communication about the goals.

The paradox of the termination of treatment is that an attachment to the therapist should have developed because it is a precondition for the therapeutic work. But it is a two-edged sword because this attachment can also become a hindrance to the clients, making it difficult for them to liberate themselves from the therapist and to develop the necessary autonomy. One of the problems is that the therapist is more talkative and active with the supportive approach than with the explorative one. This can make some therapists lose their grasp on their professional position, making it difficult for them to find the correct balance between therapeutic intervention and ordinary advisory functions. The therapeutic relationship can develop into a social relationship in which the professional status is lost. "The friendly relationship, which permits the therapist to function as an agent of support, is transformed into a relationship of friendship in which the auxiliary role of the therapist is lost" (Werman 1981: 156).

Thus, supportive psychotherapy has some characteristic techniques that provide a special "holding environment" in which the therapist establishes a space to give protection not only against external dangers, but also against the survivor's own impulses. The therapist should be able to discover external dangers even if survivors cannot do so themselves, and she should also be able to identify, openly and directly, the survivors' destructive impulses, and perhaps let them know whether or not they worry her.

SUPPORTIVE THERAPY

1. The nature of the patient's affect and cognitive problems should be carefully explained to the patients, including the methods of covering up their deficiencies in their perceptions and object and self-representations.

2. Affect tolerance must be improved. Before these patients can deal with the emotions themselves, one has to first attend to their "having" them. Handling one's emotions is a challenge in many situations in all affective disorders. However, for these patients, because of the relatively intense physiological responses, the emotions represent a special burden. What affective responses are and how one uses them to one's advantage need to be taken up in great detail by the therapist and practiced by the patients. The acquisition and practicing of the skill of "managing" one's emotions is a necessary prerequisite to utilization of affects as signals.

3. Dealing with the inhibition in self-care is another early task. The idea of affects being signals to one's self to be used and regulated to one's best advantage is not at all self-evident for these patients. Many of them use their emotions to control their love object and/or experience their emotions as emanating from their object representations, and their regulation and utilization is reserved for the maternal object representation. Before some of the alexithymic individuals dare to extend their selfhood to include their emotions and proceed to activate their verbalization and utilization of their emotions, their inhibitions in this regard have to be interpreted.

4. Affect naming and verbalization must be encouraged. Supplying to the alexithymic the words and names for emotions is a slow task, because verbalization represents just one half of the task. The other half consists in desomatization. That is why certain things must be repeated and reexperienced many times, and require time and practice. None of the statements of the patient about how he or she felt can be taken for granted as one goes through a review of his or her reactions. Since the use of dreams and utilization of the transference is limited, it is

necessary to start by pointing out the impairment in empathy and sensitivity that these patients show in their object relations. Because they do not have signal affects available to them, they also lack empathy. In particular, they have no feeling or conviction of loving anyone or of anyone loving them. (Krystal 1988: 319)

• • •

Supportive psychotherapy is more than a mere exercise in ambulatory custodial care:

"For example, a patient who comes progressively late to therapy, or frequently misses his hours, is communicating his need to avoid contact with the therapist for some reason. Not to confront this acting out is to give it tacit approval; moreover, not confronting this behavior implicitly encourages doing rather than reflecting. (But here again, the entire situation must be considered; it is possible that in a passive obsessional patient, one might encourage such behavior as a progressive step away from excessive rumination.) The therapist should ascertain if the reasons for the patient's avoidance of therapy are conscious; if they are in awareness, he should be encouraged to discuss them with the therapist as candidly as he can. Appropriate measures can perhaps be taken to mitigate the problem; this might entail, for example, spacing visits farther apart or shortening each interview. If the patient is unaware of the feelings or thoughts that prompted his behavior, the therapist may be able to grasp the sense of these acts from the general flow of the therapeutic material, and be able to discuss his conjectures with the patient." (Werman 1981: 157)

Neutrality and Engagement

The supportive attitude gets a special application when it is used for torture survivors. The reason is that torture and the Holocaust consist of such extremely terrible experiences that the therapist's work must also include a special creation of meaning. This can show itself in the explicit way in which she takes on an advocacy role vis-à-vis her clients, much more so than is usual for psychotherapists. This is a great test of the therapist's neutrality. In the field of psychotherapy, neutrality is a technical term for the therapist's ability to control her own values and prejudices in her work with the client and thus not let them become an uncontrollable part of the countertransference. Thus, neutrality has another meaning than usual when it indicates lack of color and involvement (Elsass 1994b).

Nevertheless, many therapists encounter this problem of distinguishing technical neutrality from the moral and usual meaning of neutrality, because torture in another, human-rights sense demands that one distances oneself. Many have chosen to work with torture survivors because it allows them to work in an engaged and political context; if the political aspect becomes too prominent during therapy, the therapists may go beyond the usual bounds. It may therefore be useful for some of the "advocacy" work to be delegated to the institution concerned. Most treatment centers do not hide their involvement in the fight against torture, and it is a question whether this involvement is not a necessary precondition for the neutrality of the therapist. When the treatment center has an engaged attitude, it is easier for the therapist to delegate the political elements, for which there is no room in the closed therapeutic space.

The maintenance of a neutral therapeutic approach demands intensive supervision of transference and countertransference because, among other things, the dyadic relationship between therapist and survivor is influenced by the presence of the torturer, who, like a powerful shadow, extends the relationship to a threesome. Without very thorough supervision, the therapist may put up an unconscious defense against the overwhelming feeling of helplessness, which may lead to grandiose counterreactions in the form of omnipotent helper behavior, which does not respect the survivor's autonomy. As previously mentioned, another reaction may be identification with the aggressor, which can make the therapist pursue the survivor and, like an exorcist, provoke him to relive the torture again and again, because he considers that in itself it has a cathartic healing effect (see page 64). A savior attitude, boundary transgressions, and attempts to control provocations of the survivor are typical for an insufficient analysis and understanding of transference and countertransference phenomena.

Integrity Requires a Balance between Intellect and Feelings

Integrity is the goal of reconstruction of the torture survivor's destroyed ego structures. Herman defines integrity as "the capacity to affirm the value of life in the face of death, to be reconciled with the finite limits of one's own life and the tragic limitations of the human condition, and to accept these realities without despair. Integrity is the foundation upon which trust in relationships is originally formed, and upon which shattered trust may be restored. The interlocking of integrity and trust in caretaking relationships completes the cycle of generations and regenerates the sense of human community which trauma destroys" (Herman 1992: 154).

It requires a special balance between intellect and feeling to re-create this integrity in the torture survivor. On the one hand, intellectual, opinion-forming work will strengthen the ego functions. Thus, Frankl's existential logotherapy, which developed from his own experience in concentration camps, has shown itself well suited to Holocaust survivors (Frankl 1967, 1970). But, on the other hand, searching for "the meaning of life" should not lead the therapist to emphasize the opinion-forming and intellectual aspects to the extent that she omits the emotional aspects. If the therapist exaggerates the intellectual side, it can in part be an expression of her fear that repetition and reliving of the torture experiences will make the client worse. But it can also be a sign of her fear that she herself can be influenced by gaining insight in the torture to the extent that she can no longer maintain her own creation of meaning.

Just as it is a misunderstanding to omit dealing with traumatic material, it is also wrong to focus on the torture experiences too quickly and prematurely, before the creation of a therapeutic space in which the torture survivor can feel safe and prepared.

Some therapists use crisis intervention too uncritically, push on too quickly, and fall for easy solutions. Crisis intervention was introduced in somatic departments as a reaction to an atmosphere that was far too repressive of emotions; patients and relatives were not able to relive the feelings attached to loss. Cullberg, among others, advocated the therapeutic necessity of identifying these losses, for example by means of emotion-relieving techniques (Cullberg 1983). He defined the well-known crisis phases and formulated such a simple therapeutic model that it has been accepted far outside psychotherapeutic circles. This has led to several positive developments—above all, that health workers more easily accept the feelings of grief. But crisis intervention has undergone "inflation," so that it has become a crisis industry. In certain therapeutic circles, everything, so to speak, is considered crisis and treated according to the idea that the feelings of grief must be released (Elsass 1993b). These unsound developments are due to the fact that some fundamental concepts—e.g., trauma, crisis, and loss—are too vaguely defined, so that they are not suitable for visitation to the feeling-releasing techniques (see page 30).

Thus, some studies cannot unambiguously confirm the assumption that purposeful adaptation to a traumatic situation implies that the person has worked through the trauma situation, "looked it straight in the face," and got to know its feelings, instead of having denied and repressed it (Wortman & Silver 1991).

The Stages of Therapy

The therapeutic process is long if the aim is reconstruction of the broken-down ego structures. Herman refers to a "marathon," a metaphor to counter the compelling fantasy of a quick cathartic cure. "The metaphor of a marathon captures the strong behavioral focus on conditioning the body, as well as the psychological dimensions of determination and courage. While the image may lack a strong social dimension, it captures the survivor's initial feeling of isolation. It also offers an image of the therapist's role as a trainer and coach. While the therapist's technical expertise, judgment, and moral support are vital to the enterprise, in the end it is the survivor who determines her recovery through her own actions" (Herman 1992: 174).

The therapeutic work of this marathon will proceed in stages. Herman (1992) describes them as (1) "establishment of safety," (2) "remembrance and mourning," and (3) "reconnection." She refers to successful treatment in which one may observe some changes: from working initially with the survivor's experiences of unpredictable danger to reliable security, from dissociated trauma symptoms to recognized memory traces, and finally from stigmatized isolation to regained social relations (Herman 1992: 155). Other psychotherapists, for example Cullberg (1983), Davidsen-Nielsen and Leick (1987), and Horowitz (1986), describe a similar series of therapeutic phases and suggest that the therapy changes and has stage-specificity; that one form of treatment may be inappropriate and perhaps harmful at a certain time, but appropriate and healing at another.

In the first stage, in which safety and a certain element of "basic trust" should be established, it may be a therapeutic mistake to provoke an exploration and identification of the feelings due to the torture. In this stage, the survivor has a primary need for control and safety, which the therapist can fulfill, for example, by making out a detailed therapy contract with an explicit frame. Another safety and security measure may be to introduce psycho-educative work as a teaching situation in which the survivor listens to other people's experiences of the consequences of torture and, for instance, learns various coping strategies to prevent torture's immediate dysfunctions.

The next stage, which starts the process of recalling and retelling the trauma, demands considerable therapeutic tact and understanding for "timing" and "pacing." The start of this work is often characterized by a remarkable lack of affects when the survivor again and again relates disjointed parts of his torture story. Danieli (1988) emphasizes the importance of "recreating the flow," that is, the survivor should be encouraged to relate previous important relationships, ideals and dreams, conflicts and problems, from the time before the traumatic experience (Danieli 1988). Such work establishes a context that gives a special understanding of the meaning of the trauma for the survivor.

In some therapies, the trauma story is transformed to a testimony (Agger & Jensen 1990, Mollica 1988). One of the purposes is to transform the person's story about shame and humiliation to a public story about dignity and courage. Other therapies aim more directly at getting a personal trauma story in a closed therapy room. The release of feelings is here an important part of the therapy. Several behavior therapeutic methods have been developed, such as "direct exposure," in which the survivor is guided into a controlled reexperience. Other methods use hypnotherapy, psychodrama, or other feeling-releasing techniques in which the therapist, together with the survivor, arranges the working-through of the traumatic event, for instance by working out a "script" based on the four dimensions: context, facts, emotions, and interpretations (Herman 1992: 182).

A treatment including reconstruction of the testimony story requires between twelve and twenty weekly sessions (Herman 1992: 182), but even more are required in most cases if cathartic methods with subsequent reconstruction and reintegration are chosen. Herman (1992: 183) mentions that intensive therapies have their limitations; it is quite true that the intrusive symptoms may improve, but there is not necessarily an improvement of the more negative symptoms such as numbing and social withdrawal, manifested by matrimonial difficulties and social and occupational problems. Thus, intensive and cathartic work is a necessary part of the therapy, but it is not always sufficient. Again it should be stressed that much experience is necessary with these methods.

Some survivors feel worse in this period, and Herman (1992: 182) describes how the deterioration can be so bad that hospitalization is necessary. In a preceding psychoeducative part of the treatment, the survivors should be prepared for this deterioration.

The last stage of the treatment includes reintegration and return to a daily routine, possibly with work and family. The torture has caused some basic changes in the person, and he will often be aware of how vulnerable he is and how little is needed for him to recall the traumatic situation. But with this understanding it is easier for him to orient himself and try to plan a new life. He needs partly to regain trust in himself, partly to establish relationships with others whom he dares to trust and have confidence in. The reestablishment of social relations may take its starting point in an understanding of not being the only one to have been tortured. The perception that the trauma also has a universality and a meaning in a larger social and political context can give the survivor an engagement in a case of human rights. The gradual absorption into supporting and self-help groups, in which the survivors find safety and security among equals, often with the same cultural background, may be an important way in which the therapist can finish his work and hand it over in another context outside the treating institutions.

These stages, just described, do not have any common theoretical background but are a pragmatic way of bringing order into some clinical therapeutic experiences. For the therapist, they have rather the character of a managing principle and do not always correspond with what has been shown by systematic studies (Wortman & Silver 1991). Davidsen-Nielsen and Leick (1987) therefore consider the stages as "projects" that can be worked with at various periods during the therapy, regardless of their sequence.

Cognitive Treatment Methods and Pharmacotherapy

The psychodynamic and often psychoanalytic-oriented approach is typical for the treatment of torture survivors, perhaps for historical reasons. Holocaust survivors from the Second World War were treated in the psychoanalytic tradition, and the first torture survivors to be treated were Latin Americans, with a psychiatric tradition strongly influenced by psychoanalytic thinking.

However, there is a reaction that emphasizes that behavioral, cognitive therapies are more efficient, and describes the psychodynamic psychoanalytic-oriented method as too slow (Basoglu 1992: 402).

It is, however, difficult to compare two different therapeutic methods whose goals are different. Roughly speaking, the psychodynamic method puts more emphasis on insight and veracity, the cognitive on symptom relief and efficiency (Elsass 1993a: 437).

No method can in general be said to be better or more "true" than another. The challenge for the psychotherapist is to develop knowledge and skills within several theoretical movements, and to understand their goals and views on the personality and be prepared to use them according to the client's own wishes and standards.

Several exposure-based behavioral and cognitive techniques have been used in the treatment of various conditions associated with post-traumatic stress disorders (see, for instance, the review by Keane et al. 1992). These methods belong to a research tradition with systematic, empirical studies of the results, and several studies have been published showing the effect of these methods (Fairbank & Brown 1988, Keane et al. 1989, 1992). The characteristics of these effect studies are that their systematism and validity are strictly limited to defined behavioral changes measured by means of more or less standardized questionnaires and rating scales. But a treatment with restructuring of cognitive schematizations and establishment of new coping mechanisms may, in its own rationality and optimism, have a built-in problem: it is rare for a cognitive therapy to evaluate both "cost" and "benefit" even though any redistribution of a psychodynamic, ecological situation will always involve costs, and not only benefits. Thus, Schönpflug and Battmann (1988) have shown how effective coping and solution of a work-psychology problem may have a positive result in the short term but still lead to several problems in the long term. In the same way it is also seen that some concentration camp survivors may have very articulate opinions about their traumatic situation, a source of inspiration and existential context for them in their middle age, but nonetheless they commit suicide when they become old, as, for instance, Bruno Bettelheim and Primo Levi. Torture survivors will also have a potential suicide risk even though they have been through an apparent maturing and cognitive restructuring of their traumatic situation.

Cognitive behavioral therapy of traumatized clients has been developed by Janoff-Bulman (1988, 1989), McCann and Pearlman (1990), and to some extent by Horowitz et al. (1984). Specifically for torture survivors, Foa et al. (1989) made an information-processing model and, based on conditioning theories, explained how the combination of fear and behavioral avoidance can provoke some PTSD symptoms. Chemptob et al. (1988) developed a cognitive action theory about PTSD conditions.

The methods have included desensitization treatment and relaxation techniques combined with a graduated and hierarchically arranged exposure to traumalike situations to which the client has developed a phobia. Keane et al. (1992), based on a review of several studies, conclude that exposure has the greatest effect on anxiety-based and observable positive symptoms such as nightmares, irritability, anger, and physiologically increased arousal. By contrast, there was less effect on negative symptoms such as numbing and emotional anesthesia. Keane et al. (1992) have developed a "stress management package" consisting of relaxation training, cognitive restructuring, and training in problem-solving skills. In their review of the five controlled studies using behavioral treatments for PTSD (none in torture survivors), Solomon et al. (1992) state that all exhibited improvements in intrusive symptoms after treatment (McIvor & Turner 1995: 707).

One essential ingredient in cognitive and behavioral therapy appears to be that of direct therapeutic exposure (DTE). This may be in the obvious form of systematic desensitization, implosion, graded exposure, or flooding. DTE is based on behavioral principles used in the treatment of anxiety disorders, where exposure to the anxiety-provoking stimuli in a supportive setting, either imagined or in vivo, results in arousal, attenuation, and symptom reduction or habituation, particularly where there are marked avoidance or phobic symptoms. Even in the therapies that are not explicitly behavioral, the process of retelling does contain elements of exposure (McIvor & Turner 1995: 709). Finally, it should be mentioned that there is increasing evidence that severe trauma can produce lasting neurobiological changes. No controlled trials examining the efficacy of medication in the treatment of torture survivors have been published, but a few studies of medical treatment of nontortured PTSD have been. Positive outcome predictors have been depression, neuroticism, trauma intensity, and anxiety (see review in McIvor & Turner 1995).

In summary, these cognitive treatment methods work best in combination with other forms of treatment. When the treatment alliance and the first goal of "basic trust" are established, supportive therapy can be supplemented with cognitive therapy, stress management, training in social skills, and pharmacotherapy (Mørch et al. 1995).

Combination of Cognitive and Psychodynamic Viewpoints

Cognitive therapy's viewpoints about how behavior often tries to confirm cognitive schematizations are in agreement with other psychological theories that our behavior is directed by some basic assumptions. Parkes (1975) uses the term "assumptive worlds," Bowlby (1969) "world models," and others "structures of meaning," "theories of reality," and so on. All mean that we have a perceptual system to guide our perception, thought, and action. We want to maintain this system and are often ignorant of its basic content. Our assumptive world provides us with a stable conceptual system that affords us psychological equilibrium in a constantly changing world. But because we perceive the world through these assumptive "lenses," it is very difficult to invalidate them. They generally persist and are resistant to change. Based on empirical studies, Janoff-Bulman (1989) categorized the basic assumptions into three organizing principles: the assumption of the goodness of the world, another about its meaningfulness, and a third about the value of the self. These are the basic assumptions that are challenged by a traumatic experience. Davidsen-Nielsen and Leick (1993) express the same ideas by saying that traumas hurt the ego, because we, quite unexpectedly, are confronted with the existential basic conditions: death, meaninglessness, loneliness, and our "unlimited" freedom (see page 40).

Torture survivors have their basic assumptions crucially challenged in such a way that they can no longer trust or believe in these conceptual systems. Torture leads to a potential breakdown of "the assumptive worlds"—assumptions of the goodness of the world, its meaningfulness, and the value of the self.

The cognitive approach does not exclude a psychodynamic viewpoint. Thus, Haan (1977), Horowitz (1976), and Lazarus and Folkman (1984) were among the first to present a conceptualization of the coping mechanisms. It is interesting that all of these psychologists have a psychoanalytic background which they have used as a springboard into the behavior and cognitive therapies. They have worked operationally and stuck to an empirical description in which clinical data have been grouped and categorized. An example is a study by Horowitz et al. (1984) in which some patients were given the task of describing in detail how they had overcome traumatic crises, in particular giving an account of the resources from which they had consciously been drawing. These descriptions were subsequently put together in categories which later formed the basis of Horowitz's treatment of clients in crises.

In practice, treatment can very well work with cognitive restructurings of schematizations and at the same time have an object-theoretical starting point, for instance in attachments and "basic trust." The supportive emotional approach of validating the clients and emphasizing the reestablishment of their perception of control is such a combination. Several therapists have stressed the importance of helping the severely traumatized client regain control in a warm, supportive atmosphere (see, for example, Herman 1992: 134).

The precondition for the therapeutic goal, increased autonomy, is that the client has a feeling of control. Within the framework of cognitive understanding, it means that the individual establishes some schematizations that can give him a better predictive value. For traumatized persons, just the experience of not being able to predict the misfortune, the torture, and their own reactions has been an important part of the trauma. Therefore, the aim of cognitive therapy is to focus on the aspect of predictability in such a way that, even if the survivor experiences the torture as meaningless and unpredictable, it can be included within the wider framework of understanding in which it gets its meaning. In a cognitive sense it involves replacing incongruent schematization with congruent ways of experiencing.

Incongruence and dissonance have been described as important sources of stress. In the severely traumatized event, these sources can be isolated as being meaningless things outside the survivor's goal and meaning.

"The Meaning of Life": Reality or Self-Deception

In work with the cognitive structures in the torture survivor, it may be difficult to place various schematizations and coping mechanisms in a larger existential context. Opinion-forming work is sometimes made difficult by the fact that some torture survivors have become so disillusioned that they have to establish new illusions in order to regain the lust for life. One illusion is to believe in something that cannot be confirmed in an external reality. Too many illusions that are not shared with others and cannot be corrected are called delusions and can lead to psychiatric disease. But if one is able to share them with others, one does not necessarily have to be marked as mentally ill. The problem with the difficult demarcation of illusions toward the external reality has been studied, among others, by the constructivist movement "New Look," which, by means of some experimental studies, has supported the view that humans create their own reality. Within the therapeutic methods, constructivism has been expressed in the so-called logotherapies, for instance as presented by Frankl (1967, 1970) (see page 77). Victor Frankl survived in a concentration camp where he observed that the prisoners died when they lost the meaning of life. Some were able to live for a long time, and even to survive, even if their physical condition was very poor, just because they saw a meaning in life. The purpose of the concentration camp was to deprive the prisoners of this meaning in such a way that the terror became a threat to their will to survive. In order to survive, prisoners had to give their sufferings a meaning, and they had to find a meaning in a meaningless world. Frankl later extended his experiences from Auschwitz to the therapy room. The therapy became a sort of benefice of survival in which he, through carefully planned therapeutic sessions, made clients see their own personal values and in this way regain the meaning of life (Frankl 1970).

Another psychiatrist, Bruno Bettelheim, who also managed to survive a period in a concentration camp, made personal integrity the precondition of survival. He claims that concentration camp prisoners could do very little to secure their survival, apart from hoping for the allied forces' victory over Hitler. The prisoners' sole chance of surviving was to cling to their individuality. Only by keeping their individual and spiritual morals high could they fight the disintegration of their personality and then hope for some of it to be left if the impossible should happen—if they got out alive (Bettelheim 1979, 1986).

Frankl and Bettelheim's theories that survival is dependent on the meaning of life and on high individual spiritual morals can thus be said to be a creation of appropriate coping mechanisms in a behavioral and cognitive sense. But it was shown later that coping, including creation of "the meaning of life," has sometimes been a self-deception, not in agreement with the experiences that have later emerged from the camps. On the contrary, some survived by cooperating with their torturers, by informing against others, and by stealing from the dying and the sick. The sociobiologist de Press

(1980) wrote that survivors were as a rule either strongly dogmatic fundamentalists, such as Jehovah's Witnesses, or, on the other hand, petty criminals who cooperated with the guards, sacrificed their friends, or entered into a sexual relationship with the torturers.

Old-fashioned heroism thus failed as an appropriate coping mechanism for survival. It was not always the spirit that conquered the body; on the contrary, the experiences from the death camps showed that one sometimes had to surrender to one's biological and animal instincts and repress the spiritual values about morals and ethics.

The psychologist Festinger (1957) developed these experiences in an experimental and sociopsychologic field in his theory about cognitive dissonance. One of the conclusions was that a person cannot contain two different and incompatible pieces of information without having to construct an overall structure that may be unrealistic and illusory but nevertheless creates harmony. Festinger showed that there are great individual variations in our ability to contain self-contradictions.

In summary, it can be said that we all have illusions, but in the utmost sense it may be difficult to know how far the illusion can reach. The consequential reality testing is seldom present, and many are able to maintain mental health even if there are elements of self-deception in their perception of themselves and their surroundings. Thus the paradox is that illusions and self-deception may be appropriate adaptation mechanisms on the one hand, while on the other hand they can fling some people into mental disease. Thus, self-deception can be both health promoting and disease provoking.

Some studies, for example, cannot unambiguously confirm the assumption that it is necessary to identify and relive the feelings of the trauma. The few systematic studies on the stages of crisis have, for instance, not been able to demonstrate in a convincing way that clients always react with grief and sadness following loss (Wortman & Silver 1991: 391) (see page 78). A study of patients paralyzed by spinal injury has shown that absence of sadness and depression was sometimes associated with a strong ego feeling and with the therapist's evaluation of successful adaptation to the paralysis (Malec & Neimeyer 1983). Other systematic studies have also shown that absence of grief reactions is not necessarily a problem. Many people have the ability to continue life after serious loss with good psychological function without suffering grief and without going through the prescribed stages of grief therapy (Wortman & Silver 1991: 403).

A therapist, therefore, needs a broad, overall understanding of torture and its conditions. It is not enough to adopt the usual existential cognitive attitude in which the goal may be to obtain causality understanding, control, congruence, and an overall meaning of life. The work with torture survivors is itself a challenge to the therapist's own existential beliefs, since the essential quality of torture is the meaningless and the unpredictable.

In therapeutic work with torture survivors, the doctrine about the importance of reality and self-knowledge must be taken with reservations, because illusions in this field may be difficult to demarcate and break down.

Causality understanding is not necessarily the same as finding a meaning, and one can, like Molin Jørgensen (1992), distinguish between the meaning of life and the meaning of the event. The nature of the traumatic situation can therefore rightly lead to the development of some negative basic concepts, in which, for instance, an attitude of mistrust and rejection can be considered as a "good" adaptation. But the therapy's goal is that this attitude should include only the meaning of the torture, not the more general "meaning of life."

Summary and Clinical Applications

• Therapy may not simply focus on post-traumatic stress disorder (PTSD), although this may be one of many elements in an individual response. Retelling the trauma story is a common element that is independent of the particular therapeutic orientation. But it is essential not to overwhelm the patient by covering too much material in one session. Often other aspects are more important.

• The work with relationship and attachment bonds between client and therapist is of the greatest therapeutic importance, more than the content between the parties, the interpretations and the clarifications.

• Psychotherapy of torture and Holocaust survivors is difficult and may give limited results because of the destruction of the survivors' "basic trust" and their inability to relive and describe their traumatic situation. The survivors' way of blocking and suppressing the overwhelming traumatic affects by means of psychological "closing off," "affective anesthesia," "psychic numbing," and "psychic death" might especially create problems in a therapeutic context. Other therapeutic difficulties are due to the survivors' retroactive idealization of their childhood, their feelings of guilt at having survived, and their continuous aggressions, which are often managed by a rigid, political, or religiously oriented superego. When a survivor starts to reflect back on his life, he is often prone to anhedonism, and this makes him particularly difficult to work with.

• Survivors might identify with their torturers in a traumatic bonding in order to reestablish a fixed point in their destroyed identity. But this "hate dependence" can cause new experiences of guilt that make survivors distance themselves even more from dependence on others and from retaliation and revenge. The therapist should be warned against such features of a strong, emotional bonding, potentially full of conflict. It is possible to protect oneself only by being precise and strong, by making borders and showing tact, both when rejecting the client's idealizations, and when receiving hateful devaluations.

• In visitation, the therapist must evaluate how the survivors' premorbid psyches was formed, and how their developmental potentials have been able to resist the destructive sequelae of the trauma. This may help balance the therapy between supportive and explorative techniques.

• Survivors are not borderline patients of deficit, but parts of their psychological makeup are characterized by deficit. In resemblance to borderline patients, the survivors' pathology of lack of object constancy, identity diffusion, tendency to splitting, and lack of a capacity for emotional bonding are placed more on defined islands, because they do not have the fundamental developmental basis.

• Supportive techniques that aim to reorganize the dynamic forces through experiences rather than through insight should be favored. The therapeutic approach should be a provider of something that the client lacks, and the traditional analytic approach, characterized by objectivity, patience, stability, and tolerance, should be supplemented by an attitude that focuses on establishing, together with the client, a meaning, on finding out. It is not a matter of finding something else, but to feel that something has the quality of being. This approach does not involve being warmer and in closer contact, more empathic than therapeutic neutrality otherwise requires. Torture survivors should of course have a very empathic response to understand that they are not alone, but the therapist should point out their aloneness and confirm their needs, but not necessarily satisfy them.

• Some torture survivors can often obtain considerable and lasting help from a short course of therapy using abreaction and manipulative techniques. These techniques can give immediate relief of symptoms, after which the survivors' otherwise healthy personality will be able to take over and continue the remaining work. But the severely traumatized survivors have had such fundamental parts of their personality destroyed that psychotherapy may take a long time and perhaps result only in modest improvements of function. The therapist must therefore resist an omnipotent position from which she gives too much optimism with respect to the effects of treatment. This may have a positive supportive effect in the first part of therapy, but it will quickly be replaced by despair in the survivor, which may make him stop the treatment.

• The technical neutrality must be distinguished from the moral and political neutrality. Many therapists have chosen to work with survivors because it allows them to work in an engaged and political context. But if the political aspect becomes too prominent in the therapy, they may go beyond the bounds. It may therefore be an advantage for some of the "advocacy" work to be delegated to the relevant institution. The treatment center's involvement in the fight against torture may be a necessary precondition for the neutrality of the therapist.

• Just as it is a mistake to avoid dealing with traumatic material, it is also wrong to focus on the torture experiences too quickly and prematurely, that is, before the creation of a therapeutic space in which the torture survivor can feel safe and prepared. The therapeutic work must therefore proceed in stages, decried as, for example, (1) "establishment of safety," where the therapist fulfills the survivor's need for control and safety; (2) "remembrance and mourning," which starts the process of recalling and retelling the trauma with tact and understanding for "timing" and "pacing"; and (3) "reconnection," which includes reintegration and return to a daily routine.

• Cognitive therapeutic methods with desensitization and relaxation techniques combined with a gradual and hierarchically arranged exposure to traumalike situations may work when the treatment alliance and the first stage of "basic trust" are established. But the work with cognitive structures such as various schematizations and coping mechanisms is difficult to place in a larger existential context. The work of meaning is important.

• The importance of reality and self-knowledge must be taken with reservations, because illusions in this field may be difficult to demarcate and break down. Old-fashioned heroism has often failed as an appropriate coping mechanism for survival. It was not always the spirit that conquered the body;

on the contrary, experiences from death camps show that one sometimes had to surrender to one's biological and animal instincts and repress the spiritual values about morals and ethics. This is a challenge to the therapist's own existential meaning, since the essential quality of torture is meaningless and unpredictable.

4

The Cultural Psychology of the Torture Syndrome

A Distinction between What Is Universal and What Is Culture-Bound

Forced migration because of war and political persecution leads to a confrontation with cultures that are often quite different from the Western context, in which psychotherapy was created and developed. More than three-quarters of the world's population live in non-Western cultures, and more than 90 percent are not familiar with our psychotherapeutic constructions.

Torture survivors come mainly from non-Western cultures, and the problems that we have dealt with in the previous chapters may therefore be fictive. The demarcation of the torture syndrome from post-traumatic stress disorders, the special supportive method, and the treatment stages is based on a dubious assumption, that is, that the main principles in the psychodynamic and psychoanalytic-oriented approaches are universal.

The few who have dealt with the problem of cultural insensitivity in the psychodynamic approach (Dahl 1989, Devereux 1980, Kleber et al. 1995, Prince 1980) have claimed that only a small and exclusive group will benefit from psychotherapy, and that many cultures will not live up to the visitation requirements in general. Many cultures take no interest in the form of introspection that psychotherapy takes for granted; they are ashamed of talking about psychological problems and do not speak about intimate personal matters with strangers outside their family. Usually they do not have the understanding of a "professional friendship," which psychotherapy implies.

Some of the difficulties that arise during treatment courses for torture survivors may be due to our cultural conventions of how one should "express one's problems," rather than being a result of traumatic and developmental difficulties. But on the other hand, not all therapeutic problems can be ascribed to culture specificity. Ordinary human understanding is based on a wide cultural fellowship, and psychotherapy can become a focal point at which cross-cultural understanding becomes one of the most important features of treatment.

Meeting of Two Different Explanatory Models

The precondition for "effective communication," as often described, is that the client and therapist must share the same perceptions of health and disease. Improvement in compliance and therapeutic results will depend on whether the health worker and the client acknowledge and respect each other's viewpoints of disease, even when these are not in complete agreement (Pachter 1994).

Most consultations can be analyzed with respect to compliance between two cultures, each having its own explanatory model, that is, the way in which a disease episode is perceived. It is an individual model, a conglomerate of ethnocultural, personal, and idiosyncratic perceptions, but also of biomedical concepts. It is rare to have exclusively popular, layman explanatory models or exclusively professional, scientific, and biomedical ones. There will always be a conglomerate of both, a continuum of perceptions between these two extremes. In Western Europe, for instance, asthma and diabetes are considered by both laymen and professionals as belonging to scientific and biomedical models, whereas more lay perceptions apply to the common cold and depression. In fact, we place in the lay part of the continuum the diseases we hear about from other cultures and are unknown to us. Strange phenomena that foreign cultures call *empacho* and *ataque de nervios*, as examples, are considered as culture-specific symptoms, and it is in the treatment of these conditions that we find cross-cultural understanding necessary. Some of the symptoms in torture survivors that we do not know in our culture may easily be given this status of lay, nonscientific character. We seem to be able to understand them only if they are translated into our own culture and science.

The difference between us and the others is in general based on the egocentricity of Western psychotherapy; psychological problems are ascribed more to forces of the ego than to external social and cultural conditions. However, most parts of the world have a sociocentric ideology that places individual experiences in a network of social relationships, which are the source of self-esteem, self-realization, and self-control. In other cultures, interhuman obligation and loyalty are far more important than individual personality features. According to their ideology, a social network influences the development of the personality through strengthening the features that the culture appreciates.

Another of our culture-bound Western conceptions is based on the dualistic viewpoint that diseases have either an organic or a psychological cause. We have of course developed a bio-psycho-social therapeutic concept that is removed from the monocausal viewpoint of the past. But many other cultures do not have a historical tradition that distinguishes between psychological and somatic experiences.

The third Western assumption is that the health concepts of foreign cultures are often based on lack of medical physiological knowledge. We tend to think that foreign cultures distort the real cause and veil it with superstition and prejudices. But many non-Western cultures do not isolate the cause of disease or health in a narrow formal scientific sense, but apply a much wider approach.

Even if it is important to know the concepts of disease and symptoms of various cultures, it is equally important to understand how to negotiate and communicate between the two different systems of values and perceptions. Reaching a common cultural understanding in psychotherapeutic work takes more than the therapist's knowing about the survivor's culture and respecting its peculiarities. To a certain extent it is just this difference between the two parties that should be used as an active therapeutic ingredient. Cultural psychology is thus able to reflect about the relationship between cultures rather than have a concrete detailed knowledge of the one culture.

Culture: A Position from Which We Talk

"'Culture' is not something one talks about, but a position from which one talks. In other words, it is something one sees with, rather than what one sees" (Hastrup 1992: 41). Cultural psychology therefore has a difficult task if it is confined to making foreign cultures comprehensible. Behind this attitude lies ethnocentrism, which assumes that other cultures become comprehensible only when they can be translated into our language and grasped by our scientific logic. Therefore it may sometimes occur to us not to translate words and phenomena because this forces us to see foreigners as they are, and not to transform them into something we can understand. Cultural sciences are therefore not aiming at a word-for-word translation, but rather on showing the relativism—the differences between the parties. The attempt to grasp what is fundamental to "aboriginal reality" by cloaking tradition with the mantle of "reality" can be a way of creating cultural stagnation and alienation (Bruner 1990: 27).

The term "culture" is too vague and ambiguous. It is rather a magic formula that omits some concrete problems: foreigners behave like this because they have another culture (Højholt 1992: 83). Cultural psychology is therefore something quite different, for instance, from making statistical descriptions of common psychological features in people of a specific culture or across cultures. Cultural psychology is a way of reflecting with the people who know their lives and culture best.

Cultural psychology and anthropology have been called "the uncomfortable sciences" (Kleinman 1988a: 145), because they often challenge daily knowledge, question values, and find hidden meanings in daily life. Cultural psychology has, for example, shown how other cultures' expressions can disturb our Western diagnostic concepts in such a way that some diseases are underdiagnosed and consequently treated too late, while other common conditions are defined as diseases. There are many examples of how clinical communication is disturbed and treatment becomes inadequate because of a lack of cross-cultural understanding (Estroff 1981, Kleinman & Good 1985, Kleinman 1988a, b, Rhodes 1984, Scheper-Hughes 1979).

However, the cultural theory of psychopathology and treatment does not aim at eliminating the psychodynamic way of thinking about, for example, the ego and the organization of the inner personality. Unfortunately, our Western therapies are interwoven with an individualistic concept that seldom emphasizes the social and cultural context.

The cultural psychologist wants to introduce the cultural world closely into the therapeutic context, and understand, for instance, the ambiguity of guilt and shame, instead of transferring the inner psychological descriptions from our society of guilt to foreign societies of shame. She wants to see depression and anxiety as much more than endogenous and psychodynamic features—as a culturally acceptable way of expressing one's difficulties—which, in their direct form, may be too problematic and humiliating to express in one's own culture. The foreigner is not only more family-oriented, emphasizing concepts of honor, and perhaps prepared to repay humiliations with acts of revenge; the sociocentric foreigner can also be very individualistic. Cultural psychology will therefore try not to make pathology out of every statement; it will not, for example, interpret physical complaints as somatizing and as expressions of the foreign culture's exotic and perhaps hysterical way of reacting.

Astonishment as a Motivation for Working with What Is Foreign

Cultural-psychological therapy involves curiosity about what is foreign, with both emotional and cognitive aspects. "Astonishment and the assortment of feelings that it brings with it—surprise, curiosity, excitement, enthusiasm, sympathy—are probably the affects most distinctive of the anthropological response to the difference and strangeness of 'others'" (Shweder 1991:1). It should be possible to make use of this astonishment in our treatment work to pose general cultural-psychological questions: What can we deduce from the apparent strangeness of a person's experiences and from his concepts of reality? What justifications are there for our own concepts of reality seen in the light of the apparent difference (Shweder 1991: 3)?

The principle of the cultural-psychological viewpoint is to widen the perspective and to place us in a position that demands reformulation and rethinking of our science. The cultural-psychological viewpoint can be necessary for both biologically oriented psychiatry and for humanistically oriented psychotherapy, just because it forces science and its field to become involved in other, different contexts. The cultural-psychological viewpoint thus presents a new perspective of scientific theory and a new way of thinking by means of the cultures instead of thinking about them, "thinking through cultures" (Shweder 1991).

But even though most researchers on cultures can agree on this goal, an element of seduction nevertheless sneaked its way into their practice, which has led to the fact that several important subjects have never been studied. Violence, war, and hunger should have been the most important fields of research, but hardly any studies have been published on them. It is as if the cultural sciences have been hit by the very same repressive mechanisms they try to fight.

One of the reasons is that the concept of culture may easily dangle in the air as a strangely vague entity. Thus, the cultural sciences encourage a sensitivity toward the "context" but in practice they find it difficult to define what it is. External factors become involved in a detached and haphazard way, and their interconnections are not conceptualized.

But in general, actions and meanings are something individual, and culture can be looked at as the condition and meaning structures between which the individual chooses and orients himself in his individual realization. Thus, "culture" is what is developed when together we realize our conditions as important and meaningful (Mørch 1991: 41). Culture is not something passive; it is created through individual human actions.

Culture-Bound Disease Entities

Based on cultural psychology, the previous chapter's focus on symptoms and treatments will be replaced by a consideration for the possibilities and action.

If a hypothesis is to be advanced about the existence of a torture syndrome as a diagnostic category, one has to start with the definition of a diagnosis in the cultural-psychological perspective. Is it possible, for instance, to have a diagnosis with different meanings in various cultures?

A diagnosis is a semiotic action in which the client's perceived symptoms are interpreted as signs of a certain pathological condition. By convention, all diagnoses are made in the same way, regardless of whether the condition is a stomach ulcer, a fractured knee, or a post-traumatic stress disorder. In practice, therefore, it means the transfer to mental diseases of the same attitude that is applied to medical diseases, namely, that the diagnosis refers to an "underlying" process. Even though diagnostic activity is said to be based on a "hypothetico-deductive" method (Kleinman 1988a: 8), there is an element of self-confirmation because as a rule the diagnosis is tested within the same diagnostic system as that in which the clinician has been brought up, to get order into his or her observations.

Some of the symptoms we consider to be signs of mental disease are ascribed in other cultures to moral and religious problems. But with us the diagnostic interpretation is an activity limited by the taxonomic system, with which we have been brought up, and we will therefore make interpretations within the same ordinary taxonomy. In practice, it has led to the medicalization of social problems; for example, many forms of alcoholism and criminality are labeled diseases. Despite the possible existence of some genetic and physiological factors in such processes, the problem is that increased medicalization, whether or not scientifically founded, may become a form of social control. The social system has been accused of medicalizing poverty problems, unemployment, and lack of education, and the therapeutic institutions of replacing some of the legal and religious institutions that used to function in society (Kleinman 1988a: 9, Stone 1984). In the same way, psychiatric diagnoses have been used by state authorities to control dissidents.

Culture is the unwritten social and psychiatric dictionary that we have memorized and then repressed. Increasing cross-cultural understanding, then, becomes the two-part task of bringing our own dictionary to the level of a fully conscious awareness, and then memorizing the dictionaries of others so that we can shift easily from one to another (Landrine 1995: 744).

Reactions that are specific for a certain culture have often been interpreted as distorted expressions of basic psychiatric diseases. This is known from clinical work with torture survivors when the complaints have been considered a "cultural disguise," for instance of a depressive condition, or when the torture syndrome with its flashback is taken for being a reactive psychotic condition. The problem with this paraphrasing is the hiding of the fact that the condition is more complex than is shown by these reductionistic diagnoses. The pattern of complaints is an expression of cultural complexity, a recognized behavior that can refer to anything from a medical disease to a normal aspect of grief.

There are several examples of how culture speaks through disease. Good et al. (1985) describe how complaints of "heart problems" in Iran are a condensed expression for several problems, a culturally sanctioned way of expressing difficulties both in the ill person's body and in his social and psychological relationships. Just the descriptive term "heart distress" opens the way for negotiations about changes in matrimony, family, work; thus, difficult life conditions are expressed metaphorically by using this term. The anthropologic literature is full of this kind of description of cultural expressions for diseases (Kleinman & Good 1985).

In particular, the metaphors in relation to the body are the subject of transcultural research. In all cultures, the body represents a symbolic source for the communication of problems and difficulties at the personal, social, and political levels (Turner 1985, Taussig 1987). In the case of torture it is the body that is exposed to mutilations; this makes expression with words difficult because the body is used as a metaphor and symbol of some very important fields, which often cannot be mentioned by means of language.

The Search for Absolute Disease Entities

There has been interest in developing standardized interviews and rating scales to examine the distribution of symptoms and syndromes in various cultures. The aim has been to draw conclusions about the nature of such phenomena in various parts of the world.

But it may be a source of error to believe that it is possible to study a disease category that has been developed in a certain part of the world and subsequently transferred to another culture in which the same disease may lack relevance and not be understood. For example, Landrine (1995) argues that the only culturally sensitive and professionally appropriate diagnosis we can give to minorities is "adjustment disorder," until an alternative taxonomy is constructed. In other words: the development of standardized tools for transcultural studies may lead to improved reliability of psychiatric diagnoses, but not necessarily to improved validity and understanding of the nature of the disease.

This discussion about methods in the study of culture-bound syndromes reflects the debate about universality or relativity and about the dichotomy between "ethic" and "emic" (Bracken 1993, Flaherty et al. 1988).

From a transcultural viewpoint, these discussions cover fundamental questions about what is considered normal in the culture in question, about how a disease is perceived and expressed, and whether a treatment succeeds or not—in short, about fundamental premises for the treatment system.

Already at the end of the 1960s, WHO started several studies using standardized methods to compare the occurrence of schizophrenia in various countries. Roughly speaking, it was found that schizophrenia was in general equally distributed, but that there was a difference in the occurrence of diagnostic subcategories, and that the course was better, shorter, and less chronically incapacitating in developing countries than in the industrialized world (Bleuler 1978, Harding et al. 1987, Kleinman 1988a: 47).

In the nonindustrialized parts of the world, there are more acute psychoses that are associated with serious traumatic situations in persons without premorbid features and in whom normal function returns in a matter of a few days (Murphy 1982, ref. from Kleinman 1988a: 36). One should therefore be prepared to see a larger number of short reactive psychoses in foreign cultures; they do not have the features of misdiagnosed schizophrenia or borderline psychotic outbreaks, but may sometimes be part of normal behavior, a culturally recognized trance condition that responds quickly to the treatment of local healers.

WHO's studies on depressive disorders in different cultures show that these do not have the same universal distribution as schizophrenia (Sartorius et al. 1983). However, the rates of depression and neurotic disorders are higher in refugees and immigrants (Beiser 1985, Beiser & Flemming 1986). In several psychiatric epidemiological studies, depression has been described as a sequela of exodus and deculturalization (Kleinman 1988a: 38).

It is only recently that scales have been developed for specifically documenting PTSD following the experience of torture, although the psychometric properties of these instruments have not yet been elucidated (Mollica & Caspi-Yavin 1992, McIvor & Turner 1995: 706).

In general, epidemiologic data do not support a radical, relativistic viewpoint that psychiatric diseases are not comparable across cultures. The main diagnostic categories are found everywhere.

It is mainly the smaller psychiatric problems that are expressed in culture-bound syndromes. Examples such as *latah*, *amok*, and *susto* occur only in non-Western cultures. By contrast, anorexia and agoraphobia are confined to the Western industrialized world. In the same way, there are also some cultures that resist certain problems such as alcoholism, which occurs very rarely in Middle Eastern Arabs but is very common in American Indians and Eskimos.

Though such epidemiologic studies are important for future research, it is remarkable that they have led to nothing but biological theories about diseases. This in itself should not be criticized, but the way in which the research has been carried out has created an interpretation of data that can become self-confirming and tautological for work with clients from foreign cultures. Thus, this type of epidemiologic study assumes homogeneity of the client material; clients with the greatest difference between the cultures were therefore excluded. But just these heterogeneous patient populations have great interest from a culture-psychologic viewpoint because they can throw light on the great diversity of cultures.

In the search for absolute disease entities, psychological, social, and cultural aspects have an important function concerning the biologic processes. The professional "disease" category becomes the proper unit, the object that is hidden in the cultural and popular "illness" disguise. Thus the diagnosis becomes a reduction, a semiotic interpretation of the disease process's vague contradictory and changing symptoms of illness. Endogenous depression is therefore assumed to arise relatively independently of social and psychological conditions, as a biological disorder, in contrast to reactive depression, which to a larger extent is a reaction to the demands of the surroundings and personal experiences. By contrast, in a culture-psychologic context, the starting point will be the popular "illness" experience from which the culture can be understood (Elsass 1988).

The solution is not to give preference to one model at the expense of the other. There are studies, for example, that show that the social and psychological component of the illness experience of chronic pain is a decisive factor in whether the client goes to work, independent of the existence of a biological abnormality (Osterweis et al. 1987). However, there are also studies that show that biological abnormalities and genetic dispositions make some clients more vulnerable than others to schizophrenia and depression (Kleinman 1988a: 25).

A usable model must contain a dialectic interplay between biological and cultural processes. Sometimes one of them will have more influence on the disease's manifestations than the other, but it is the relationship between the two factors that is more important than the factors separately. The dialectic interplay changes the view of disease physiology in such a way that it becomes an inseparable part of the personal experience and the social and cultural interaction.

Cultural Psychology: More Than Direct Translation

Unfortunately, psychiatry is a theoretically underdeveloped area that has had difficulties in integrating anthropological theories and concepts (Kleinman 1988a). The cross-cultural field has therefore been characterized by very prosaic translations. Questionnaires, rating scales, and psychometric instruments have been translated by bilingual experts, and the validity has been examined by translating "blindly" back to the language from which they originated, to see if there was still agreement. The reliability is checked by examining whether the correlation coefficients are the same in the new version and in the original, and the validity by conducting some thorough qualitative interviews (Flaherty et al. 1988).

But in anthropological and cultural-psychological research, the translation work has another priority: it is, in a much wider sense, a description of ways of thinking, categories, types of communication, and behavior patterns that are always placed in a context that will give a valid understanding. It is much more than linguistic translation; it is an attempt to place observations and structural categories in a context in which the translation itself adds to increased theoretical knowledge. In the research interview it is therefore necessary to operationalize one's concepts and transform them into a series of questions in which the phenomenology and meaning of the symptoms are examined and not only crossed off on a check list (Mishler 1986).

There are several examples of how questionnaires lose their validity and meaning through translation without additional culture analysis (Kleinman 1988a: 29). Some ethnic groups, such as Latin Americans, southern Europeans, and Asians express more pain, anxiety, and depression than is the West European standard (Kleinman 1988a: 31). But it is difficult to draw conclusions as to whether such foreign cultures are more expressive and symptom-producing. There are, for example, epidemiological studies that show that blacks in the United States, despite their socially worse situation, report fewer complaints than whites, perhaps because it has become part of their survival strategy to reach a higher frustration tolerance (Dohrenwend 1966, ref. from Kleinman 1988a: 31). Other studies have focused on the social context of the interviews; for example, blacks in the United States expressed more symptoms when interviewed by blacks than by whites (Dohrenwend 1966, Kleinman 1988a: 31). The finding that many people from non-Western cultures are more liable to react with somatic symptoms for psychological problems is more frequent when the client is examined at the doctor's office or in treatment institutions, whereas the frequency declines when the clients are interviewed in their own homes. The clients complied with the doctor's wishes by presenting physical symptoms, whereas their complaints in their own surroundings are different. Thus, foreigners often exaggerate our cultural conventions when they come to us for treatment while their symptoms have another form and meaning in their own culture (Helman 1990, Sachs 1989: 125).

Anxiety and Depression

Several previously mentioned aspects of the torture syndrome change between, on the one hand, fitting uniquely to the person, and, on the other hand, being parts of general features of the culture. Culture-bound symptoms are individual features that take shape from the special culture of which the person is a part. In practice they are seen in the torture survivor when several complaints, such as anxiety, depression, and experiences of guilt and shame, sound differently to the Western therapist when compared with the concepts in the survivor's own culture.

The somatic component in particular can be culture-bound, and studies have found a predominance of somatic symptoms in depressed and anxious clients from non-Western cultures, though these symptoms are also common in Western societies (Kleinman & Good 1985, Kleinman 1988a: 41).

Furthermore, there is also a difference in disease behavior, for example in the referral pattern. There is a greater readiness in Western cultures to consult professional therapists; in other cultures, psychiatric diseases can be something one tries to hide from others, something that is preferably treated within the family (Kleinman 1988a: 45).

The combination of culture-universal and culture-specific symptoms of depression and anxiety has been described in Iranians (Good et al. 1985) and Chinese (Kleinman & Kleinman 1985). The experience of guilt in combination with depression is mainly a Western phenomenon (Murphy 1982), and suicide is less common in depressed clients in the Third World (Headley 1983, Kleinman 1988a: 43). Persons with psychological depression are preoccupied with guilt and negative ego experiences, which lead more easily to suicide than in the client with somatic symptoms. One can therefore suggest the hypothesis that somatization per se protects against suicide, and that somatized depression has an easier course than psychological depression.

One of the big problems in working with torture survivors is to know whether their anxiety and depressive symptoms are signs of pathology (Torture 1993). Western psychiatry has made great progress in demonstrating well-defined biochemical changes, in particular in depressive conditions, and has developed several very potent psychoactive drugs. It would be irresponsible not to use this knowledge in the therapy of the culture-foreign client. But developments within biological psychiatry should not lead to culture-conditioned arrogance on the part of Western therapists.

Transcultural research shows considerable variation in depressive emotional levels, symptoms, and diseases in different cultures (Kleinman & Good 1985). The biologically orientated psychiatrist in particular would be interested to know whether her nosological categories are the same in different cultures. But if we have only established psychiatry as the professional starting point, we run the risk, as mentioned before, of arguing in tautological circles, because we describe the disease with the same machinery of concepts toward which we turn later to make it more likely that our treatments are correct (see page 30). It will be of more interest for the cultural psychologist to investigate how depressive symptoms reveal a person's relationship with society, and the influence of society on the individual. Here, for instance, depression will manifest itself as grief, which has to be translated and interpreted in order to identify a hidden meaning in a hidden system, that is, a sort of social arrangement that produces its own meaning in a society. In this perspective, the medical treatment of depressive symptoms presents a problem because it isolates the client from his social and cultural context.

Learned Helplessness and the Meaning of Symptoms

Many torture survivors describe how they were broken down by the unpredictability of the torture and its lack of consistency (see pages 10 and 43). Among the most frustrating aspects were the unpredictable changes in attitude of the torturer, between anger and friendliness, and the continuation of the torture, whether or not the victim confessed. This uncontrollable situation provokes the anxiety and helplessness that are the basis of the subsequent depression. The external traumas are transferred and changed to inner personal feelings. Single specific events become internalized to a generalized helplessness, with a negative self-concept and overdimensioned experiences of guilt and shame.

But it is difficult to attribute depression in the torture survivor to a learned helplessness. There are, for example, no studies to show that one can simply add up a person's negative experiences and show that the more often he has experienced a lack of relationship between action and result, the more easily he becomes depressed. It is not the negative events per se that are important for the depression, but rather the meaning given them by the individual.

Depressive symptoms often have a quite different meaning for torture survivors than for Westerners. It is, after all, doubtful whether, outside the European-American psychiatric tradition, one can apply symptoms such as feeling low, decreased interest, decreased energy, or increased tiredness as symptoms of depression.

Depression is associated with feelings of sin and guilt in only a few societies outside Judeo-Christian culture. Buddhism even claims that generalized hopelessness is one's personal lot, and that salvation consists in understanding and reliving this hopelessness (Kleinman & Good 1985: 134). To the Buddhist, life is suffering and grief, and the cause of grief is attachment to wishes and demands; it is only recognition of the ultimate hopelessness that makes transcendence and salvation possible. In the same way, grief is a religious experience for Shiite Muslims, for whom the ability to experience intense dysphoria is a sign of deep understanding and maturity. By contrast, Balinese people, in particular from Thai-Lao, consider it a virtue to balance emotional heights and depths; only this leveling can maintain a stable and harmonious life.

In Western society, however, depressive feelings exist in a more freely flowing form and are not in the same way tied to a cosmology and context (Obeyesekere 1985: 138). This is one reason why depressive symptoms are easier to identify and treat as disease. But in other societies, depressive feelings have become articulated within religion, and in many places the suffering is the beginning of religious transformation and liberation. In such a context, depression is not part of professional treatment work, but rather part of "culture's work." Depression is outside pathologizing and is managed via displacement of the inner private world to a social ideology and further on to a public world of meanings and symbols.

Even though depression in the Western world has a looser attachment to a social context than in other parts of the world, Western ideology has also been gradually developed with respect to its treatment. Within crisis therapy intervention, we often consider depression as the result of an unfinished and unsuccessful grief-work. Loss is followed by grief, but if it does not come to an end, it leads to pathological grief reactions with weakening of the ego-feeling and subsequent hopelessness. Quite correctly, there is a difference between grief and depression, but if grief becomes chronic, pathological reactions will follow. Reactive depression arises because the client is no longer able to identify the real loss. In a psychodynamic sense, the client must compensate for an object loss by transforming his or her previous attachments to new objects. In a certain way it can be said that the person's inner and original object relations will always be the same, but that their shape changes. An object is exchanged with another, the shape changes; but the inner psychodynamic balance remains the same.

Grief therapists in Western cultures must appeal to this inner constant in the person, because there is no external constant as in other cultures, for example in the shape of a conviction about something immortal and reincarnated. Depressive symptoms, particularly according to biomedical concepts, are interpreted without any reference to internal or external constants. By surrendering to the biological treatment, which can be very effective in certain contexts, one of the great costs will be renunciation of the meaning-giving in the "culture work."

Guilt and Shame Cultures

Terms relating to feelings appear so often in our language that it is tempting to date them to Adam and Eve; this is widespread in all cultures. Such widespread terms include guilt and shame, but to try to uncover the phenomena to which they refer, and look at them in a cultural context, provides a key to the understanding of foreign cultures.

Psychological problems such as bad conscience, suicide attempts, introverted depressions, and lack of self-promotion are seen as the result of the "culture of guilt" in Christian, Western culture. By contrast, Middle Eastern and Arab societies have been called "the culture of shame," with psychological problems that are characterized by somatic expressions, fewer suicides, but more extrovert actions to make good one's esteem in the family and the local society (Shehadeh 1989, 1991).

To start with, the feeling of guilt can be considered an internal phenomenon, whereas shame is an external phenomenon caused by a need to obtain recognition by other people. Guilt can be felt as a gnawing tension between our ego and our conscience, but it does not present specific external features that other people can notice. By contrast, shame can express itself by a specific physical sign that others can interpret, such as blushing. Shame is a fundamental human feeling that arises when others, or we ourselves, evaluate ourselves in relation to society's ideals and determine that we are weak, insufficient, worthless, and unloved (Vanggaard 1991: 161).

In West European culture we know guilt well from the suffering, conflict-ridden, and depressive person. Hamlet is an example of how the feeling of guilt arises from an unhappy situation, which is transformed to an inner continuous fight characterized by indecisiveness and paralysis of action. We experience an inner power, which rules us with strength and authority, and to which we can be either faithful or unfaithful, obedient or disobedient (Vanggaard 1991: 165). According to which side we choose, we have a clear or bad conscience, but only we ourselves need know something about our inner harmony or disharmony, about our inner clashes and our pangs of conscience.

Benedict, who studied the differences between so-called shame and guilt cultures, mentioned Japan as an example of a shame culture (Benedict 1979), which has another concept of being faithful to oneself. To have self-respect means that you are obliged to make sure that others respect you and you should abstain from all that can provoke the disapproval of other people. It is meaningless to refer to a clear conscience vis-à-vis the Japanese; they have no conscience in our sense of the word. Their self-respect comes from a comparison of their surroundings—that is, as a result of this overview, they shrewdly evaluate and weigh all the factors in a situation. We say, "Listen to your conscience"; in Japan they say, "Guard your reputation" (Vanggaard 1991: 165).

The experience of sin and guilt can be neutralized by remorse, confession, and forgiveness in Christian cultures, but something similar does not hold for the Japanese. They do not feel inner tension when others know nothing about their actions. A confession will not ease them; on the contrary, it may lead to feeling further insulted. For them, the abolition of shame takes place by the restoration of honor, possibly by revenge.

We find this kind of life in the old Nordic sagas, in which shame, revenge, and honor were the basic elements of one's life but Christianity led to another attitude. Before Christianity, a man had full command over himself and his body, but after the Fall came uncontrollable instincts and desires. Today this unruliness is seen particularly in relation to our sexuality, which has become full of problems and a source of guilt and remorse. In Japan and several other cultures, sexuality is not an area that can generate guilt and shame in the same way; nakedness is not shameful, and erotic lust is quite legitimate when it is kept in its correct place. The Japanese language has no word for perversion (Vanggaard 1991: 167).

Differences such as this between guilt and shame cultures may have a decisive influence on psychotherapeutic work with torture survivors. People from guilt cultures depend on an inner power. They can feel relief for their bad conscience by revealing it to others, for instance if they have informed against friends under torture. People from shame cultures depend on the attitude of the surroundings and may feel it is unimportant or at worst defamatory to have to find some inner motives and feelings for a situation in which they have been humiliated during torture, for example.

Aggression, Suicide, and Morals

The different attitudes toward guilt and shame are reflected in relation to aggression. Open person-to-person aggression will more often be conscience-ridden and cause inner conflicts in guilt cultures than in shame cultures. Thus, the demand of psychotherapy to work with inner conflicts in a closed, confidential room is more in agreement with West European culture and with torture survivors who belong to the educated middle class and are used to our psychologized ways of interpretation.

In a comparative study of Greek and Danish women who had attempted suicide, the Greek group was more marked by shame, and their suicidal actions were directed toward others in a more aggressive or appealing way. By contrast, the Danish women were a less visible group, marked by guilt feelings and self-reproach, and the suicidal attempts were to a much lesser extent directed toward others (Arcel 1986).

The feeling of shame is used as a tool of child-rearing in the Arab world. The child is brought up to unconditional acceptance of parental and teacher authority and is sometimes untouched by the content of what is taught, because he is busy reproducing and repeating. If the child says or does something wrong, he may be corrected by being ridiculed. The effect of being laughed at is just as painful as being beaten, and it is an effective way of being made to feel humiliated. Part of self-consciousness is thus created by loss of self-confidence and fear of being laughed at. The child is trained to feel shame, though not necessarily by an inner understanding of having done something wrong. The ability to self-criticize is not promoted as in Western culture; instead, a social feeling is built up toward the pressure and criticism of others (Shehadeh 1989: 16). One can certainly say in Arabic, "I am ashamed of myself" ("ana khajlan min nafsi"), but "I" and "myself" do not refer to the same thing; the meaning is rather, "Please excuse me if I hurt your feelings" (Shehadeh 1989: 17). Shame is produced more by what the person thinks that others think about him, than by what he thinks of himself. Thus, the child may not feel responsible and guilty of a wrong action.

The morals codices reflect the various attitudes toward guilt and shame. Within the ethics of honor/family, the values are concrete; honor and shame are the most important values, and they are interpreted by the family and the local society. Within the ethics of fairness/individual codex, the values are abstract and interpreted by institutions such as schools and universities in parallel with the family.

An important value is the right of the individual to shape his or her own life; control takes place by making others feel guilt and by rewarding "appropriate" performance. No society is controlled exclusively by one code of ethics or the other; both feelings are part of ethical control, but occur in different forms in different societies. The code of honor/family is attached mainly to agrarian, patriarchal societies with feudal elements. The fairness/individual codex is connected with middle-class, industrialized societies (Arcel 1986: 172).

The Public and the Private Room

In the eyes of west Europeans, Arab and Islamic societies are marked by a form of ambivalence that we do not know in the same way. In the culture of shame there is a tendency to look at the state as a legal person, and it is not necessarily disgraceful to cheat that person. But at the same time, the state is shown a loyalty similar to the loyalty shown to one's family. The state is an authority one serves, and whose needs and wishes one follows—not as in the West, where the state is at our service and has become an administrative vehicle almost without identity, given the task of fulfilling our demands. The task of the citizen in Islamic society is to guard the honor of the nation, for example by not publicizing its weaknesses, such as the use of torture. The ethnic minorities can think as they like in private, but when they go public they must be careful not to break their loyalty toward the state.

Shame presents different faces in the private and in the public room. For example, there are two terms for honor in Turkish: *Namus*, which is similar to our word for "virtue," and *sjeref*, which is similar to our "sense of justice." If a girl is raped, she loses her virtue and honor but is not considered shameful. She is considered shameful, however, if she relinquishes her virtue on her own initiative. But regardless of whether the girl is losing her *namus* voluntarily or by violation, the other concept of honor is involved and demands punishment of the guilty. If this does not happen, it means dishonor for the person involved and for the family. The guilty one must therefore be executed, and the same applies to the girl if she lost her virtue voluntarily.

This distinction between public and private ideas of honor may be the reason why some torture survivors do not want to talk about their trauma, because in their minds they have been deprived of their honor. They do not understand that, by giving words to the torture, they can be helped in a psychological sense by doing something to bring them out of the situation in which their ability to act was paralyzed. Instead, they think according to public concepts of shame, that mentioning the trauma will only create even more shame. In the same way, people are willing to tell a lie when their personal honor is involved, since they consider it more dishonorable to admit the act than to carry it out. Some civil servants thus deny in public that torture takes place in their country, though they know very well that it does. They consider it more dishonorable to admit to it than that it is there, and they consider it disloyal of others to publish information to that effect.

The desire for revenge is more attached to the conception of justice than to anger, and what paralyzes torture victims subsequent to torture is more a feeling of powerlessness and paralysis of the ability to act than an inner psychological blocking of anger and rage. Therefore, if the therapist primarily appeals to torture survivors in order to make them identify so-called suppressed feelings, the therapeutic effect will be nil. Instead, it may be better to appeal to the "construction of meaning" and to the restoration of honor by asking them to do something. The helplessness and inactivity will be considered dishonorable by others, whereas their attempts to become active persons, again trying to join the family and the circle of friends on equal terms with other members, can make them avoid the feeling of shame.

In the West European therapy room, the survivor's helplessness can thus be increased if focus is put only on the inner psychological forces without seeing the shame and dishonor attached to the revelation to others of his defeat and trauma. Treatment is only appropriate if the therapist is able to give the survivor an understanding of the therapy room as one from which shame is excluded. The testimony method can therefore be a very dubious treatment in certain Islamic cultures, just as psychotherapy may be. The testimony method has been developed in Latin American contexts and has been very effective there, but it cannot be applied immediately in other contexts.

Individual Cultural Expression

Finally, some reservations are necessary. The relationship between guilt and shame, which manifests itself in so many different combinations, is specific for each individual in such a way that it is impossible to talk about a culture as being either a "guilt" or "shame" culture. Furthermore, within the same country, there are such big differences in the concept of cosmology and in cognition between uneducated villagers and educated academics that they are sometimes larger than the differences between representatives from different countries. The difference between a middle-class citizen from a Middle Eastern country and one from the United States may be much smaller than between a poor villager and a well-educated academic within the same country. The distinction between guilt and shame cultures therefore provides only guideline categories for transcultural understanding.

More recent concepts of culture challenge the validity of the viewpoint that culture comprises some cognitive schematizations that are generally widespread in a minority. Instead, culture is today considered a form of value orientation, an attitude and some ethical principles that are embodied in and experienced by the people of a community at a certain place. This viewpoint respects the fact that there may be great mutual differences, even within the same cultural group, based for instance on sex or on social and political standpoints.

The realities of health and illness are shaped by ongoing interpersonal interactions—negotiations at the levels of perception, cognition, expressed emotions, and values, all of which are involved in strategies for daily coping that may be constrained, but certainly not determined, by human psychophysiology (Lewis-Fernández & Kleinman 1994: 68). The interpersonal process combines the social world and the body. The individual reality is a lived experience of all these perceptions, opinions, and feelings at many different levels. In this context a depression becomes something that can be referred to only as an inner clash between body and self, which also takes place at social levels, for instance as an expression of demoralization because of a political regime, of conflict at a work site or in marriage, or of the loss of a social network.

A therapist must accept that self and personality are more pluralistic and changeable than our departmentalized thinking can understand; only the changeability is culturally determined. The self and the personality are more ambiguous than previously assumed by both the egocentric and the socio-centric concepts, and society is a unique mixture of egocentric and socio-centric traces.

In short: in the understanding of the torture survivor we have to be prepared for complexity.

Summary and Clinical Applications

• War and political persecution lead to forced migration and a confrontation with cultures that are different from the Western context, in which psychotherapy was created and developed. More than three-quarters of the world's population live in non–Western cultures, and more than 90 percent are not familiar with our psychotherapeutic constructions.

• Astonishment and the assortment of feelings it brings with it—surprise, curiosity, excitement, enthusiasm, sympathy—are among the emotions that can well describe the differences and strangeness among "others." This "astonishment" should be used in our treatment work to pose general cultural-psychological questions: What can we deduce from the apparent strangeness of a person's experiences and from his concepts of reality? What justifications are there for our own concepts of reality seen in the light of the apparent difference? The principle of the cultural-psychological viewpoint is to widen the perspective and to place us in a position that demands the reformulation and rethinking of our science—thinking by means of the cultures instead of thinking about them, and thinking through cultures.

• Many cultures take no interest in the introspection that psychotherapy takes for granted; they are ashamed of talking about psychological problems and do not speak about intimate personal matters with strangers outside their family. Usually they do not have the understanding of a "professional friendship," which psychotherapy implies.

• Western psychotherapy is based on egocentricity; psychological problems are ascribed more to forces of the ego than to external social and cultural conditions. However, most parts of the world have a sociocentric ideology that places individual experiences in a network of social relationships, which are the source of self-esteem, self-realization, and self-control. In other cultures, interhuman obligation and loyalty are more important than individual personality features. Furthermore, many non-Western cultures do not isolate the cause of disease or ill health in a formal scientific sense, but apply a wider approach.

• Reaching a common cultural understanding in psychotherapeutic work takes more than the therapist's knowing about the survivor's culture and respecting its peculiarities. To a certain extent, it is just this difference between the two parties that should be used as an active therapeutic ingredient. "Culture" is not something one talks about, but a position from which one talks. In other words, it is something one sees with, rather than what one sees.

• The cultural psychologist wants to introduce the cultural world closely into the therapeutic context, and, for instance, to see depression and anxiety as much more than endogenous and psychodynamic features. Mental symptoms may be a culturally acceptable way of expressing one's difficulties, which, in their direct form, may be too problematic and humiliating to express in one's own culture.

• The foreigner may be prone to diagnostic problems because some of the symptoms that we consider to be signs of mental disease are ascribed in other cultures to moral and religious problems. Reactions that are specific to a certain culture have often been interpreted as distorted expressions of basic psychiatric diseases. Until an alternative taxonomy is constructed, the only culturally sensitive and professionally appropriate diagnosis we can give to minorities is "adjustment disorder."

• It is particularly the metaphors in relation to the body that are the subject of transcultural differences. In the case of torture, it is the body that is exposed to mutilations; this makes expression with words difficult because the body is used as a metaphor and symbol of some very important fields, which often cannot be mentioned by use of language. In the clinical interview it is therefore necessary to operationalize one's concepts and transform them to a series of questions in which the phenomenology and meaning of the symptoms are examined and not, for example, just crossed off on a checklist.

• Depression is associated with feelings of sin and guilt in only a few societies outside Judeo-Christian culture. It is, after all, doubtful whether, outside the Euro-American psychiatric tradition, one can apply symptoms such as feeling low, decreased interest, decreased energy, or increased tiredness as symptoms of depression. But in other societies, depressive feelings have become articulated within religion, and often the suffering is the beginning of religious transformation and liberation. In such a context, depression is not part of professional treatment work, but rather part of "culture's work." By surrendering to Western grief therapy and especially to biological treatment, one of the great costs is renunciation of the meaning-giving in the "culture work."

• The difference between guilt and shame cultures may have a decisive influence on psychotherapeutic work with torture survivors. People from guilt cultures depend on an inner power. They can get relief from their bad conscience by confessing to others, for instance if they had informed against friends under torture. People from shame cultures depend on the attitude of those in their surroundings and may feel it without importance or, at worst, consider it defamatory to seek inner motives and feelings for a situation in which they were humiliated, as during torture.

• Shame presents different faces in the private and in the public sphere. The task of the citizen in Islamic society, for example, is to guard the honor of the nation, for instance by not publicizing its weaknesses, such as the use of torture. The ethnic minorities can think as they like in private, but when they go public they must be careful not to break their loyalty toward the state.

• The distinction between public and private ideas of honor may be the reason why some torture survivors do not want to speak about their trauma—because they have been deprived of their honor. They do not understand that, by talking about the torture, they can be helped in a psychological sense, because in that way they are doing something to bring them out of the situation in which their ability to act was paralyzed. Instead, they think according to public concepts of shame, that is, mentioning the trauma will create even more shame. Treatment is only appropriate if the therapist is able to give the survivor an understanding of the therapy room as a place from which shame is excluded. The testimony method can therefore be a very dubious treatment in certain Islamic cultures, just as psychotherapy can be.

• The desire for revenge is more related to the concept of justice than to anger. What paralyzes torture victims from foreign cultures is more a feeling of powerlessness and paralysis of the ability to act than an inner psychological blocking of anger and rage. Therefore, if the therapist appeals to torture survivors primarily to make them identify so-called suppressed feelings, the therapeutic effect will be nil. Instead, it may be better to appeal to the "construction of meaning" and to the restoration of honor by asking them to do something.

5

Cultural-Psychological Treatment

Examples of Psychotherapy Showing Respect for Foreign Cultures

Meeting a foreigner gives rise to some fundamental considerations with respect to the effect mechanisms of psychotherapy. Change occurs, as Mead said, when two cultures intervene in each other, such as "another's image of myself incorporated inside me and opposed to my own image of myself" (Mead 1932). Thus, the therapeutic session with a foreigner is not a collision between different explanatory models, but rather an interplay in which one sees oneself in the light of the other.

But consideration should be given to whether psychotherapeutic assistance to torture survivors is a transference reaction due to our bad conscience, when we only react to parts of their traumatized situation without paying due respect to their foreign cultural background. Our treatment system ignores the fact that more than three-quarters of the world's population do not belong to Western culture. Perhaps the offer of psychotherapeutic help is an ethnocentric reaction to political violence, one where the assistance consists in introducing them to Western ideas of treatment.

Psychotherapy therefore implies an answer to some fundamental questions: Will the torture survivor be able to understand that the intimate relationship that goes with the therapy is not friendship, but performance of professional assistance? Can the torture survivor accept that the relationship that develops between him and the therapist in the confines of the treatment room is confidential, and that it does not necessarily require that his family and friends be informed and involved in the same way as he may be used to in his home country? Does the torture survivor understand that he himself must help to create the therapeutic story that has a healing effect, or does he believe that the therapist should be the active one who delivers the healing lecture, as may be familiar to him in his own culture? Are there subjects such as sexual experiences or criticism of his parents that cannot be put into words because they can cause taboo-like experiences of guilt and shame?

In answering these questions, cultural psychology cannot be required to act as a data base, to be consulted every time a foreign culture is approached. To a certain extent, the client himself should function as this data base, and the way in which the questions are put should reflect the therapist's own lack of knowledge; in an honest way the role of the therapist should be "the ignorant knowing one."

There are very few publications in which cultural psychology deals with methods of treating foreigners (see review in Sue et al. 1994). Some papers, such as that of Hiok-Boon (1983), suggest how the therapist can respect the foreigner's individuality:

1. Train each member of the therapeutic team in the cultural perceptions of disease and health and the treatment traditions that are typical for the ethnic group from which the clients come.
2. Learn their language or be sure to have good interpreters.
3. Find out how much the clients know about your culture, and how much they have become "deculturized" from their own.
4. Spend more time with the clients.
5. Search for the clients' explanatory models and their expectations of the treatment.
6. Examine your own therapeutic practice together with the clients and be ready to stop the treatment if the difference between yours and the clients' concepts is too large.

But even though prescriptive rules express respect toward a client's particular cultural background, they are too vague. Cultural psychology has developed beyond the stage of being an invitation to be more knowledgeable and to show more respect.

The Cultural-Psychological Method

Earlier it was thought that it is possible to get rid of culture-bound concepts by studying how demarcated ethnic groups perceive health and disease, and what are their specific concepts about the self regarding one's body and health. But today the science of cultural psychology is characterized more by a special attitude toward foreigners, a method close to that employed in anthropologic fieldwork (Hastrup & Ramløv 1988). It involves home visits, participation in some of the group's common activities, visits to their own gathering places such as restaurants, clubs, and perhaps their religious centers. The interview can take the form of a mini-ethnography (Kleinman 1988a: 155), which reveals the family's history and studies its ethnic culture, for instance based on its myths and religion. The way of constructing a history and a meaning is central—with all its metaphors, its twists and plots, and its progressive change between the illness narrative and the local context.

The fieldwork method demands a theoretical foundation. To understand the meaning and significance of the disease, it may be necessary to supplement the therapeutic method with anthropologic theories about language, metaphors, interpretation, and representation (Clifford & Marcus 1986, Geertz 1973, Hastrup & Ramløv 1989, Lakoff & Johnson 1980, Rosaldo 1980). One may also need more general information about ethno-medical and culture-specific subjects within the social sciences, and obtain some leads from journals such as *Social Science in Medicine, Medical Anthropology, Culture, Medicine and Psychiatry*, and *The Medical Anthropology Quarterly*.

But if the treatment's goal is to bring about an understanding that makes use of the differences between the two explanatory systems, the most obvious is to use the clients themselves. The differences should appear in the therapy room, in which the very comprehension of the differences is an essential therapeutic effect mechanism.

The working method is not necessarily the nondirective way of questioning with open questions such as "Tell me more about that" or by emphasizing and underlining the last statement from the client. Some of the clients from non-Western cultures will simply not take part in this form of conversation and will block and repeat the same statement again and again. Sticking to one's traditional psychotherapeutic nondirective attitude may make a very large part of the world's population appear alexithymic. They are not prepared to expose their feelings in a dyadic professional situation opposite a passive therapist (Prince 1987: 116).

Cultural psychology's method is to build up sensitivity toward what is implicitly taken for granted, and to accept that the meeting with the foreigner will lead to a reexamination of one's own categorizations. In the interview, the questions should always center on why the foreigner thinks the way he does about the surrounding world and about his problems. The method focuses strongly on the other's viewpoints, and compares them with one's own in such a way that one systematically becomes aware of one's own prejudices and attitudes. For a period, therefore, one may have to be actively talking about and explaining one's own attitude and practice. The point of reference is a respectful attitude to the alternative knowledge, which is considered comparable with, though different from, one's own understanding—a constant swinging between lay perspective and scientific thinking, between the foreigner's self-understanding and one's own, between the lived experience and the scientific observation. It is therefore the cultural perspective rather than a specific content that is cultural psychology's fundamental contribution to treatment.

But this demand for relativism and continuous negotiations between lay and professional knowledge across the cultures should not change the therapist into a romantic chameleon that "goes native." The work with torture survivors requires one to stand firm and to take a moral and ethical standpoint against repression, degeneration, destruction, violence, and suffering.

Comparison of Non-Western and Western Treatment Practices

In general, psychotherapeutic work has the character of symbolic healing with a mutual verbal exchange that takes place with the help of illness narratives, metaphors, and rituals, sometimes followed in parallel with body language. If psychotherapy is considered a symbolic negotiation with respect to the client's symptoms and illness narrative, with the aim of relief and possible cure, it is practiced in all cultures.

Thus, it is in use in most non-Western cultures under the terms of "shamanism" and "healing," usually within the popular sector, the family, and the local society, that is, in nonbureaucratic and private contexts. In Western culture, however, it is used within the public professional institutions, often without direct links to the local society and the family.

With us, psychotherapy is usually linked with psychiatry and clinical psychology, and implicitly with their scientific approach, from which it gets prestige and recognition. In other cultures the treatment's ideology and theory are based on a mentality that reaches far beyond diseases and penetrates large parts of the culture. The idea of disease may be connected with a general cosmology, as in the balance between Nature's individual parts, such as Yin and Yang, cold and warmth.

This distinction between a narrow Western scientific, possibly biomedical, way of thinking and a broader non-Western cultural mentality is perhaps more obvious. Analyses of the Western health system have shown that culture is expressed also in its medical system, and that treatment is a manifestation of social control and social cosmology (Helman 1990, Kleinman 1988a). In the West, social and cultural problems are medicalized and transformed from moral and legal difficulties into therapeutic questions. Our treatment ideology also exceeds its limits by making various interhuman difficulties the subject of therapy and clinical psychology; medical and psychological viewpoints vis-à-vis humans have become an all-embracing practice (Michelsen 1989). Some typical differences between Western and non-Western treatment practices have emerged.

In our institutionalized treatment, the meeting between therapist and client takes place in a dyadic way in a closed room; the therapist may perhaps encourage the client to bring a few family members. In other cultures, treatment is often public, for example as part of religious rituals within the local society. Many others can hear what the client and the therapist are talking about, and diagnosis and treatment are of public concern. In Western society, we aim at an egalitarian exchange in which the client's autonomy and self-determination are emphasized. This contrasts with other cultures, in which the therapist usually takes on an authoritarian and actively talking and acting position. It can therefore be said that the Western way of treatment is egocentric and the non-Western is sociocentric (see page 92).

The clinical exchange between healer and client in non-Western cultures may be somatic, psychological, moral, and religious; it may include ways of speaking that specify the social roles for therapy and care. With us, the exchange often takes place in the public health system and is more limited in its expressions; we can find similarities with non-Western healing only within the alternative sector. Non-Western healers often use supportive techniques, sometimes based on suggestion and charisma. In the local society, the healer is an authority who cannot be fitted into a larger public system. He will often try to avoid regulations and public state control, and is thus working on the fringes of what is legal. The client has no guarantee of confidentiality and is powerless if anything goes wrong. In Western society, however, legal issues are of great importance, and there are clear laws on right of access to documents and duty to inform, and there are committees, including lawyers, that deal with patients' complaints.

Referential versus Indexical Self: Egocentric versus Sociocentric Treatment

Many concepts are so basic in our thinking and behaving that we do not even imagine that they might have other connotations. Time is taken for granted as a valuable and natural resource that should be used wisely, managed, and saved (Landrine 1995: 745). But in other cultures, the experience of past and present is so different from ours that the psychoanalytic attitude is almost impossible to incorporate into a therapeutic attitude. In other cultures, punctuality has a different significance than in ours, and belief in reincarnation—life after death—for example, may have a fundamental influence in blaming a former, earlier trauma on the current behavior.

The self is perhaps the most basic of such culturally shaped concepts, which are difficult to make explicit. In Western culture, "the self is presumed to be a cognitive and emotional universe, the center of awareness, emotion, judgment, and action" (Landrine 1995: 747). Fundamental in Western psychopathology is that one's thoughts and feelings are experienced as emanating from somewhere other than the self, and that they are controlled by someone other than the self.

The self is the final explanation for behavior and is responsible for behavior (Landrine 1995: 748). In this referential construction of the self, social units are presumed to exist in order to meet the self's needs. But this referential conception of the self is unknown among the vast majority of the world's people. The alternative concept of the person is the indexical self, a sociocentric construction that does not have traits or needs of its own in isolation from its other relationships and contexts. In a therapeutic setting, for example, it implies that the self is not a separate entity that can be referred to or reflected upon in isolation. The non-Western client has difficulty with "tell me something about yourself" and instead gives long, detailed descriptions about concrete interactions with others. Externalization and projections are more evident. Family and communities are given priority over individuals, and therapy may entail or necessitate a renegotiation of the construction of the self by and for all members of the relationship. Treating the minority client in isolation is perhaps the most frequent cross-cultural, psychotherapeutic error.

Group therapy has not been widely used partly because groups in countries of asylum may lack cohesiveness, if they consist of people from differing political, ethnic, and linguistic backgrounds (McIvor & Turner 1995: 708). Only a few attempts have been made to use such therapy. Fischman and Ross (1990) have developed a model for time-limited group therapy for exiled torture survivors. Landrine suggests a "cultural triage model" of intervention to prevent the Western isolation of the self. In this approach, a Western clinician, a folk healer from the culture and/or an authority from the community in question, and the family meet and agree on several conceptualizations of the problems. Then a multicultural/multilevel course of treatment can take place with the Western clinician, the indigenous healer, and the family (Landrine 1995: 759).

Thus in sociocentric cultures, the self tends to be seen as not responsible for one's behavior. "Once again, it is clear that effective psychotherapy with people from sociocentric cultures must entail treating the relationship—the marriage, the family, the relationship between the person and various immaterial beings—through which the individual has or is a self at all" (Landrine 1995: 760).

There is an aspect of social control in both systems, but in the non-Western system there is greater public involvement. The public takes a direct part in the individual treatments and is familiar with them. The healer is the center of greater attention and may, for instance, lose his prestige and be expelled from the local community if his treatments are without effect. In both Western and non-Western systems there is a mutual form of control, in which the parties are held together in a dialectic interplay. But it is only in the Western context that the consultation can be considered part of a rhetorical power struggle, in which the parties—the professional and the layman—both fight for the recognition of their own perception of "illness" or "disease" (Elsass 1993a: 331). In the non-Western system, the client submits to the healer, who represents the culture; if the healer is not its mouthpiece, he will lose his power and healing abilities. There are, however, variations. Certain Buddhist forms of treatment are based on an egalitarian exchange between therapist and client in a confidential relationship similar to our treatment ideals about reciprocity and nonforced insight. By contrast, other forms of treatment, for example in Latin America, have more of the character of charismatic healing, where the client is required to submit in public to the healer's prescriptions and cosmology.

In some contexts, local healing systems have been described as a political opposition to Western colonial power that has penetrated the native society. The traditional healer here creates disorder and encourages a mental political force against colonialism's demand for order, predictability, and straightforwardness. The shaman's task is to create images of unpredictability, in which he becomes unruly and wild in his rituals, not in order to eliminate wildness, but to regain it (Taussig 1987: 391). Some of these ways of thinking may be an expression of romanticizing what is foreign, where healers are ascribed qualities that may be an expression of our own need to clear our bad conscience with respect to our imperial past (Kleinman 1988a: 128). The political struggle which we cannot undertake ourselves is delegated to others, and we project our motives into healing rituals that we perhaps do not understand, for example, of the neocolonial restoration of the bad conscience; an ennobling of the primitive (Elsass 1992a: 114).

In all cultures, the content of treatment depends to a large extent on interpretation. Outside of psychoanalysis, the healer must take part in interpreting the client's complaints and illness narrative in agreement with an underlying theory. This background is exposed more or less explicitly and is very different in various cultures. In some cultures, the treatment consists of teaching the client a disease taxonomy that is part of a complex ethno-theory about healing herbs in an ecological system. In other cultures, for example in our own psychoanalytic practices, the theoretical reference point for interpretations is more implicit. In many non-Western healing rituals, emphasis is put on emotional arousal with catharsis, psychophysiological changes, and religious manifestations, prayers, persuasion, and confessions. Exorcism is used in many places as a symbolic expulsion of evil, thus giving a concrete expression of hope and expectation with respect to healing. Introspection is also considered, but in contrast to our insight-giving therapies, it more often makes use of irony, paradoxes, and rhetorical questions as effect mechanisms.

Translation and Cooperation with the Interpreter

Language is an important tool in psychotherapy, and it has great importance even in most of the nonverbal therapies. However, translation, both in diagnostic work and in treatment, is a great problem, and wrong diagnoses and treatment occur frequently because of problems in interpretation (Westermeyer 1990).

There are many examples of how misunderstandings can arise from language problems. Psychiatric practice has many standard terms, which are completely misleading if they are translated word for word. Thus, the question "Do you hear voices?" may be misunderstood by the client, who may think that her hearing will be tested. Furthermore, there are several abstract ideas that are difficult to translate, but which nevertheless may be essential for the understanding of the torture survivor's situation and subjective condition. Pain, for instance, may have many more different meanings in languages other than our own, and may refer to both mental and somatic conditions. By contrast, several psychological conceptions are more differentiated in Western Europe than in other cultures, and many circumlocutions may be needed to explain the difference between sadness and depression, or between anxiety, fear, and being afraid. The psyche is called *avron* in Iran, but the adjective *avroni* is a form of abuse, that is, use of the term "psychological problems" is a serious taboo. Therefore, "bad nerves" or possibly "neurotic" is used if, for instance, one thinks that a stomach ulcer is due to mental disorder. Furthermore, there are interpreters who think that it is more difficult to translate the remarks of the therapist to the client than vice versa (Jørgensen 1991)—yet another manifestation showing that therapeutic intervention and our psychological formulations are to a large extent a west European product.

The traditional anthropologic literature contains several descriptions of such misunderstandings between cultures. They are rarely a result of translation problems in themselves, but should be seen in the cultural context in which the translation takes place. Cultural codes cannot simply be translated from one language to another; they are only understandable when they are put into larger contexts, in which there is a description of how different cultures can have divergent conceptions, for example, of authorities and power relations in the client/therapist relationship (see, for example, Ben-Ezer 1985), or of one's environment, as for example time, light, and darkness (see, for example, Sande 1991).

The problem is not only that linguistic nuances are lost through the interpretation, but also that the client's transferences are disturbed by the presence of the interpreter, because direct contact is not possible. Høglund (1988), for instance, thinks that for the same reason it is impossible to conduct a long-lasting, insight-giving therapy. Others, however, such as Jørgensen (1991), have had good experiences with psychoanalytically oriented therapy when a special technique is used by both interpreter and therapist.

In psychotherapy that has more limited goals, linguistic communication is less complicated than in long-lasting insight therapies, in which the transference is an important part of the effect mechanisms. When pathological conceptions are transferred to the therapist, they can become the object for processing. But while ordinary psychotherapy consists of a dyadic relationship, the interpreter's involvement introduces a triadic relationship. One of the interpreter's difficult tasks is to remain neutral; she must at the same time be active and translate, but should also be able to stay withdrawn in such a way that contact is primarily between client and therapist. This neutral position can be emphasized if the interpreter translates everything in the first person, and if she makes it clear from the start that alliances with the client are not possible.

Some transferences to the interpreter will also take place, and the feelings that are engendered will form important informational material. For this reason, among others, it may be necessary to have a meeting after each session, when the therapist and interpreter discuss the linguistic problems and also exchange experiences about the therapeutic events. It may then be possible for the therapist to have the cultural standards for different events and statements clarified.

The triadic relationship can cause divisions in the transference. Jørgensen (1991: 27) and Mirdal (1987) describe how the nation becomes personified and symbolically identified for clients in exile. The interpreter is considered the person through whom help arrives, and the therapist as the one who understands the client only because of the presence of the interpreter. Since the interpreter usually comes from the same country or culture as the client, she will activate a motherly, careful, and understanding attitude. But at the same time the client is also ambivalent toward this mother object and may react against dependence by questioning the interpreter's trustworthiness and reliability. This may lead to the client's rejection of the interpreter on the grounds that he cannot trust those from his own country and that there may be spies and informers among them due to the political conditions. In the same way, the therapist may represent the fatherly aspect, a representative of the reality principle and the approach to "the new world." Implicitly, there is in this a wish for progression and cure through therapy that can provoke the client's ambivalence by his testing of the therapist and his setting of limits. This division of transferences can lead to competition between interpreter and therapist in relation to the client.

The Psychodynamic, Psychoanalytic Approach to the Culture Encounter

The relationship and the transference between client and therapist are best described within the psychoanalytic tradition. But, as already mentioned, psychoanalytically oriented psychotherapy is to a large extent a treatment phenomenon of the West (Kleinman 1988a: 122, Rycroft 1986). Nevertheless, some of psychotherapy's nonspecific elements, such as empathic support, contain essential effect mechanisms in all cultures, even if they appear in different contexts and with different content. Psychoanalytic thinking has been chosen as the reference point because it constitutes one of the best described treatment forms with a common theory and system of ideas. And when one ventures into the troubled waters between two cultures, it may be important to have some fixed and well-defined points for orientation.

There is need for clarity about reference points and identity in the culture encounter, but it does not necessarily mean that one has to stick to them rigidly and inflexibly. Psychoanalytic therapists who work across cultures must be ready to deviate from their reference point; but they should be able to get back by means of their own theories (Roland 1980). The journey between cultures may become the seesaw of the identity on which one swings between oneself and being lost in foreign waters; if one is on the side of forfeiture all the time, one will disintegrate and perish. The therapeutic process will then stop, since the dialectic interplay disappears; instead of the client meeting another, he meets nothing.

If the psychoanalytic approach is applied, the relation-oriented aspects should be clarified to a larger extent than the content-oriented aspects vis-à-vis the client from a foreign culture. First and foremost, one must note the psychotherapeutic working method, with its confidential room and professional relationships. Many clients will have come from a culture in which treatment gives no guarantee of confidentiality and where it forms an integral part of the local society's control. It is particularly important for the torture survivor to feel secure and to know that he is not again entering a system of agents and informers. It is therefore important, already at the first visit, to explain to him the position of the institution and the type and content of the treatment.

The clients have usually had no experience with treatment as part of a public institution. They will sometimes be ignorant about what the public social and health systems can do for them, and they will therefore not be able to distinguish between the psychotherapist and social advisers. The torture survivor often continues to seek advice about financial problems over and over again in the hope of having them solved, together with other psychological problems.

Clients often have a culturally supported expectation about the therapist as an active, advisory, and charismatic person. If the therapist practices only psychotherapeutic neutrality, it may be experienced by the client as, at best, incomprehensible and, at worst, as lack of therapeutic skills, and a signal that the treatment is useless (Neki et al. 1985). When, finally, the clients discover that the treatment relationship is based on a mutual exchange of words, they find it hard to understand that the relationship is professional and not a friendship that can be incorporated into the rest of the client's family and circle of friends.

Only by putting these differences into words and by making them the subject of mutual research may it be possible to establish the cooperation in which the parties see themselves in the light of the other.

Rather than simply stressing the necessity for therapists to be culturally sensitive and to know the cultural background of clients, some researchers, such as Sue and Zane (1995), have specified intervention strategies, for example to provide structure, guidance, and direction rather than nondirectedness in interactions. Therapists are therefore advised to be direct and specific, rather than giving nonspecific, empathic support.

STRATEGIES FOR CULTURE SENSITIVITY

Instead of learning how to be authoritarian, directive, or structured, the therapist should first of all learn how to become credible with clients.

Achieved credibility can be examined in terms of three areas in which cultural issues are important. These are stated as hypotheses:

1. *Conceptualization of the problem.* If the client's problems are conceptualized in a manner that is incongruent with the client's belief systems, the credibility of the therapist is diminished. Directly or indirectly, therapists often convey their understanding or conceptualization of the causal links in the client's problems or situations. If therapists are antagonistic to clients, they may not gain credibility.

2. *Means for problem resolution.* If the therapist requires from the client responses that are culturally incompatible or unacceptable, the achieved credibility of the therapist is diminished. For example, a therapist may encourage an Asian client to directly express anger to his or her father in family therapy. The response (expression of anger toward father) may be quite ego dystonic because of cultural values.

3. *Goals for treatment.* If the definitions of goals are at odds between therapist and client, the credibility of the therapist will be diminished. D. W. Sue (1981) cited the example of an Asian American client who saw a counselor for vocational information. The counselor's goal in working with the client was to facilitate insight into the deep underlying dynamics concerning motives and decisions. This was not the goal of the client, who felt extremely uncomfortable in the session. In such situations, the therapist and client tend to judge the effects of treatment by different criteria. One may feel treatment is successful; the other, unsuccessful. [Sue & Zane 1995: 777]

Three Culture-Sensitive Treatment Methods

The most important aspect of "culture-sensitive" treatment is not to search for common features in the clients of a foreign culture but to look at the clients as individuals in a foreign context. Instead of being trauma fixated and looking at the foreigner as a client *with* problems, the therapist should rather try to understand him as a person placed *in* a problem situation. The sessions should deal with possibilities and resources instead of problems and symptoms. The therapist should emphasize the clarification of her own and the client's expectations; the context of the referral should be made explicit, together with a detailed working outline (Reichelt & Sveaass 1994a, b).

But it is not sufficient to use this "culture-sensitive" approach as a "recumbent" reflection on our psychodynamic working method, and to leave it at that. One way might be to establish cooperation with a traditional healer from the culture in question (see, for example, Peltzer 1995, Williams 1994). But the cross-cultural approach must also produce some visible proposals for treatment of the torture survivor; we must therefore be prepared to step outside our usual therapeutic contexts.

Descriptions of three methods follow.

1. Psychoeducation

The aim of psychoeducation is to teach the clients, perhaps together with their relatives, about the client's psychological problems, especially with the purpose of promoting conscious problem-solving strategies (Goldman 1988). The education is structured by a pedagogic training program arranged beforehand and adapted to the special learning conditions allowed by the clients' specific situation. Psychoeducation is a method that respects the foreign culture, because the Western therapist presents her knowledge in an open and direct way, without any therapeutic "ulterior motives." It was developed particularly for psychiatric patients and their relatives (Ascher-Svanum & Krause 1991, Brown et al. 1987, Gent & Zwart 1991, Goldstein 1992, Leff et al. 1984). No programs are particularly adapted for torture survivors, but use of the method can be recommended as a form of user influence in which professional knowledge is presented to the client. Publications such as WHO (1996) can be used as background material for setting up a program.

Psychoeducation has its professional reference point in the vulnerability model, which, briefly, is based on the fact that stress situations can make a disease worse (Zubin & Spring 1977). The method can often be used together with the other cognitive treatments that have gradually become well-developed treatment methods of traumatized clients (see for example Basoglu 1992). Both methods are based on the assumption that strengthening of conscious mechanisms, such as coping and competence, functions as an antidote against stress and vulnerability.

The subjects of the training include theories about psychological problems, variations of symptomatology, and the rationale for various psychosocial support measures and ways of coping with symptoms. Furthermore, some adjacent subjects can be included, such as teaching/training about the client's legal status, and the possibility of using the social and health systems as resources. This training does not require any special psychotherapeutic competence, but can be delegated to various professions according to the subjects that are being covered.

Psychoeducation in itself is not psychotherapy, but it represents an essential aspect of the thinking behind cognitive therapy, and it is a special offer that does not demand particular psychotherapeutic skills. Psychoeducation has similarities with the practice in which the client is involved as a kind of coresearcher who is actively sharing one's professional knowledge and is encouraged to supplement it. The attitude is to emphasize that the client is a self-reflecting individual who can also be brought to reflect about the professional's knowledge.

Psychoeducation has many features in common with the type of patient information that is used within somatic disease. The experience here is that the more information the patient has about his disease and treatment, the more his compliance improves.

A course in psychoeducation typically involves twelve to eighteen sessions. It cannot therefore be expected to have any significant, lasting influence in itself.

Studies on the psychoeducation of psychiatric patients agree in general with other research findings concerning the usefulness of information about the prevention of diseases and about risk factors, that is, behavior does not necessarily change even when knowledge is increased. In the same way, psychoeducation in itself does not lead to changes, but creates more awareness about risk factors—an awareness that, together with other forms of intervention, may produce an effect. Studies on effects also show that clients express great satisfaction after a course, singling out the sharing of professional experiences, a field from which they have all too often felt excluded. Although the clients do not apply the newly learned ways of reacting, and perhaps cannot remember so many concrete details from the teaching, most of them are well satisfied because of the reduced distance between professionals and laymen (Cozolino et al. 1988, Orhagen 1992).

The group may consist of ten to twelve torture survivors, preferably from related cultures with a common language, taking part in one weekly two-hour session with a break of fifteen minutes—a total of ten to eighteen sessions. The setting may be a conference room with a table and teaching materials such as a blackboard and overhead projector.

The teachers should be sensitive to the length of time the torture survivors can keep their concentration. It helps to take small pauses or to ask questions about the subject, such as "Do you know this about yourself?" or "Do you think the description fits your situation?" The presentation is therefore short and precise, with overheads and handouts of working papers. Overheads must be simple and contain key words to help memorization. Working papers and homework must be easy to understand and must be explained in detail before they are given out.

One of the great risks in using this model is that one may take too superficial an approach for the individual client, and forget his individualism because of the highly pedagogical situation.

PSYCHOEDUCATIVE PROGRAM

1. *Orientation.* The purpose is to present the group members to one another and to introduce the meaning of psychoeducation. The method may be called "psychology teaching" or "a course in health promotion." The headings of the various sessions are briefly described, and the participants are given a written program.
2. *Symptoms and post-traumatic stress disorders.* A description is given of symptoms that may follow severe traumas. The torture syndrome is explained without mentioning the nature of the trauma; torture methods are not described.
3. *Worsening of symptoms and coping.* Identification and coping with stress are covered, with cognitive therapy and its methods as reference points. Examples of how symptoms can get worse under stress are given, and how to deal with these symptoms in various appropriate ways.
4. *Therapy and treatment.* The rationale behind psychotherapy is introduced, and, with group participation, various examples from daily life are brought forward to illustrate the psychotherapeutic way of thinking.

(*continued*)

5. *Emigration and flight.* The difficulties of the refugee are mentioned and examples are given on how to deal with them.
6. *Cultural resources.* The participants introduce their own culture, and examples are given on how it differs from the new culture.
7. *Social resources.* A social adviser introduces the local social system and explains the rights and obligations of the torture survivor.
8. *The body and physiotherapy.* A medical doctor and a physiotherapist give a talk about the somatic symptoms and signs that are caused by torture, and mention various relaxation methods.
9. *Creating a meaning in life.* Examples are given of how torture survivors may try in various ways to create a new meaning in life, in particular by appealing to the rational side of the survivors' mental functions. The group may be visited by a well-functioning survivor who can describe how he handled his situation.
10. *Conclusion and evaluation.* Important subjects from the sessions are repeated, and the course is evaluated.

2. The Testimony Method

The testimony method is based on South American experiences, mainly from Chile during the period following the 1973 coup. Here, risking their lives, psychologists collected testimonials from previous prisoners in order to document the effects of the suppressive regime (Cienfuegos & Monelli 1983). The treatment method consisted of putting the political engagement in focus; for many of the tortured the ideology had a great importance for their integrity. Cienfuegos & Monelli (1983: 44) consider political work as a special type of object relationship, and see the treatment's purpose as reestablishment of the object that torture has tried to eliminate.

The testimony method may consist in tape recording the torture survivors' description of their torture, in reprinting it, and reading it through several times with the clients, in order to process the experience. The document functions as a form of memory that can be read again and again; it can be transcribed and analyzed together with the therapist. The purpose is to create a historic, public document that accuses the suppressive regime of its violation of human rights, and also to create personal material with which the client can re-create his or her political consciousness and, to a larger extent, a meaning in life.

Agger and Jensen (1990: 116) point out that the word "testimony" has a double meaning: on the one hand, it is something objective, legal, and political; on the other, something subjective, private, and cathartic. Many cultures have healing rituals in which the testimony and the confession have an essential position. Agger and Jensen (1990: 116) quote the anthropologist La Barre: "Testimony as a way of getting rid of the internal 'evil' would seem to be a universal phenomenon." The experience of guilt and shame, self-reproach, the feeling of being rotten, dirty, and evil, are essential features of the survival syndrome in many torture survivors, the so-called survivor guilt (Danieli 1988). Here the testimony might be a healing and purification ritual that is common to both the therapist's and the client's cultural context— a transcultural psychotherapeutic tool and a united advocacy against political suppression.

The testimony method is important because it goes beyond the traditional psychotherapy room and gives it a political importance that has been of great importance to the survivors. Creation of a meaning has been very important for the mature person. Based on his experiences in concentration camps during the Second World War, Frankl described how important it was for survival to maintain a spiritual and ideological consciousness and to have a purpose and a meaning (Frankl 1967, 1970) (see pages 77 and 85, respectively). The testimony method gives such a possibility of reestablishing a meaning to a painful and destructive torture experience, thus giving the survivor political and spiritual dignity.

The method requires therapeutic experience. As previously mentioned, some of the survivors may experience retraumatization if the therapist insists rigidly that the trauma story must be brought forward (see page 77). Another difficulty is that the method cannot immediately be supplemented with traditional psychotherapy because they take place in different spheres of intimacy. When the political public dimension has been introduced first, it can be difficult for some therapists to change to the closed, confidential room that is otherwise known to the therapist.

If the therapist and client come from the same nation and have had the same political attitude to the suppressive authorities, the method can lead to mutual seduction and idealization in which it may be difficult to express aggressive feelings toward the therapist, who has perhaps risked her life to help the client (Agger & Jensen 1994: 282).

Another reservation with respect to the method is that it is more easily applicable in some cultural contexts than in others. As mentioned, it was developed in a South American context, but in other cultures it may provoke a humiliating feeling of shame in the client because it exposes weakness and humiliation, which, according to the "culture of shame," should have a private and inner status (see page 104). Agger and Jensen (1990), however, have used the method to great advantage in clients from Middle Eastern and African cultures, and Weine and Laub with Bosnian survivors of "ethnic cleansing" (Weine & Laub 1995). In such cultural contexts, it should be particularly stressed that the purpose is to establish political documentation that will humiliate the others and create shame for their actions, and thus liberate the client from the same experiences.

3. Fairy Tales as a Therapeutic Instrument

Through the centuries and within all cultures, people have gathered together to tell fairy tales, often the same ones, perhaps because they are poetically entertaining and because they speak directly to the unconscious. They give hope and courage to the listeners because they offer order and solutions to conflicts, which in real life we are often not able to solve (Brun 1992, Brun et al. 1992).

When one has a fairy tale in common with the torture survivor, one can indicate that one is exchanging symbols for the feelings that may be so difficult to speak about. The foreign language clients may feel frustrated by not being able to express themselves in their mother tongue, and the expressions for their problems may be interpreted in a much too simplified and banal way. But in a fairy tale, the linguistic difficulties may sometimes be overcome, because the fairy tale, in poetic form, communicates symbols for the feelings that may be so difficult to put into words.

Many psychological core conflicts and traumatic solutions are generally made available by a fairy tale. Only the archetypal and the universal decrease any suspicion. The resistance can feel less heavy, and the client has the opportunity to work with essential conflicts without having to do so strictly according to the traditional psychotherapeutic working method.

Many have worked with fairy tales and psychotherapy (see review article, Brun et al. 1992). The tradition is strongest within the Jungian school (Kast 1991, von Franz 1989), but the Freudian tradition has also worked with fairy tales (Bettelheim 1976, Lotz 1988). The Jungian school, with the archetypes and its often visually produced world of symbols, may be the most suitable to give a psychological understanding of fairy tales.

The following points are based on Brun's overview (Brun 1992, Brun et al. 1992) of the use of fairy tales in psychotherapy.

The naive method. Therapist and client are together with a fairy tale, and one of them reads aloud to the other. The therapist refrains from real interpretations, but one talks about what one has experienced; the hope is to be able to stimulate the client's inner imagination. In a sense, they go on a journey together, but it is for the client to decide if he wants to continue with his experiences. The therapist does not put them in relation to the client's situation.

The interpretation-oriented method. The client relates his associations with the fairy tale. The tale functions as a sort of transitional object, and the therapist tries to give insight to the most important effect in the same way that dreams are used in insight-giving psychotherapy.

Fairy tales as play therapy. The client is given the opportunity to identify himself with a fairy tale figure, from which he may create a world. Therapist and client remain in the make-believe world and use the protection that may come from using fairy-tale language, even if both know what it is all about.

Fairy tale production. The client writes his own fairy tale, and, as in drama therapy, the therapist is an instructor who helps to narrate it. The client may choose to play the hero's role and will be helped by the therapist with questions about his clothes, which room he is entering, etc. The therapist can also introduce various supporting characters and give them an entry line on the fairy-tale stage.

The associative technique. Brun describes how this technique can be used with brain-damaged patients, and how she develops symbols with a group of patients. One of the exercises is about a tree; the client must recount his first memory of a tree and the qualities he thinks of when he hears the word tree, and what the tree can symbolize.

There are thus various ways in which work with fairy tales can liberate energy and create better contact with the unconscious. For torture survivors the fairy tale is a good way to establish a culture-specific form of treatment and to create a distance from the traumatic situation, which may be very difficult to talk about.

Constructing a Meaning

The ultimate goal of psychoeducation, of the testimony method, and of work with fairy tales is to construct a new meaning and story for the torture survivor. Psychoeducation can be said to be the construction of the professional's story in a very direct and unmasked way vis-à-vis the client. The testimony method is the political story construction, and the fairy tale is culture's person-oriented construction.

Based on cultural psychology, humankind's participation in culture and their way of realizing themselves through culture are based on the individual's way of sharing meanings and concepts with others. A central research subject in cognitive psychology's "folk psychology" is the construction of meaning, which becomes sense because others understand it and can share it with the client (Bruner 1990).

This meaning-centered cultural psychology deals with the ways in which people construct a meaning—not with what they do, but rather with what they say they do and what others say about it. The method is introspective, but it has ingredients from anthropology's fieldwork. It is context-oriented and an instrument for the ambiguity of different cultures.

When one studies people's constructions and reconstructions, fact can become stranger than fiction. This happens when people construct good stories that are not necessarily true, but contain some elements of truth that can be shared by others, and will make the listeners characterize their tale as "the good story."

The very distinction between "the good story" and "the true story" demarcates the psychotherapeutic content of the testimony method from the work of political documentation. The testimony documentation work that is made during the therapy must be true, but it is the way in which it is constructed that decides whether it has therapeutic importance. The fairy tale has no reality, but nevertheless it has a meaning as "the good story" for the storytellers and their listeners. Here it is the sequence of the story's parts that make it meaningful rather than its truthfulness.

Life Story Research: Narratology

Because meaning and story construction are so important for the torture survivor, it may be of value to seek information for one's therapeutic work within humanistic cognitive psychology about traumatic memory research (e.g., *Journal of Traumatic Stress*, 1995).

Fact and fiction, as mentioned, have the same form, and the question of which came first is irrelevant and impossible to answer. The important thing is how meaning constructions—stories—get their form, regardless of whether they are fact or fiction.

The function of a story and a narrative is to unite separate parts into a whole, with a beginning, a middle, and an end. Later years have seen the development of a discipline about the story as a phenomenon: "narratology," derived from "narratives." "Story" or "narrative" also mean the structure and the way in which the story is told; "narrative" means both life story and life within story (Cox & Theilgaard 1987: 8).

There are various ways of characterizing a narrative structure. Some have stressed its inherent sequential character, where the interpreter must get hold of its central "plot" in order to get an understanding of its separate parts (Bruner 1990: 43). Another important quality is that it can be both "realistic" and "imaginative" without the force of the story being lost. As already mentioned, it is the sequence and the plot of the structure that are decisive for the story, rather than its so-called truth or falseness.

Within semiotics, various contributions have been presented to this perception of the story: "Life stories can be told because they are lived, and they are lived because they are told. Life's actions and sufferings can be seen as a process in which we ourselves tell stories and listen to stories, live them out, and live through them" (Carr 1986: 126). "Time becomes an experienced and human time to the extent it is organized based on a way of telling a story; on the other side the story only becomes meaningful to the extent in which it reflects the qualities of a temporal experience" (Ricoeur 1984: 13).

Based on the fact that we are to some extent the stories that we tell about ourselves, therapy can be looked at as the work of telling a story, as a way of telling and retelling the life and trauma story together with the therapist. It is a creative process in which different perspectives and incomplete short stories gradually take shape and become a complete, coherent, and understandable entity. The creation of a new story structure involves a change of the client's experiences. During therapy, the trauma story becomes a narrative about the torture, which is more complete, more consistent, understandable, and convincing—a story that stretches out and catches the client and sometimes his family's relevant past, his present, and his potential future. This common construction of the trauma story gives relief when it gives context and understanding, and when it increases the social support and care and leads to mastering and control. A trauma story that creates meaninglessness, social isolation and helplessness will produce the opposite effect (Brody 1987: 185).

The Trauma Story as Explanatory Model

The process in which the story is structured, interpreted, and told is called an "explanatory model." It is usually the explanatory model that forms the plot of the narrative presentation and is the important structure from which the rest of the story is constructed. If it has a disease or trauma as a central subject, the life story will turn into an illness narrative or a trauma narrative. Such an explanatory model is created both by clients and by therapists; it "gives explanations about the trauma and treatment that provide guidelines as to which therapist and treatment one should choose, and which furthermore gives the trauma a personal and social importance" (Kleinman 1980: 104).

Seen from the professionals' position, the client's explanatory model may often appear vague with many-sided meanings, be variable, and have unclear limits between idea and experience. When speaking about their disease and trauma, many clients include professional psychological terms, but they use them in other, flexible, and sometimes irrational ways from those used by the therapist. The clients' self-experience does not have the character of a theory and model, which the professional can use as a fixed given feature. For the therapist, however, the descriptions are clearly structured and built up around scientific causal relationships. The meeting between client and therapist may thus be seen as an exchange, a transaction between the explanatory models of laymen and professional. This exchange depends on several psychological, social, and cultural conditions. Sometimes a power struggle will arise between the two types of explanatory model, when the therapist's model intermingles with the client's and makes the professional concept part of the client's self-experience, rather than the other way around.

One way of understanding the explanatory models of laymen is to start with the types of question they pose when they feel ill or traumatized. The answers to these questions are often interwoven into a life story context (Helman 1990: 96):

1. What has happened? The answer results in the organization of the symptoms in recognizable patterns with a name and an identity.
2. Why did it happen? The answer suggests the etiology of the condition.
3. Why did the trauma hit me? The answer results in making an association between the trauma and the client's behavior, for instance in relation to personality and social conditions.

4. Why just now? Considerations about "timing" of the trauma, its initial symptoms and speed of development.
5. What will happen to me if the problems are not tackled? The answer leads to considerations about course, outcome, prognosis, and risk.
6. What will be the possible effects on other people? The answer results in considerations about how the trauma might affect the relationship to family and friends and conditions with respect to job and income.
7. What shall I do about the problems, and whom shall I contact for help? The answer may result in consideration of strategies for treatment of the symptoms such as self-treatment, seeking advice from family or friends, or contacting a doctor.

The torture survivor's story develops as an answer to such questions. If the therapist is unable to bring them up during the therapy, it will not be possible for her, together with the client, to construct a coherent story that gives meaning and thus relief.

Self-Respect and Life Plan

In order to make it a story, some narratologists will assume that the person has the experience of being able to make a life plan. "To have a life plan" is closely related to wanting one's life story to be determined by one's personal wishes (Brody 1987: 49). Thus one has some ideas about what would be desirable and one should be able to choose a path that should give as many benefits as possible, all depending on the direction one takes under the given social and cultural conditions and on how one evaluates one's own qualities and skills (Sachs 1981).

Self-respect involves having such a plan that forms one's life story. It is a social and psychological concept in which friends and family, network and social surroundings are important factors that can both decrease and increase self-respect (Brody 1987: 54).

Precisely this self-respect is an important reference point for the understanding of the full significance of torture. The life plan for the torture survivor should preferably be in agreement with the realities enforced by the trauma. A life plan that assumes a perfect and harmonious existence and that does not accept even minor problems is not appropriate. For example, a life plan is irrational if its fulfillment requires a much longer life than the average.

It is the breaking point at which the life story changes that is important for the understanding of torture's influence on the victim. Torture trauma usually causes a radical revision of the life plan, and the clients' task is to establish a certain degree of continuity with their original life plan, and with the values and attitudes which they had before they were tortured.

By focusing on the point at which the life story becomes a disease or trauma story, it is possible to give a more nuanced picture of the trauma experience. There are various general types of such breaking points between life story and disease and trauma story:

1. *Trauma as an isolated island in one's life story.* When the trauma is over, one restarts one's life plan where it was left off, as if nothing had happened. This method is most suitable for the acute diseases, but there are also patients with chronic diseases who do not accept that they always have to live with the disease. They look at their treatment as a duty, something to be got through, so that they can restart their previous life as soon as possible. Some torture survivors also have this "island concept" on an unrealistic basis, and will cling to it until they die.

2. *Trauma as a denial.* Serious life-shortening diseases such as cancer can particularly start with total denial. In the same way, this denial can continue in torture survivors for such a long time that they never get around to telling their trauma story because it will always threaten their identity. Some continue to live as if nothing had happened, even if they have been extremely influenced by the torture.

3. *Trauma as a career.* Here clients take on their trauma as a new career, denying their previous life plan and formulating a new one, with the torture as the main object. The survivor becomes so fixed on the disease that all aspects of daily life are associated with the torture. Sometimes the trauma itself can give the clients a kind of satisfaction; especially if their previous life did not have a particular meaning, they can obtain long-awaited attention and importance because of the torture.

4. *Trauma as the fatal outcome.* Here the trauma is accepted but it does not influence the person's life plan. The survivors may try to get various treatments, but only in the hope of a short prolongation of life before death. They unconcernedly continue their tasks in life, in an attempt to finalize them, and may for example work in order to finish a book or a house. Some torture survivors consider suicide the unavoidable end result.

5. *Trauma as an accident.* Here torture is considered a factor that puts a sudden and unhappy end to the life story. The person may have always

worked hard, and just when life was supposed to get better, the torture came, raising the question of what use has it all been. The client becomes depressed and sees a wasted life, feeling a loss and an awareness of the importance of something never obtained.

Behind such types of trauma and disease stories is the assumption that life can be seen as a story, and that to some extent the main actor has a life plan that he or she shares with others. But the concept of "self-respect," of having a rational life plan, is a psychological simplification. It is not exclusively a conscious and rational formation; it also consists of some unconscious and person-related factors that act together and make the persons formulate, often vaguely, their meanings of life in various ways. One can have self-images at many different levels, and even if one expresses apparently openly that one accepts the traumatized situation, at another level one may not at all have overcome the injustice of having been tortured. In this interpretation, in which both conscious and unconscious feelings are accounted for, no life story is necessarily better than any other. Each has its own logic, which may be the most appropriate adaptation to a difficult situation for the individual.

Many theories have been developed about the occurrence of these various types of trauma story. Some authors, such as Siegler and Osmond (1974), believe there is a tendency to reproach either oneself or others for the trauma. But since such accusations and reproaches quickly become a destructive element in a society in which traumas are as common as in ours, the trauma story has become a way of controlling the hostility. The therapist's role is to confirm and strengthen this story, and just because the tendency for accusations and reciprocal reproaches is so large, there must sometimes be a figure of authority to resist it. That is how the therapist gets authoritative status. But if the therapists strengthen their power by making the open and individual life story a standardized and fixed way of treatment, the therapeutic neutralization of the hostility does not occur, and the underlying anger and destruction from the torture can again burst into flames.

It is inappropriate in transcultural work to search for one presentation that will satisfy both therapist and client. There is no reason to think that the whole truth exists and that it will be able to liberate the client. Truth has many faces, and knowledge in itself does not lead to liberation. The goal of therapy must be the same as that of fieldwork: a dialogue in which cooperation is the most essential feature. The dialogue must create its own meaning, and the goal should be both order and chaos, unity and fragmentation, stagnation and movement.

Despite different cultural contexts, this cooperation is based on some generally accepted healing factors such as mutual confidence, empathy, and various social systems of support. They are the preconditions for bringing the explanatory models of therapists and clients closer together, so that at a common point they create "the good story" that respects the standards for disease and health of both the torture survivor and the professional.

Summary and Clinical Applications

• The therapeutic session with a foreigner is not a collision between different explanatory models, but rather an interplay in which one sees oneself in the light of the other.

• It is impossible to consult an anthropological data base every time a foreign culture is encountered. To a certain extent the clients themselves should function as this data base, and the way in which the questions are put should reflect the therapist's own lack of knowledge; the role of the therapist should be "the ignorant knowing one."

• In Western countries the self is the final explanation for behavior and is responsible for behavior. In this referential construction of the self, social units are presumed to exist in order to meet the self's needs. But this referential conception of the self is unknown among the vast majority of the world's people. The alternative concept of the person is the indexical self, a sociocentric construction that does not have traits or needs of its own in isolation from its other relationships and contexts. In a therapeutic setting, for example, it implies that the self is not a separate entity that can be referred to or reflected upon in isolation. Treating the minority client in isolation is perhaps the most frequent cross-cultural, psychotherapeutic error.

• The non-Western client has difficulty in complying to "tell me something about yourself" and will instead give long, detailed descriptions about concrete interactions with others. Externalization and projections will be more evident. Family and communities come before individuals. Therapy may entail or necessitate a renegotiation of the construction of the self by and for all members of the relationship.

• A "cultural triage model" of intervention can be suggested to prevent a Western isolation of the self. In this approach, a Western clinician, a folk healer from the culture and/or an authority from the community in question, and the family meet and agree on several conceptualizations of the problems. Then a multicultural/multilevel course of treatment can take place with the Western clinician, the indigenous healer, and the family together.

• The interview can take the form of a mini-ethnography, where the meeting with the foreigner will lead to a reexamination of one's own categories. In the interview the questions are always centered on why the foreigner thinks the way she does about the surrounding world and about her problems. The method focuses strongly on the other's viewpoints, and compares them with one's own in such a way that one systematically becomes aware of one's own prejudices and attitudes. For a period, therefore, one may have to be actively talking about and explaining one's own attitude and practice.

• The working method is not necessarily a nondirective way of questioning with open statements such as, "Tell me more about that," or by emphasizing and underlining the last statement from the client. Some of the clients from non-Western cultures will simply not take part in this form of conversation. By sticking to one's traditional psychotherapeutic nondirective attitude, a very large part of the world's population may appear alexithymic. They are not prepared to expose their feelings in a dyadic professional situation opposite a passive therapist.

• Rather than simply advocating the necessity for therapists to be culturally sensitive and to know the cultural background of clients, therapists are rather advised to be directive, to provide structure and guidance. But instead of learning how to be authoritarian, directive, or structured, the therapist first of all should learn how to become credible with clients.

• The differences between the Western, egocentric system and the non-Western, sociocentric system should be put into words between therapist and client. In our institutionalized treatment, the meeting between therapist and client takes place in a dyadic way in a closed room; the therapist may encourage the client to bring a few family members. But in other cultures, treatment is often public, for example as part of local religious rituals.

• In all cultures, the treatment content is founded to a large extent on interpretations that are in agreement with an underlying theory or ideology, which is exposed more or less explicitly. In some cultures, the treatment consists of teaching the client a disease taxonomy, which is part of a complex ethno-theory, such as healing herbs in an ecological system. In other cultures, as in our own psychoanalytic practices, the theoretical reference point for interpretations is more implicit. In many non-Western healing rituals, emphasis is put on emotional arousal with catharsis, psychophysiological changes, and religious manifestations, prayers, persuasions, and confessions. Exorcism is used in many places as a symbolic expulsion of evil, thus giving a concrete expression of hope and expectation about the healing. Insight is also dealt with, but in contrast to our insight-giving therapies, it more often uses irony, paradoxes, and rhetorical questions as effect mechanisms.

• Only by putting the differences between the foreign client and the therapist into words and by making them the subject of mutual research can it be possible to establish cooperation in which the parties see themselves in the light of the other. One should emphasize the clarification of one's own and the client's expectations; the context of the referral should be made explicit, together with a detailed working contract.

• Translation, both in diagnostic work and in treatment, is a great problem. The interpreter should be able to stay neutral and withdrawn in such a way that contact is primarily between client and therapist. This neutral position can be emphasized if the interpreter translates everything in the first person, and if he makes it clear from the start that alliances with him are not possible. It may be necessary to have a meeting after each session, when the therapist and interpreter discuss the linguistic problems and also exchange experiences about the therapeutic events. It may here be possible for the therapist to get a clarification of the cultural standards for different events and statements.

• Examples of culture-sensitive treatment methods outside the usual therapeutic contexts might be as follows.

Psychoeducation. A structured pedagogic training program with the purpose to increase the client's knowledge about psychological problems and especially promoting problem-solving strategies. The program may consist of ten to eighteen sessions with a group of ten to twelve clients. Psychoeducation is not itself psychotherapy, but has many features in common with the type of patient information that is used within somatic disease.

The testimony method. The purpose is to create a historic, public document that accuses the suppressive regime of its violation of human rights, and also to create personal material with which the client can re-create his political consciousness and, to a larger extent, a meaning in life. The method is important because it goes beyond the traditional psychotherapy room and gives it a political importance that has been of great importance to the survivors. It requires therapeutic experience, because some of the survivors may experience retraumatization if the therapist insists rigidly that the trauma story must be brought forward. In cultures such as the Middle East, it may provoke a humiliating feeling of shame in the client because it exposes weakness and humiliation, which according to the "culture of shame" should have a private and inner status.

Fairy tales as a therapeutic instrument. Studying a fairy tale together may help overcome linguistic difficulties, because the fairy tale, in poetic form, communicates symbols for the feelings that may be so difficult to put into words. The resistance can feel less heavy, and the client has the possibility to work with essential conflicts without having to do so strictly according to the traditional psychotherapeutic working method.

• The ultimate goal of this culture-specific method is to construct a new meaning for the survivor. The function of a story and a narrative is to unite separate parts into a whole. The narrative structure develops as an answer to some questions: 1. What has happened? 2. Why did it happen? 3. Why did the trauma hit me? 4. Why just now? 5. What will happen to me if the problems are not tackled? 6. What will be the possible effects on other people. 7. What shall I do about the problems, and whom shall I contact for help? The torture survivor's story develops as an answer to such questions. If the therapist is unable to bring them up during the therapy, it will not be possible for her, together with the client, to construct a coherent story that gives meaning and thus relief.

• Despite different cultural contexts, therapeutic cooperation is based on some generally accepted healing factors such as mutual confidence, empathy, and various social systems of support. They are the preconditions for bringing the culture-specific methods in use.

6

Postscript

The Torture Survivor's Perspective: A Follow-Up Examination Combining Supervision with Research

The torture survivor's perspective may be distorted when it is processed and filtered by the professional. The considerations about the specific torture syndrome and supportive treatment have all been developed within a closed therapy room. The culture-psychologic approach certainly tries to put the psychodynamic working method into a larger perspective that respects the client's cultural background and can recommend some culture-specific treatment methods. But all these reflections are those of the professional, and it cannot be taken for granted that they respect the clients' interests. If one is unable to involve the torture survivors in the development of professional knowledge and let them have a sort of user influence, the result may be institutional self-confirmation. Treatment centers that want to avoid stagnation and development in the wrong direction must be open to ideas from outside, for example, in the form of supervision and research.

In order to obtain a form of reflection in the daily routine, an "atmosphere of inquiry" (Main 1957), a follow-up examination, has been carried out. Its starting point was the situation that many therapists desire but rarely achieve; namely, to call the torture survivors back about six months after their treatment and ask them to give an account of "what they got out of the psychotherapy." The study was carried out as a combination of supervision and research.

Supervision

Supervision can be defined as an intensive, interpersonally focused, one-to-one relationship in which one person is designated to facilitate the development of therapeutic competence in the other person (Loganbill et al. 1989, ref. from Lansen 1993). The overall purpose is to protect the client's interests. The supervisee is responsible for the client, and the supervisor for the supervision.

Supervision is different from teaching in the sense that it is adapted to the individual's situation and needs. Teaching focuses on transmitting the same information to all the students regardless of differences in their levels of knowledge. The purpose of supervision is to give the therapist a knowledge and an understanding that makes him or her more independent in solving different treatment situations. In order to obtain the necessary skills, therapists must learn to observe their own behavior and to evaluate it in relation to some criteria that they have learned and which they understand as necessary. The supervisor's role is to help with this observation and evaluation of skills, in such a way that the therapist/supervisee will add to and improve his or her possibilities for taking initiatives and actions.

Few descriptions have been published about the supervision of those working with torture survivors (Lansen 1993, 1994). The professional opinion is, among others, that the nature of the survivors' traumas can make a narcissistic wound to the fabric of the self that shakes the survivors' idea about predictability, control, and mastering. It is this overwhelmed ego function that may also shake the therapist, and which she must consider. In this process, the supervisor should reflect the same combination of cognitive and emotional support as the therapist does vis-à-vis the client during therapy. From the cognitive point of view, it is the supervisor's task to contribute professional knowledge in the form of introductions to theories and concepts that give structure and perspectives (Wilson & Jacob 1994: ix). Furthermore, it is the supervisor's task to focus on the emotional aspects, for instance by making conscious the complex transference and countertransference phenomena that arise in the work with the "unbearable traumas."

Many therapists are influenced by the work to such an extent that they sometimes risk not being able to tolerate it; they get involved in a form of "vicarious" or "transmitted" traumatization. Some writers, such as Fischman (1991) and Comez-Diaz & Padilla (1990), consider that these countertransference phenomena are specific to work with torture survivors. Lansen (1993), using questionnaires, contacted some treatment centers for torture survivors and found that 10 percent of the therapists, about three hundred people, reported symptoms of vicarious traumatization. The most frequently preferred precaution against these symptoms was supervision. Another study by Hafkenscheid and Lansen (1992 ref. from Lansen 1993) showed that 20 percent of the therapists who mentioned vicarious traumatization as a problem scored just as high as the average of the traumatized clients on an "impact of event" rating scale.

Thus, apart from the fact that the therapy itself can be a threat to the integrity of the therapist, many psychotherapists often have to carry out post-traumatic therapy under the very same conditions as those endured by their clients when they were traumatized (Agger & Jensen 1994: 263). More and more therapists are working in countries in which torture is practiced, and many are therefore exposed to the same traumatizing situations as their clients.

Therapists who have survived the same traumas as their clients are called "wounded healers" (Agger & Jensen 1994: 264, Comez-Diaz & Padilla 1990). This metaphor has two perspectives. One is based on the fact that the "wounded healer" is expected to have greater empathy with the clients, in the same way that a wounded saint and the Christ crowned with thorns may have healing powers because of their own sufferings. Many shamans heal on the assumption that, by taking on the suffering themselves, they take it away from their clients. The other perspective is that the "wounded healer" has a need to help others, because she herself was a victim of trauma. She has an unconscious need to help and, by getting involved in a close relationship with the traumatized client, she gets a kind of satisfaction; by helping others, she helps herself. Neither of these perspectives needs to be a bad starting point for treatment, but they require an outside supervisor to call attention to them.

The precondition for successful treatment is that the therapist knows how she can handle her own subjective reactions to the torture survivor's problems. There are no solutions to this problem other than supervision; as Jung said, "Even the Pope has a confessor" (Jung 1963; Agger & Jensen 1994: 265). Supervision can take place between colleagues, but in order to prevent the institution from being hit by the very same repressive mechanisms that it tries to fight (see page 25), it is recommended that the supervisor comes from outside.

Research

One of the most important aims of the supervisor is to protect the interests of the clients, and one of the aims of research is to contribute different perspectives of the client experience and make sure it is respected.

However, studies on client experience have been criticized because they focus too much on the encounter between client and therapist, and because the research is exclusively derived from this encounter (Dreier 1993, Højholt 1994, Nissen 1994). Maluccio (1979) in particular calls attention to these limitations and therefore involves the framework of the treatment situation and the client's so-called extra-therapeutic conditions. Several of his interviews show that clients are to a large extent influenced by and conscious of factors outside the therapy room, while the therapist looks at them as unimportant "matters of course." In the same way, Højholt (1994), in a study of a counseling practice, mentions that professionals have little insight into what otherwise is happening in the clients' lives and rate such factors as less important than the clients themselves.

The desire to obtain a systematized insight into the clients' daily lives, and to get to know about their own processes and suggestions for solutions, demands that they get involved as coresearchers and become explorative themselves with respect to their own experiences and daily events. Some of these formulations are in agreement with psychotherapeutic practice; thus, psychoanalytically-oriented therapy has some explicitly formulated goals to support the clients' autonomy, and offers some techniques to give more opportunities for action, both within and outside the therapy room. Nevertheless, the practice of involving the client as coresearcher can lead to a basic criticism of psychotherapy, because the involvement of the user's perspective, in the utmost sense, can result in a different view and theory of science (Dreier 1993, Nissen 1994). The user's perspective is not satisfied by including only more variables about extra-therapeutic conditions, but implies a meta-perspective in which the influence of research on psychotherapeutic practice and professional development is studied.

With respect to practice, the question has been asked whether systematic research of psychotherapy has had any influence on psychotherapeutic work. Psychotherapists are not big users of research literature, but they acquire knowledge, for instance, in supervisory contexts and in the literature that relies on cases and examples of clinical material (Haynes et al. 1987, Lazarus 1990, Strupp 1981, Tyler & Clark 1987). Finally, seen from a user perspective, it can be said that psychotherapy research in itself puts a filter on the client experience in such a way that it becomes self-confirming (Nissen 1994).

It is therefore necessary to get a better understanding of psychotherapy's effect mechanisms vis-à-vis torture survivors, but in a way that improves the relationship between scientific activity and practice.

Problems, Method, and Materials: A Case Study

The follow-up examination was carried out as a combination of supervision and research. The starting point was that the therapist wanted to know what the client and therapist focused on when they talked about psychotherapy, and what they meant by effective and noneffective mechanisms.

The Problems

Does the "torture syndrome" exist?

Do torture survivors demand a special supportive therapeutic approach in which, for instance, establishment of "basic trust" is more important than identification of the trauma?

Are the cultural differences between therapist and client so large that they constitute an essential hindrance to psychotherapy?

The Method

The method was to let the client's story be an independent, externally anchored voice. The method may be seen as a combination of the classical case study, as known from other supervisions, and the resource-demanding empirical and controlled design (Elsass et al. 1995).

The assumption was that the client himself was able to talk in a nuanced way about the therapeutic yield, and to evaluate the personality of the therapist and the progress of the treatment—that he had grasped many features that can give the therapist essential information. Use of the client's account, understood as a "narrative" about the psychotherapy, made it possible to present his perspective without unnecessarily reducing it with a scientific method, which is a risk in using standardized questionnaires and rating scales (Elsass 1994a, 1995).

The Materials

The materials consisted of twenty torture survivors and ten therapists, all of whom were interviewed after the end of treatment. Each therapist chose one or more clients, and the participants were interviewed using the same method. The results were compared with those from similar interviews of forty-eight other patients with anxiety and their twenty-four therapists.

The qualitative analysis focused on collecting wide-ranging material, which should show the variation between different statements. Some of the therapists therefore included more than two clients. By contrast, the quantitative analysis was subject to strict exclusion and inclusion criteria (see appendix, page 162).

Data Collection and Analysis

Data collection was carried out by the author. It was necessary to have an independent observer in order to give these narratives scientific value. Since the therapists were involved in the process under study and were interwoven in the transference, the retrospective description would be exposed to mutual distortion had they interviewed the clients—the "Hello-goodbye effect." However, the author was also part of the process because he was the therapists' supervisor.

The analysis was made by a combination of quantitative and qualitative methods. The representative value of the material may have some shortcomings. The quantitative analysis was therefore only used as a guideline for the qualitative analysis. By means of "grounded theories" (Strauss & Corbin 1990), important text cores have been deduced, based on a systematic reading and assisted by quantitative analysis. With respect to method, therefore, the study is placed between quantitative natural science's demands for being representative, and the humanistic science's use of qualitative methods.

The materials and methods are described in more detail in the appendix.

Examples of statements by torture survivors and therapists follow here. The interviews were read with the aim of finding those parts of the texts in which the parties talk about the same subject.

Clients' Statements

Symptoms of the Torture Syndrome

In the quantitative study (see appendix), by and large, torture survivors had the same number of complaints as Danish anxiety patients, but the qualitative study showed that they had another character. They rarely had the same symptom-fixation as psychiatric patients. By contrast, some of the complaints were vague and unspecific. They were often existential in character, similar to the numbness of Holocaust survivors. The therapists said that some of the torture survivors were somatising at the start of treatment, but that cooperation between psychotherapist and physiotherapist often managed to break the symptom fixation.

"Anxiety." THE CLIENT: Though I was aware of having problems I didn't know their nature. Until I found out that it was anxiety. My therapist said so, at any rate.

"Depression." THE CLIENT: I suffered from depression. Before I started therapy I was so depressed. I was sitting at home in front of a mirror and talked to myself, I had nobody to talk to, so you can understand how important it was for me to get somebody to talk to. I was almost going mad from loneliness. I didn't feel I could be together with others after what I had gone through in prison.

"Pain." THE CLIENT: I have severe pain in my legs. My physiotherapist is helping me but I haven't improved much. My great wish is to be able to walk normally, to be able to ride a bike.

"Do not feel the love of people." THE CLIENT: I do not feel the love of people, it is just the same to me whether the weather is good or bad, whether my conditions are good or bad. I have reached a kind of indifference, I cannot feel the love of another person. The only feeling I have left is to cry, simply. And then the complete hopelessness.

"Dead inside." THE CLIENT: My great problem is that I feel dead inside. I can't remember, and forget everything.

The Therapeutic Process

In describing the therapy, the clients were more matter of fact than the therapists, who were more occupied with psychological processes. In general, the parties agreed that improvement depends on work with "deeper-lying" problems.

"A deeper-lying problem." THE CLIENT: Though I knew I had problems, I didn't know what sorts of problems they were. Until I found out it was anxiety.

Since being in prison I have been very unwilling to talk about it. I have been hiding and afraid of everything. It made me transfer my anxiety to some persons. When I started therapy, for instance, I was very afraid of my husband. But in reality I had an anxiety problem that I transferred to real persons. But now I have had a talk about my real problems and also with my husband, and that has helped.

I discovered by degrees that my problem was a deeper-lying anxiety. When I found that out, and when I revealed it, it was like waking up from a nightmare that had lasted many, many years.

THE THERAPIST: There was a long introductory phase when she was on guard vis-à-vis me and help in general, and when we worked hard on the subject of asking for help for problems. It was my feeling that another problem lay hidden behind the torture trauma, namely that her main problem was seeking help.

I then started to talk with her about the torture method and her time in prison. But I did not feel that this in itself changed her condition. Putting her torture experiences into words did not produce any change. What did bring about a change was when we started to talk about her dilemmas before her time in prison and the start of therapy, and during her time in Denmark.

It was only then that we started to talk about the torture and how to ask for help. I think this helped her to become more free and to have it out with her family about her servile and silent role.

"A regression to the kindergarten age." THE CLIENT: When they killed my two brothers I was completely shocked. And that was what we talked about during therapy. I had never talked with anyone about what had happened. It was a great help to talk about it and to find out that I had done nothing wrong. Just to be able to talk about it to somebody that I trusted helped me. It took a long time and it was hard, but it helped.

I was really more open with her than with my family. It was not love I felt toward her, but rather trust.

THE THERAPIST: I realized very quickly that the biggest problem was not the imprisonment and the torture, even if it had been extremely traumatic. But his dilemma and problem was really that he had never been fully accepted by his family.

I made a regular regression with him, and via dreams we got all the way back to kindergarten age. And only when we had been through all that work did we arrive at the torture experiences, which he was then really able to live through—a very difficult course. And then all of a sudden one day he got around what I call "the sharp corner." Then he came smartly dressed, and suddenly he could see what was happening around him—he could see the world. He could speak about his anger, he could control himself, and his nightmares disappeared. The only remnant was that he would occasionally dream about the sham executions he had been through.

Basic Trust

The torture survivors were very concerned about trust and safety in their contact with the therapists. They were thus more occupied by the form than the content of the therapy. It was very rare for any of them to give a description of the psychodynamic content of the therapy, for example the work with transference, such as the therapists did. By contrast, the survivors found it important to mention the setting of the therapy and the feeling of safety it gave. They often mentioned how important it was for the treatment center to create this atmosphere of safety.

"The place meant a lot." THE CLIENT: The place itself meant a lot to me. Just to go through the door to a place where I knew that some Danes were working for us torture survivors—that helped. It is not because one gets friends from coming here, but still one feels one gets a new family. As a refugee it means a lot to have a place to come to and to feel welcome.

THE THERAPIST: It took time to establish an atmosphere of safety so that he could work during the therapy. But when trust had finally been established, he worked well, almost too well. We got into a period during which he developed a strong transference to me, and I had to bring it up several times. He had become too dependent on the therapeutic process, which of course meant an improvement, but rather as part of a transference reaction. Only when this reaction had been discussed did he become more free, and could to some extent liberate himself from the dominating influence of his psychological symptoms.

"To have a fixed appointment." THE CLIENT: What was so good with the therapy was the fact that I had a good therapist who was always there. She was always waiting for me when I came. Just to have a fixed time was a help—the fact that I knew that this one time every week was for me, and it was my time. During the week it was easier for me to solve my problems, because I knew that it was quite certain that I had an appointment with my therapist.

THE THERAPIST: He said it was important for him that nobody within the system got to know anything about him, and he also said that he didn't dare to speak so much about certain concrete situations in his home country because of fear about how it could be used.

After about half a year, I felt that he gradually attained more and more understanding for the reactions he had shown during his torture and for those he showed today.

We worked of course a lot with the torture situation, but also with his childhood experiences, and how he transferred some of his previous and inappropriate reactions to me. He had had a very dominating father and had probably been sexually violated. This we worked with a lot, and an important precondition was that I became of great importance to him and that he felt safe in the process.

Reliving the Trauma

Most torture survivors and therapists emphasized that the torture experience, "the trauma story," should have a specific placement during the therapeutic course. One should be careful not to place it too early during therapy. A good working alliance has to be established before the clients can start to speak about their torture experiences, if indeed they are ever able to.

"Feeling worse." THE CLIENT: Talking is very, very important because one empties oneself and spreads everything out. But sometimes after a talk, everything inside me felt very intense, and it felt like a new crisis. That kind of crisis was a great strain to me because I remembered everything, and these crises obsessed me. Each time, I had to go back and start analyzing everything from the beginning. It was during that time I felt worse, and I was about to give up.

THE THERAPIST: When I started with him, I did as one was supposed to do, that is, I began to talk about the torture. First I focused on the events he had been through. But he felt so bad that we had to leave the subject, and I began again as with all other types of clients, that is, I listened to his background, the story of his life, and thus I found out what kind of life he had had before. It gave me an understanding of what resources he had. And I could now evaluate his situation.

"Regression to the baby stage." THE CLIENT: We were sitting there and talking about matters I had never mentioned to others, and gradually I got to like her very much, and when a patient likes her doctor, she feels better. It was

very difficult, but at the same time a big help. But when I left and had finished, I felt very bad, because I missed her.

THE THERAPIST: She had been exposed to severe sexual torture and had been raped daily in the prison. She resisted talking about it. One of the big problems is that men know that when a woman has been raped, she will be rejected by her husband. Even if the rape took place in prison, she is later at the sexual disposal of all the other men in her surroundings. Therefore she was raped by several men in her own family.

She took the stand that she would not talk about it before she could do so in Danish, but she could not live up to this goal and started to talk about it.

And she cheated me in that process, because she regressed to the stage of being a baby, in which she curled herself up like a fetus, sucked her thumb, and lost her language, and I could not make contact with her at all. And she did so several times, both with me and during physiotherapy, and sometimes it took hours before we could get her back to normal.

The Supportive Attitude

Most therapists mentioned that the kind of psychotherapy they practiced on torture survivors was different from other types of psychotherapy. The traumatic experience must be introduced with great care and be handled in a way that fits the rest of the person's psychodynamic setup. The result becomes a special kind of supportive psychotherapy that demands great experience.

"To take steps in another direction." THE THERAPIST: It is my experience in connection with torture that the most traumatic experience takes the longest time to unearth and set straight. Survivors may feel that their family let them down after they came back if a mother or father says: it was your own fault.

I think it may be harmful to stir up too much by talking about the torture more than is absolutely necessary. It is necessary to make contact with the experiences and touch them and put them in their place, and the same principle applies to traumas in general. I think that in some cases it may be directly harmful to relive experiences over and over again with all the feelings switched on. According to my way of working, one runs the risk of re-traumatizing instead of putting things in their right place. One risks making the footsteps in the snow deeper instead of taking steps in another and new direction.

"To give advice and to make demands." THE THERAPIST: It led to many things when she started to talk about the torture. When she applied for something from the social system, the answer was always no, exactly the same as when she asked the torturers to stop beating her. And she also asked for something from the therapy to which I had to say no, as for instance drugs and more frequent sessions.

Another thing was that she slightly felt she was a special case, but I had to tell her that this was absolutely not so in the sense that she was not the only one who had been exposed to torture.

It became a long course in which my role as container was replaced by one of a father who gave advice and demanded something. I supported her as part of a liberation process, and left her slowly to take care of herself, also during our sessions. It was very complicated and I had to include her in the supervision.

"To get the client on his or her feet." THE THERAPIST: It is difficult to say what had helped, but I didn't work as with my other patients. For instance, I rang him and asked him to come when he felt bad. Perhaps I should have left him alone without exceeding the therapeutic framework. I would never have done so with my ordinary clients. But I believe that he needed good advice and somebody to get him onto his feet. This kind of concrete and practical interference never became a problem.

Cultural Differences

Compared with the therapists, the torture survivors were more occupied with cultural differences. In practice, it was a question of language problems, different concepts of time, and different approaches to political and religious matters. The political matters were regularly mentioned as a problem. But after successful therapy several torture survivors said that the good result was due to the fact, among others, that the therapist was one of the few Danes with whom the survivor had felt something in common, a kind of similarity.

"The cultural difference that made therapeutic work difficult." THE CLIENT: You had better ask the therapist, because I can't remember anything.

I said over and over again that the police were after me and wanted to kill me, and he told me that there was no reason to be afraid. The police are always after me and look for me in the streets, and I think they are planning to put me in prison. But he didn't want to listen to me. Neither was he interested in hearing about the political problems of my country right now. But then there were so many other things we talked about, and that was good.

"Time was a problem." THE CLIENT: Perhaps she was a bit too pedantic about time, and when an hour had passed, there was nothing to do. But she was always there and tried to put questions to me in many different ways. She always tried to reach an understanding.

Time was a problem. In the beginning I felt that two hours once a week would be better than one hour twice a week. The time was not always sufficient. Sometimes I could feel that she had no more time, and then of course one stopped talking. But if nothing else, I learned to watch time a bit more and that is certainly something you are very concerned about here in Denmark.

(The therapist did not mention time.)

"Two people on equal terms." THE CLIENT: European and non-European, to be a refugee and not a refugee. I didn't know how it would be to be here before I was here. I didn't know anything about Denmark. Slowly I was able to put a face to the Danes, and I must admit I didn't trust these pale faces. I was ambivalent because on the one hand I had found a place in Danish society, on the other one does not feel 100 percent welcome here.

But I felt on equal terms with my therapist, as two human beings without any connection by nationality and religion. One had different conceptions of the other. But there was something apart from being two people, and that was being a person around whom I did not feel inferior. That helped me.

THE THERAPIST: And then I also learned something about his culture and religion. That made me happy.

The Extra-Therapeutic Room

It is well known from other psychotherapy studies that the clients are more occupied than the therapists by conditions outside the therapy room.

The quantitative analysis showed that the differences between torture survivors and their therapists were larger than with other groups of clients (see appendix). These are often very concrete matters, not mentioned by the therapist, such as a death in the family, breakup of a marriage, or political changes in the home country.

"Sexuality." The client: Sometimes my children say that it was my fault that we came to Denmark. For instance, my daughter was raped. A Danish boy came and raped her. I was very angry and felt that it was my fault because if I had not been involved in politics, we would not have had to flee. It is perhaps this that hurts me most.

(The therapist did not mention this matter.)

"Politics." The client: As you know, I have been very involved in politics. I am a soldier and fighter. But my therapist has never taken any interest in this. I don't think she knew how much it meant to me to be a soldier. But then there were other things that she was good at.

(The therapist did not mention this matter.)

The Outcome

In the quantitative analysis all the clients and therapists mentioned that something positive resulted from the treatment (see appendix). However, three of the twenty clients thought that the treatment had resulted in little benefit.

Negative Outcome

Two of these three clients were critical of the therapy because they had not been helped in some concrete matters such as housing and finances.

The therapists said that the torture survivors had misunderstood some fundamental preconditions for psychotherapy and only looked at it as a kind of social advisory assistance. In the third case, the client mentioned that his therapist was not interested in hearing about political problems, but wanted rather to talk about psychological problems.

"Social problems." The client: I got nothing out of psychotherapy. My mental state has not improved. I have so many problems in my social life and I

did not get any help at all. The memories of the past, what happened to me, get worse when I don't have a good place to live in. My very greatest problem is my housing problem, and it still has not been solved.

THE THERAPIST: She was not at all ready for psychotherapy at that time. I was in a dilemma because she was referred to me for psychotherapy and I was expected to treat her so that she would feel better. But for her, the problems were exclusively social and not mental.

The whole therapeutic course was influenced because she had some expectations that were not compatible with my role as therapist. And as a matter of fact, she was convinced that if she improved mentally she could not ask for financial compensation and better housing conditions.

"Political problems." THE CLIENT: We victims, who have been through great isolation and torture, are always afraid of expressing ourselves; we are afraid of our loneliness, and we are afraid of trusting someone. It also applied to the therapy.

When, for instance, the prison was mentioned as something I should talk about, and when a sensitive issue was touched, I relived the happenings in the prison. It would have been better for me to talk about my political work, but my therapist did not have any understanding of this.

THE THERAPIST: I asked him several times about his thoughts of what he got out of entertaining me with political matters. And just as in so many other questions, I was not sure that he understood me at all. And it should be added that he knew many Danish words, and even if an interpreter was present he seldom listened to me but continued to talk in his own fashion.

He was the first really "foreign" client I had from that area, and their upbringing is of course different. They are not used to talking about feelings, especially deep feelings; perhaps it was this cultural difference that made the therapy difficult.

Positive Outcome

Seventeen of the twenty torture survivors evaluated the treatment results as extremely positive. However, many of them added that they were not completely cured. Some therapists also mentioned that the survivors were still affected by the torture, but that they became more able to live with their symptoms. It was only the therapists who referred to the results as "insight," "autonomy," "maturing," and "development." The torture survivors mentioned the benefits in a more concrete way, that is, they could again experience feelings, control their anger, and they no longer suffered nightmares and anxiety.

"To know one's own illness" / *"Master of one's own life."* THE CLIENT: I got to know my illness and have learned how to live with it. I am almost living normally again. In a symbolic way, it was like waking up after an operation and not feeling pain any more.

THE THERAPIST: She started to make decisions about how she wanted to live instead of being influenced by external circumstances. And she started to have ideas about what happened in her life. She became mistress of her own life. But I look at it as the beginning of a process.

"To get the brain working again" / *"To value wife and children."* THE CLIENT: His method aimed at making me sit down quietly, whereas I am used to running around and not sitting quietly for 5 minutes. I can tell you that I can now sit for hours in one place without running around as I used to do before the therapy started.

Sometimes my brain could not at all follow what happened, but he was a man who could control me during the treatment. He got my brain working again.

THE THERAPIST: Gradually his symptoms disappeared and he had a more realistic attitude. He was very suspicious, almost paranoid, and that disappeared. He attained a better relationship with his wife and children, and came to appreciate them more.

"To understand oneself better" / *"Freedom and autonomy."* THE CLIENT: The most important thing I got out of it was to understand myself better than before, and that really was important. I must admit that I am not completely cured and normal.

The result is not that I have all the answers to all questions. Previously I had thought: Now I give up because all my problems are too complicated. I still think it is a bit too difficult to solve the problems I have, but one of the conclusions I came to during therapy was to try to live with them.

THE THERAPIST: He got a bit more insight into his reactions so that he could distance himself from them for a time, and experience greater freedom and autonomy.

"To feel better without being cured" / "More courage to face life." THE CLIENT: I find it difficult to say what I got out of it. I don't think one can be cured by just talking to a psychotherapist. That means that my attitude is that a client can never return to his normal pre-torture condition. But looking at myself, I think I am feeling better than before. I don't think I can say what I have found out. I can only say that I feel better than before.

THE THERAPIST: My patient was both intelligent and well functioning socially, and then it usually goes well. The symptoms have disappeared and he has more insight, more courage to face life, and has fewer complaints.

Discussion

The statements of the clients and therapists support, to some extent, the hypothesis about the existence of a torture syndrome, and they point out the helpful factors in the psychotherapy, in particular a specific supportive attitude of the therapist. But this presentation of the clients' experiences is not necessarily a direct expression of what "really" happened during the therapy. The way in which the clients construct their stories about the psychotherapy—how they put it into words—may reflect many of the unspoken motives and feelings they relive when they have to talk about the therapy. Furthermore, it may give a picture of how they want to present themselves to the investigator. The same may hold for the presentation by the therapist (Finn & Sperling 1993). The clients' "putting into words" reaches far beyond some psychodynamic conditions in the therapy room.

"Putting into words" means that something does not need to exist as a real physical object but gets a presence and features that are constructed in speech. Analysis of "putting into words" usually implies a detailed and thorough understanding of how a speech and a text are built up, and an examination of the conditions under which they were produced (Elsass 1994a, Elsass 1995, Elsass et al. 1995).

One party's evaluation and selection of significant situations in the therapy must be seen in relation to the other party's, because together they constitute the conditions of the parties' choice of words. But apart from that, they should also be seen in connection with the therapy that is practiced, the therapist and her methods, and in a broader sense with the professional setting and the culture in which the therapy takes place.

It was common for client and therapist to be talking about different subjects. Though there were many common subjects in their narratives, each of the parties had their local points. Thus, torture survivors were more concerned with the form of the therapy and by conditions outside the therapy room, such as political subjects and the situation in their own country. By contrast, the therapists were more occupied by the content of the therapy, the analysis of the psychodynamic conflicts, and the transference. However, this difference was not necessarily a hindrance to a therapeutic course.

The differences between the accounts of the clients and therapists might be explained by their different positions as narrators.

In the follow-up examination the client looked at the therapeutic process as a narrative process, a retelling and processing of his or her original account. By contrast, the therapist was occupied by the case story, which not only repeated the client's story and the therapist's interpretation of it, but also told about the course of the therapy itself. Furthermore, the therapist gave a third account, the interpretative meta-story about the principles and background of the therapeutic work.

It was not possible to make a clear distinction between these three stories for the client and the therapist, respectively, because the stories were intertwined, and the essence of the therapy is that the various stories mutually create one another. When the client is more occupied by the format and by some extra-therapeutic conditions and the therapist is not, the reason is not necessarily that the client has a more "open" and "realistic" view than the therapist; the client has another perspective and another knowledge/context.

In general, all the stories are of basic importance, because the therapy does not find its data but creates them. In another context, one may criticize this construction, but it is not necessarily a question of the therapists avoiding a consideration of the context because they do not mention it. By not mentioning it, they may, paradoxically, provoke the client to bring it into the therapy room and to begin to work with it in such a way that the stories start to interplay and create new ones.

Thus, the therapy is not only a link-up of two stories, the client's and the therapist's, but also an addition of something new, all aimed at creating "the good story," the story that creates a context and a meaning of importance for the client's daily context of action.

From anthropology we know of other healing rituals in which the parties may well talk about different subjects, and the result is still healing (Elsass 1992b, Lévi-Strauss 1967). As mentioned, change will occur when two perspectives merge into one, as for instance "another's image of myself incorporated inside me and opposed to my own image of myself" (Mead 1932) (see page 113). In contrast to many of the other situations to which the traumatized refugee is exposed in the encounter with a foreign culture, the therapeutic encounter does not have to be a collision but an interplay, in which one sees oneself in the light of the other.

Summary and Clinical Applications

• Many therapists are influenced by their work to such an extent that they get involved in a form of "vicarious" or "transmitted" traumatization. More and more of them are working in countries in which torture and war occur, and many are therefore exposed to the same traumatic situations as their clients.

• The precondition for successful treatment is that these "wounded healers" know how they can handle their own subjective reactions to the torture survivors' problems. There are no other solutions to this problem besides supervision.

• Supervision can take place among colleagues, but in order to avoid the institution being engulfed by the very same repressive mechanisms it tries to fight, it is recommended that the supervisor comes from outside.

• Treatment centers that want to avoid stagnation and development in the wrong direction must be open to ideas from outside, such as those coming from research. But psychotherapists are usually not users of research literature, and there is a need for a better relationship between scientific activity and practice.

• As an example of action research, a follow-up study combined with supervision practice has been carried out. Twenty torture survivors and their therapists were interviewed six months after treatment stopped and were asked to give an account of "what they got out of the psychotherapy." The results were compared with statements from forty-eight patients with anxiety disorders and their therapists. The patients and therapists' narratives were analyzed with qualitative and quantitative methods.

• All the clients were able to talk in a nuanced way about the therapeutic process and to evaluate the therapist and the progress of the therapy, information that can be valuable for the supervisors.

• All torture survivors and therapists said that the sessions had had a positive effect on one or more of the clients' symptoms. By and large, the torture survivors had the same number of complaints as the anxiety patients, but the qualitative study showed that they had another feature: they rarely had the same symptom fixation as psychiatric patients, but were often similar to the numbness of Holocaust survivors.

• The torture survivors demand a special supportive therapeutic approach in which establishment of "basic trust" is more important than identification of the trauma. A good working alliance has to be established before the clients could start to speak about their torture experiences, if indeed they were ever able to do so.

• The cultural differences between therapist and client are not so large that they constitute an essential impediment to psychotherapy. Language problems, different concepts of time, and different approaches to political and religious matters were, as a rule, mentioned as problems. But several torture survivors said that the good result of the therapy was due to the fact, among others, that the therapist was one of the few foreigners with whom the survivor had felt something in common, a kind of similarity.

• The results show that the torture survivors were more concerned with the form of the therapy and by conditions outside the therapy room. By contrast, the therapists were more occupied by the content of the therapy, the analysis of the psychodynamic conflicts, and the transference.

Appendix

Quantitative Analysis

Materials

Ten psychotherapists and one or more clients of each participated in the study. In all, twenty survivors participated. Furthermore, twelve general practitioners and twelve psychologists participated, each with two clients, a total of forty-eight patients who had attended psychotherapy sessions.

The Therapists

The ten psychotherapists were employed by the Rehabilitation Center for Torture Survivors (RCT) in Copenhagen during the study period from 1990 to 1995. Six of them were specialists in psychiatry, and four were clinical psychologists. They had been treating torture survivors for not less than three years. All had been through postgraduate training in psychotherapy, and all the psychologists were licensed.

The twelve general practitioners (M.D.'s) were recruited from a group of general practitioners who took part in a supervision group under the leadership of the late Dr. Torben Bendix, consultant at the psychiatric hospital in Aarhus. Each had been supervised for at least six months, and each had treated at least two clients during a complete course. The psychotherapy, about which they were interviewed, was carried out while they were members of the supervised group.

The twelve psychologists were final-year psychology students at the Institute of Psychology, University of Aarhus, attached to the Center for Psychotherapy.

The Clients

All twenty torture survivors were included in the qualitative analysis, but the quantitative analysis included only one client from each therapist. The client who first finished his or her treatment during the selection period was included unless he or she could not satisfy the following criteria.

Inclusion criteria. At their first contact with the therapist, all the clients should have complaints of anxiety. Using the questionnaire of SCID, all the clients were diagnosed by the author as having generalized anxiety (Spitzer & Williams 1988). Furthermore, the clients should never have had psychotic symptoms before, had never been admitted to a psychiatric hospital, nor had ever received psychiatric or psychological treatment. The participants should not have had diseases of the central nervous system or been addicted to drugs or alcohol.

The clients were contacted by their therapist and asked if they would like to take part in the study.

The ten torture survivors were selected as the first treated by the therapists during the selection period, at least six months, and at most eighteen months before inclusion. They came for therapy once a week for at least three months, and at most eighteen months, with an average of forty-four sessions. None had panic disorders or other psychopathology. More severe psychopathology was suspected in one case, and this person was replaced by the same therapist's next client during the study period. One other client refused to take part in the study, and the next client was therefore selected. Three clients were excluded because they used an interpreter, and the next clients during the study period were included in the quantitative analysis.

The torture survivors comprised two women and eight men, aged from twenty to fifty-two years (median thirty years). Four came from Iran, two from Iraq, two from Turkey, and two were Palestinians.

Of the twenty-four patients with anxiety, half had had psychotherapy with their general practitioner, the other half with a psychologist. (See also the description in Elsass et al. 1995a.)

The GPs' clients came for therapy at least once a week for a minimum of three months and a maximum of one year. Selection was based on completion of the treatment six to eighteen months earlier. The GPs selected the first two clients under treatment in this period. In two cases in which a panic disorder or other psychopathology was suspected, the second of the therapist's two clients was selected for the study.

The psychologists' clients came for therapy once a week for three months. The treatment ended six to twelve months before they were included in the study. Each psychologist, during training, had two clients under treatment.

Methods

The author interviewed all the torture survivors and their therapists, as well as the general practitioners and their patients. Students of psychology Britta Kaplan and Helgi Rasmussen interviewed the psychologists and their clients at the Center for Psychotherapy under close supervision by the author. Everything was written down during the interview and was later transferred to a data file for quantitative and qualitative analyses.

Therapists and clients were all interviewed according to the same plan. The questions were formulated to correspond with open, unstructured answers, which were later structured by means of more specific questions.

The interview consisted of the following subjects and questions:

1. *Narrative about the psychotherapy*. After a short introduction the interviewed person was asked to "tell about the psychotherapy, and what the client got out of it." The clients/therapists were told they could say anything they wanted to, and that they had ten minutes to do so. No leading or additional questions were asked, but if the interviewee stopped talking, he or she was encouraged, in a neutral way, to continue.

2. *Helping and nonhelping elements*. Clients/therapists were then asked to describe whether "there were elements in the therapy that were found helpful, and whether there was something that was not considered a help or was a direct hindrance."

3. *The significance of the profession and the institution*. Clients/therapists were asked about advantages and disadvantages of (a) the therapist being a trained therapist, and (b) the therapist being attached to an institution for torture survivors in particular.

4. *Extra-therapeutic conditions*. Clients/therapists were asked to speak about events outside the therapy room, but during therapy, that influenced the well-being of the client and the extent to which it was thought to be caused by the therapy.

5. *Rating of outcome*. The interview ended with a rating in which both parties, on a rating scale from 1 to 5, were asked to evaluate the same topics in therapy that were used in the "outcome scale" (Malan 1976: 57): occurrence of symptoms, ability to solve problems, self-understanding, and tolerance toward others. They were asked to evaluate their well-being before the start of therapy, and again three months after it ended. Apart from this, the therapists were asked to indicate which of their two therapies had been most successful.

6. *System of belief.* Both therapist and client were asked to speak about their views on health by answering these questions: "What do you think is of general importance for staying healthy?" "Think of a person whom you know and who lives a healthy life; what is of importance for this person's health?" and "Can you give an example from your own life which you consider of importance for your health?"

7. *Torture's influence on the system of belief.* The torture survivors were asked what they considered the "most important in their lives" before they were tortured, and what kinds of changes the torture caused.

8. *Aggression and revenge.* The survivors were asked how the torture had influenced their handling of affects. More specifically, they were asked whether they experienced anger and revenge, and what their attitude was about being violent toward others.

9. *Coping.* The survivors were asked to think of a concrete situation within the previous six months which had been difficult for them, and to relate how they managed it.

10. *Global assessment.* For each interview, the author gave an overall evaluation of the following:

    a. The degree of insight, rated from 1 to 3: (1) "focusing on symptoms and little insight"; (2) "insight in a few causal relations"; and (3) "good insight reflecting psychodynamic understanding."
    b. The degree of compliance between the parties, rated as (1) "poor," (2) "fair," and (3) "good."

The data were analyzed using a combination of quantitative and qualitative methods. Based on a random sample of interviews, some empirical "data-driven categories" were formulated into which each single sentence could be placed (Strauss & Corbin 1990). Each sentence was placed in a category concerned with the content of the therapy, and furthermore was given a dimension concerned with the relationship between the parties (see table 1). When two or more subsequent sentences were given the same score, they were considered as one meaning-unit. The interviews of the psychologists and their clients, and of the general practitioners and their patients, were then scored by the author and Dr. Bent Rosenbaum; when there were differences between the scores, agreement was reached by discussion. The interviews of the torture survivors and their therapists were scored by the author, but samples of the scores were checked by Dr. Rosenbaum. These scores were the basis of the quantitative analyses.

TABLE I
Categories for the Narrative about Psychotherapy

Categories	Dimensions
1. Before therapy	1. No reference
2. Referral problem	2. Reference to both parties, neutral
3. Agreement and aim	3. Reference to the interplay, negative, resistant
4. Technique and method	4. Reference to the interplay, positive
5. Process	
6. Symptoms and problems during therapy	
7. Result and help	
8. Extra-therapeutic conditions	
9. Termination	
10. After therapy	
11. Reference to torture	
12. Reference to cultural differences	

Based on the scores of the first part of the texts, that is, "1. Narrative about the psychotherapy," it was possible to draw a "narrative signature" as several connecting lines between the scores' categories and dimensions. Furthermore, a narrative similarity coefficient between client and therapist was calculated. These similarity coefficients express the degree of agreement between the scores and their sequence when the interviews with the client and therapist were compared. The coefficient between two texts was calculated by adding the number of scores and the sequence of scores that appear in both texts, put in relation to the product of all the scores and sequences.

The similarity coefficients were calculated using the following formula: $S = (N_{1,2} + N_{2,1} + S_{1,2} + S_{2,1}) / A$, in which S is the narrative similarity coefficient; $N_{1,2}$ are scores in the client interview that also appear in the therapist interview; $N_{2,1}$ are scores in the therapist interview that also appear in the client interview; $S_{1,2}$ are sequences of scores in the client interview that also appear in the therapist interview; $S_{2,1}$ are sequences in the therapist interview that also appear in the patient interview; A is all the possible scores and sequences in the most extensive of the two interviews (Butchart & Blanche 1991).

Results

Narrative about the Psychotherapy

Torture Survivors and Their Therapists. There were no significant differences in the amount of narrative text or in the number of scores between the clients and the therapists.

Table 2 shows the distribution of categories and dimensions for torture survivors and their therapists. Both parties most often put the following categories into words: (5) "Process," (6) "Symptoms and problems during therapy," (7) "Result and help," and (8) "Conditions outside the therapy," whereas the other categories were used only to a very small extent.

The quantitative distribution was largely similar for therapists and clients, except that the torture survivors used significantly fewer categories for "process" than their therapists (Mann–Whitney $p < 0.05$). Furthermore, the torture survivors used the category of "torture" significantly less than the therapists (Mann–Whitney $p < 0.05$). With respect to the relationship between therapist and client, the torture survivors mentioned the interplay as positive more often than the therapists (Mann–Whitney $p < 0.05$), and there was also a trend to mention more often "technique and method" and "conditions outside the therapy" (Mann–Whitney $p < 0.05$, $p < 0.05$).

Each sentence of "Narrative of the psychotherapy" was given a score within a category concerning the content of therapy and within a dimension concerning the relationship between client and therapist. Table 2 shows the number of scores for clients and therapists, respectively.

TABLE 2
Ten Torture Survivors and Ten Therapists

	Clients	Therapists	Mann–Whitney
Category (content of therapy):			
Before therapy	27	17	n.s.
Application problem	5	12	n.s.
Agreement and aim	0	1	n.s.
Technique and method	25	11	0.05
Process	67	97	0.05
Symptoms and problems	50	47	n.s.
Results and help	88	49	n.s.
Extra-therapeutic conditions	29	7	0.05
Termination	0	1	n.s.
After therapy	6	12	n.s.
Reference to torture	11	25	0.05
Reference to culture	5	9	n.s.
Dimension (relationship between client and therapist):			
No reference	112	90	n.s.
Neutral reference	73	89	n.s.
Negative reference	34	58	n.s.
Positive reference	61	31	0.05

Torture Survivors Compared with Anxiety Patients Table 3 shows the scores for anxiety patients and their therapists. There were no statistically significant differences in the distribution of scores between the therapists for the two groups; but the anxiety patients and torture survivors are distinguished in that the torture survivors used significantly more statements concerning "symptoms and problems during therapy" (Mann–Whitney $p < 0.05$), and were significantly more concerned about the extra-therapeutic room, "outside the therapy" (Mann–Whitney $p < 0.05$). By contrast, the anxiety patients used the category concerning "the process" more often than torture survivors (Mann–Whitney $p < 0.02$).

TABLE 3
Twenty-four Patients with Anxiety and Twenty-four Therapists

	Clients	Therapists	Mann–Whitney
Category (content of therapy):			
Before therapy	27	13	n.s.
Application problem	14	19	n.s.
Agreement and aim	10	4	n.s.
Technique and method	53	15	0.05
Process	210	134	n.s.
Symptoms and problems	29	48	n.s.
Results and help	127	95	n.s.
Extra-therapeutic conditions	26	7	0.05
Termination	17	12	n.s.
After therapy	15	12	n.s.
Dimension (reference to relationship between client and therapist):			
No reference	139	141	n.s.
Neutral reference	4	175	n.s.
Negative reference	67	45	n.s.
Positive reference	68	18	0.05

Rating of Outcome

When the ratings before and after the therapy were compared, all the torture survivors and therapists said that the talks had had a positive effect on one or more of the subjects of "Symptom occurrence," "Ability to solve problems," "Self-understanding," and "Tolerance toward others." However, three of the ten clients considered that the treatment had resulted only in little progress (one step), whereas the rest rated the progress at seven or more steps. There were no trends showing that some dimensions were to be improved more than others, and there were no significant differences between the evaluations made by torture survivors and therapists.

Comparison of Therapeutic Courses with High and Low Outcome Scores

There were no differences in the distribution of the scores of the therapeutic course when the material was divided into two groups, that is, above the median, and below (and equal to) the median.

Narrative Signatures

The narrative course was drawn as lines between the different scores for categories and dimensions of the narrative about the psychotherapy. Figures 1–4 show such courses for the four groups: the torture survivors (A) and their therapists (B), the anxiety patients (C) and their therapists (D). The categories are numbered 1–10 (in italics), and the dimensions within each category are numbered 1–4 (in circles), as in table 1. A line was drawn for the torture survivors and their therapists between the various scores when two points were connected two or more times. The lines were drawn for the anxiety patients and their therapists when two points were connected four or more times. The more connections between two scores, the thicker the line. The arrows on the lines indicate movement from a higher to a lower category number; no arrows indicate the opposite movement.

These figures illustrate that the torture survivors move around more than their therapists between the various scores. Furthermore, the survivors were more occupied than their therapists by extra-therapeutic factors, in particular the conditions before the therapy. By contrast, the therapists were more occupied than the survivors by the process.

Though the narrative signatures for anxiety patients and torture survivors cannot immediately be compared because of the difference in number, one nevertheless had the impression that there was more similarity between clients and therapists in the anxiety group than in the group of torture survivors, a fact that was confirmed by calculating the narrative similarity coefficients. The Danish patients and therapists were more occupied by the process, while the torture survivors were relatively more occupied by the symptoms.

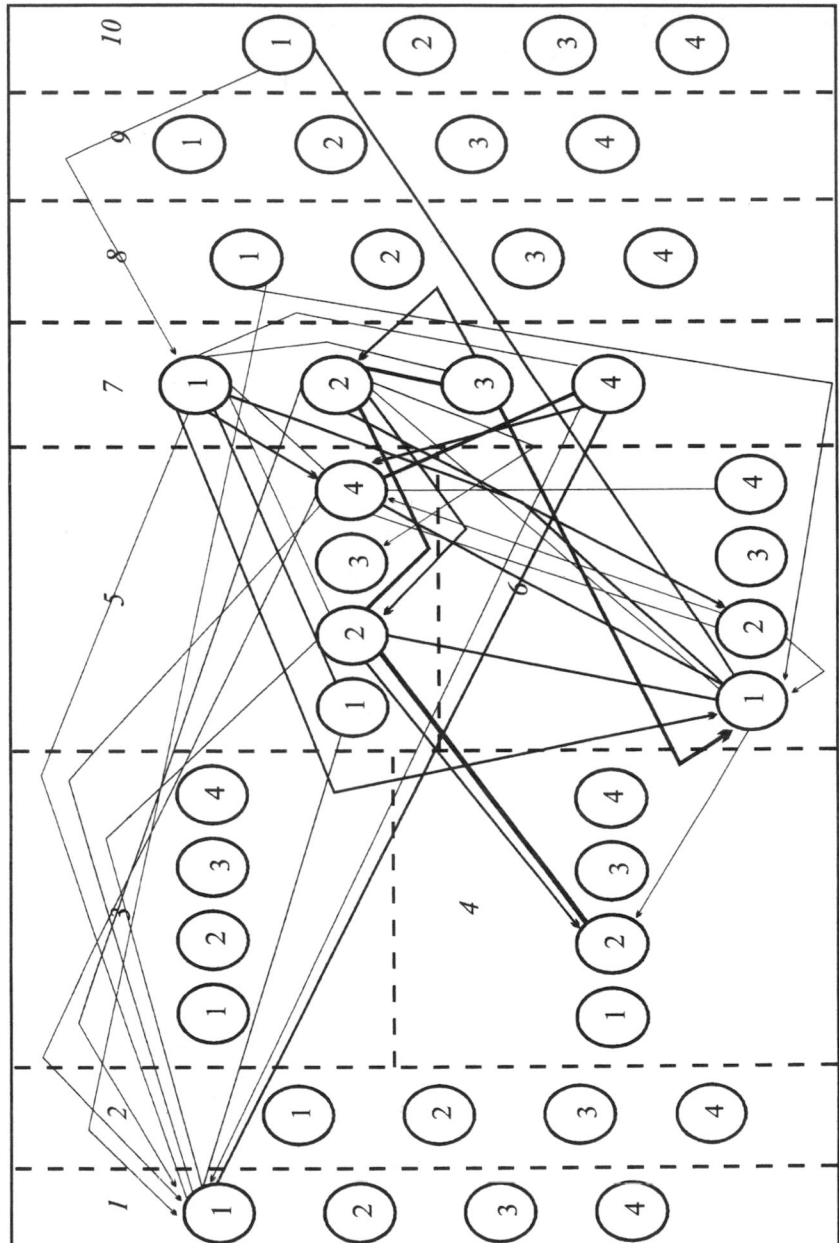

Figure 1. Group A: Torture survivors.

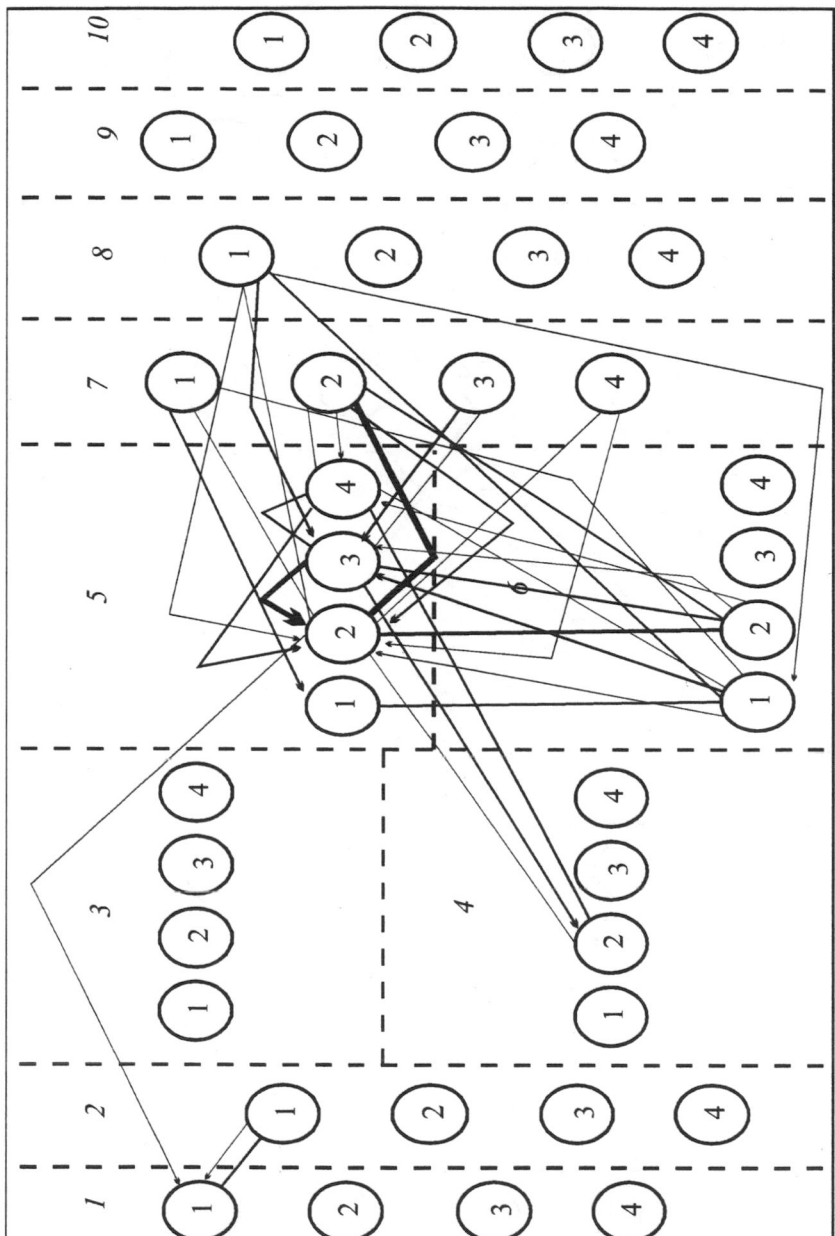

Figure 2. Group B: The torture survivors' therapists.

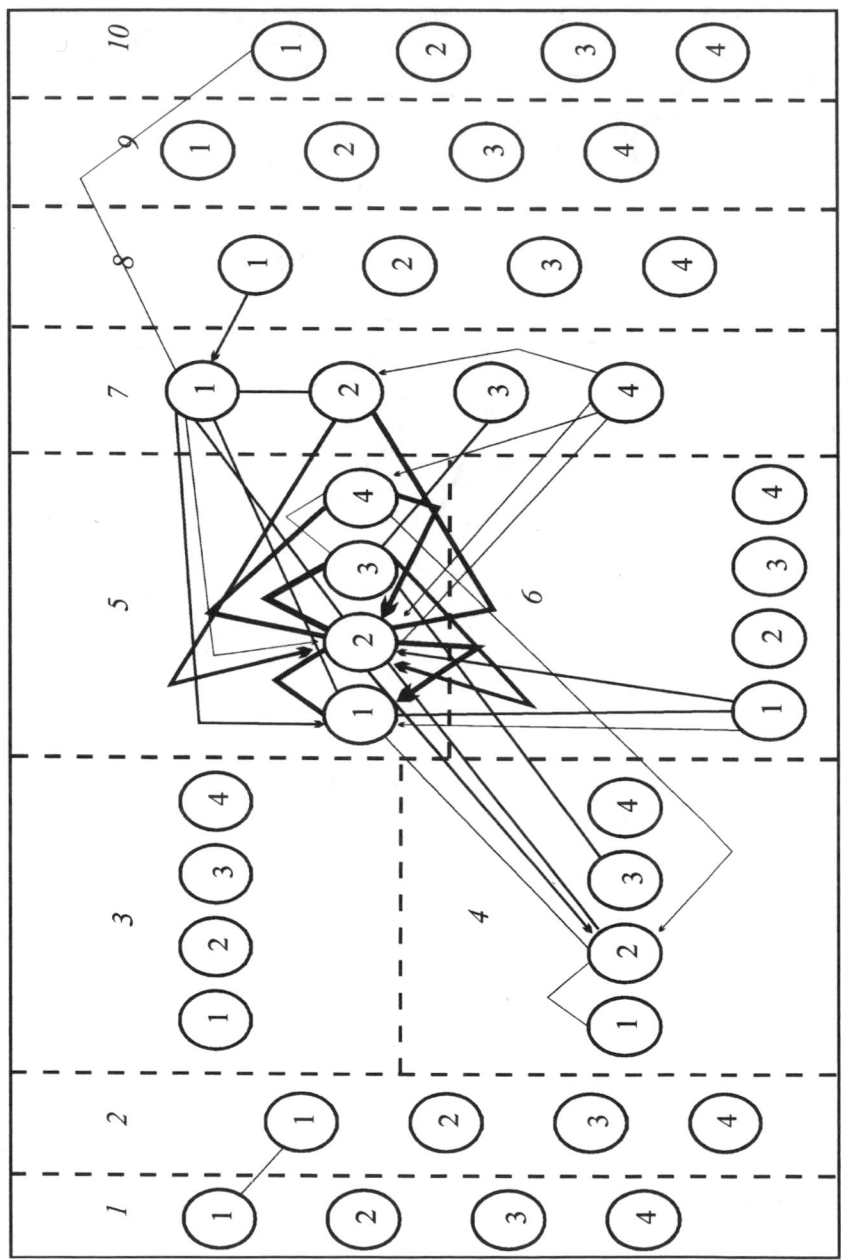

Figure 3. Group C: Anxiety patients.

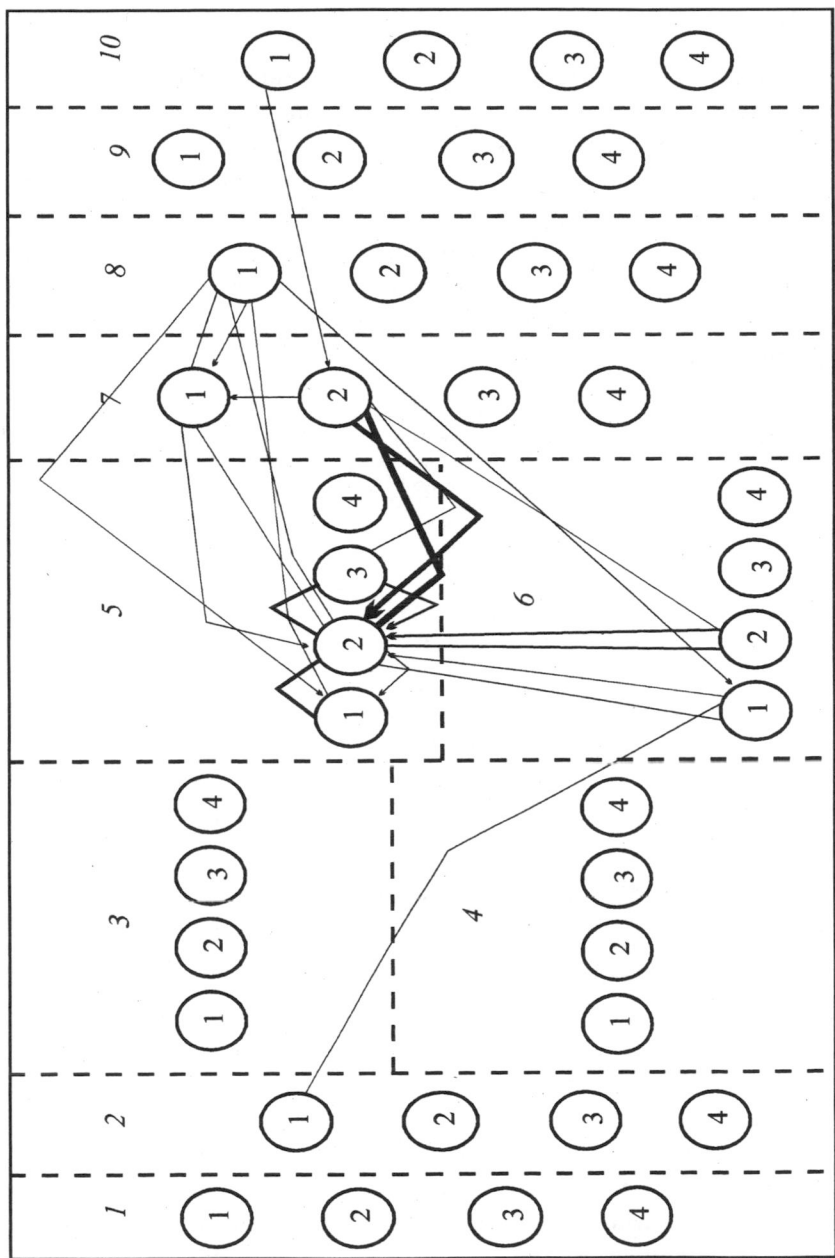

Figure 4. Group D: The anxiety patients' therapists.

Narrative Similarity Coefficients

The narrative similarity coefficients, calculated from the categories and transference dimensions, are shown in tables 4 and 5.

The similarity coefficients were not significantly different when the short narratives were compared with the long ones, or when narratives with few categories and dimensions (below or equal to the median) were compared with narratives with many (above the median).

The similarity coefficients for the torture survivors and their therapists were significantly lower than for anxiety patients and their therapists (Mann-Whitney $p < 0.05$).

TABLE 4
Narrative Similarity Coefficients
(10 Torture Survivors, 10 Therapists)

1. client/therapist	0.024
2. client/therapist	0.038
3. client/therapist	0.037
4. client/therapist	0.066
5. client/therapist	0.064
6. client/therapist	0.029
7. client/therapist	0.015
8. client/therapist	0.049
9. client/therapist	0.046
10. client/therapist	0.042

System of Belief and the Influence of Torture

The torture survivors' concepts of health were directed toward the topics of "nutrition," "a job and good financial conditions," "close relationships," and "attitude toward life." None of the torture survivors mentioned "exercise" or "no smoking" or "little alcohol intake," which were emphasized by both the anxiety patients and a representative sample of Danes aged 30 and 50 years (Elsass et al. 1995).

All the torture survivors mentioned that the torture had very much influenced their attitude toward what they considered "most important in life," compared with what they considered important before the torture. Seven torture survivors said of most importance to them now are the family and close relationships with friends and acquaintances. Three answered that it was most important to "create peace on earth."

TABLE 5
Narrative Similarity Coefficients
(24 Anxiety Patients, 24 Therapists)

1. client/therapist	0.080
2. client/therapist	0.041
3. client/therapist	0.049
4. client/therapist	0.043
5. client/therapist	0.035
6. client/therapist	0.046
7. client/therapist	0.075
8. client/therapist	0.056
9. client/therapist	0.054
10. client/therapist	0.028
11. client/therapist	0.055
12. client/therapist	0.059
13. client/therapist	0.099
14. client/therapist	0.087
15. client/therapist	0.060
16. client/therapist	0.050
17. client/therapist	0.032
18. client/therapist	0.099
19. client/therapist	0.017
20. client/therapist	0.046
21. client/therapist	0.094
22. client/therapist	0.074
23. client/therapist	0.057
24. client/therapist	0.106

All the torture survivors said that they felt revengeful against the regime and their torturers, but that after torture they could no longer be physically violent toward others.

By the conclusion of their treatment, six of the torture survivors had been exposed to a traumatic situation in Denmark, such as assault, restrictions imposed by the police, or a drastic change in their financial or housing situation. All had reacted passively, with a tendency to isolate themselves for a short period, but then regained their previous function.

Summary

The quantitative description is not suitable for a valid presentation because of its uncertain representativeness. Although an attempt was made to make allowances for this by narrow and strict inclusion and exclusion criteria, the quantitative presentation should only be taken as a supplement to the qualitative analysis that was presented in the previous chapter. The quantitative presentation suggests hypotheses that the torture survivors were less occupied than their therapists by the torture and psychodynamic process. Compared with anxiety patients, the torture survivors were more fixed on symptoms and on what happened outside therapy in the "extra-therapeutic room." Furthermore, there was less agreement between clients and their therapists in "putting into words" the psychotherapeutic process among torture survivors than among anxiety patients, possibly because of cultural differences. But all the torture survivors and therapists said that the talks had had a positive effect.

• Ten psychotherapists participated, each with one or more torture survivors, in all twenty torture survivors. Furthermore, twelve general practitioners and twelve psychologists participated, each with two clients with an anxiety disorder, a total of forty-eight patients. All interview data were analyzed using a combination of quantitative and qualitative methods.

• All the torture survivors and their therapists said that the therapy had had a positive effect on one or more of the items listed on an outcome scale. However, three clients expressed that the treatment had resulted in little progress.

• The narratives about psychotherapy showed that the torture survivors talked less about the process in the sessions than their therapists and mentioned the torture experience more seldom. The survivors gave more attention to the framework of the therapy, the technique and methods, than their therapists and also to the conditions outside therapy such as changes in their work situation and political circumstances in their homeland.

• In contrast to the anxiety patients, the torture survivors talked more about their symptoms and problems. The anxiety patients where more familiar with the psychodynamical way of thinking than the foreign survivors and gave more attention to the process in the sessions.

• The differences between the narratives of the torture survivors and their therapists were larger than for the anxiety patients and their therapists. But this cultural difference did not have any connection to how the outcome of therapy was rated.

• All torture survivors mentioned that the torture had very much influenced their attitude toward what they considered "most important in life," and said that of most importance to them now was the family and close relationships with friends and acquaintances. Only a few answered that it was most important to "create peace on earth."

• All the torture survivors said that they felt revengeful against the regime and their torturers, but that after torture they could no longer be physically violent toward others. They usually react passively and have a tendency to isolate themselves.

References

Abraham, K. 1927. A short study of the development of the libido. In *Selected papers of Karl Abraham*. Basic Books, New York.

Agger, I. 1991. Skammens magt: Kvindeligt vidnesbyrd fra exilet *(The power of shame: Testimony of exiled women)*. In P. Berliner, B. Karpatschof, and R. Kuschel, eds., *Vrede, konflikt, kultur (Anger, conflict, culture)*. Dansk Psykologisk Forlag, Copenhagen.

———. 1995. *Theory and practice of psycho-social projects under war conditions in Bosnia-Herzegovina and Croatia*. ECHO/ECTF. European Community Task Force, Zagreb.

Agger, I., and Jensen, S. B. 1990. Testimony as ritual and evidence in psychotherapy for political refugees. *Journal of Traumatic Stress* 3:115–30.

———. 1993. The psychosexual trauma of torture. In J. P. Wilson and B. Raphael, eds., *International handbook of traumatic stress syndromes*. Plenum Press, New York.

———. 1994. Determinant factors for countertransference reactions under state terrorism. In J. P. Wilson and L. D. Jacob, eds., *Countertransference in the treatment of PTSD*. Guilford, New York.

———. 1996. *Trauma and healing under state terrorism*. Zed Books, London.

Allerton, W. S. 1964. Mass casualty care and human behavior. *Medical Annals of the District of Columbia* 33:206–8.

Alvarez, F. 1988. Rio revuelto. *Semana* 325 (26 July).

American Psychiatric Association. 1994. *DSM IV*. Washington, D.C.

Amnesty International. 1993. *Amnesty International report 1993*. Amnesty International Publications, London.

Antropologicas: Violencia e informacion en Colombia y America Latina. 1988. *Antropologicas* 87 (March).

Anzieu, D. 1985. *The skin ego: A psychoanalytic approach to the self*. Yale University Press, New Haven.

Arcel, L. T. 1986. Selvmordsforsøg: En sammenligning mellem græsk og dansk materiale *(Suicide attempts: A comparison between a Greek and a Danish study)*. In P. Elsass and K. Hastrup, eds., *Sygdomsbilleder: Medicinsk antropologi og psykologi (Disease patterns: Medical anthropology and psychology)*. Gyldendal, Copenhagen.

Arcel, L. T., ed. 1994. *War victims, trauma and psycho-social care*. European Community Task Force, Zagreb.

Arcel, L. T., Folnegovic-Smalc,V., Kozaric-Kovacic, D., and Marusic,A. 1995. *Psycho-social help to war victims: Women refugees and their families.* International Rehabilitation Council for Torture Victims, Copenhagen.

Ascher-Svanum, H., and Krause, A. A. 1991. *Psychoeducational groups for patients with schizofrenia.* Aspen Publications, Maryland.

Baker, R. 1992. Psychosocial consequences for tortured refugees seeking asylum and refugee status in Europe. In M. Basoglu, ed., *Torture and its consequences: Current treatment approaches.* Cambridge University Press, Cambridge, U.K.

Barudy, J. 1989. A programme of mental health for political refugees: Dealing with the invisible pain of political exile. *Social Science and Medicine* 28:715–27.

Basoglu, M. 1992. Behavioral and cognitive approach in the treatment of torture re-lated psychological problems. In M. Basoglu, ed., *Torture and its consequences: Cur-rent treatment approaches.* Cambridge University Press, Cambridge, U.K.

———. 1993. Prevention of torture and care of survivors: An integrated approach. *Journal of the American Medical Association* 270:606–11.

———. 1995. Severity of trauma as predictor of long-term psychological status in survivors of torture. *Journal of Anxiety Disorders* 9:339–50.

Basoglu, M., ed. 1992. *Torture and its consequences: Current treatment approaches.* Cam-bridge University Press, Cambridge, U.K.

Bauman, Z. 1994. *Modernitet og holocaust (Modernity and the Holocaust).* Hans Reitzels Forlag, Copenhagen.

Beal, A. L. 1995. Post-traumatic stress disorder in prisoners of war and combat veterans of the Dieppe Raid: A 50-years follow-up. *Canadian Journal of Psychiatry* 40:177–84.

Beiser, M. 1985. A study of depression among traditional Africans, urban North Americans and Southeast Asian Refugees. In A. Kleinman and B. Good, eds., *Cul-ture and depression: Studies in the anthropology and cross-cultural psychiatry of affect and disorder.* University of California Press, Berkeley.

Beiser, M., and Flemming, J. A. E. 1986. Measuring psychiatric disorder among Southeast Asian Refugees. *Psychological Medicine* 16:627–39.

Benedict, R. 1979. *The chrysanthemum and the sword: Patterns of Japanese culture.* Tuttle Company, Tokyo.

Ben-Ezer, G. 1985. Cross-cultural misunderstandings: The case of Ethiopian immi-grant-Jews in the Israeli society. *Israel Social Science Research* 3:1–13.

Bettelheim, B. 1943. Individual and mass behavior in extreme situations. *Journal of Abnormal Social Psychology* 38:417–52.

———. 1976. *The uses of enchantment: The meaning and importance of fairy tales.* Pen-guin Books, London.

———. 1979. *Surviving and other essays.* Vintage Books, New York.

———. 1986. *The informed heart: A study of the psychological consequences of living under extreme fear and terror.* Peregrine Books, New York.

Bibring, E. 1954. Psychoanalysis and the dynamic psychotherapies. *Journal of Ameri-can Psychoanalytic Association* 2:745–70.

Bion, W. R. 1958. *Experiences in groups.* Tavistock, London.

Blackwell, R. D. 1993. Disruption and reconstitution of family, network, and community systems following torture, organized violence and exile. In J. P. Wilson and B. Raphael, eds., *International handbook of traumatic stress syndromes.* Plenum Press, New York.

Bleuler, M. 1978. *The schizophrenic disorders: Long-term patient and family studies.* Yale University Press, New Haven.

Borofsky, G. L., and Brand, D. J. 1980. Personality organization and psychological functioning of the Nuremberg war criminals: The Rorschach data. In J. E. Dimsdale, ed., *Survivors, victims and perpetrators: Essays on the Nazi holocaust.* Hemisphere Publishing, New York.

Bowlby, J. 1969. *Attachment and loss.* Hogarth Press, London.

Bracken, P. J. 1993. Post-empiricism and psychiatry: Meaning and methodology in cross-cultural research. *Social Science and Medicine* 36:265–72.

Brandt, P. Å. 1980. *Den talende krop (Body language).* Rhodos, Copenhagen.

———. 1994. Hvorfor stigende vold? (*Increasing violence—why?*) *Weekendavisen,* 1 April.

Brett, E. A., and Ostroff, R. 1985. Imagery and post-traumatic stress disorder: An overview. *American Journal of Psychiatry* 142:417–24.

Breuer, J., and Freud, S. 1895. Studies on hysteria. *Standard Edition.* Hogarth Press, London.

Brody, H. 1987. *Stories of sickness.* Yale University Press, New Haven.

Brown, C. S., Wright, R. G., and Christensen, D. B. 1987. Association between types of medication instruction and patients' knowledge, side effects and compliance. *Hospital and Community Psychiatry* 38.55–60.

Brown, G., and Harris, T. 1978. *Social origins of depression: The study of psychiatric disorders in women.* Tavistock, London.

Brun, B. 1992. The application of fairy tales in psychotherapy. In B. Brun, E. W. Pederson, and M. Runberg, *Symbols of the soul: Therapy and guidance through fairy tales.* Jessical Kingsley Publishers, London.

Brun, B., Pederson E. W., and Runberg, M. 1992. *Symbols of the soul: Therapy and guidance through fairy tales.* Jessica Kingsley Publishers, London.

Bruner, J. 1990. *Acts of meaning.* Harvard University Press, Cambridge, Mass.

Brunvatne, R., Lysgaard, K. H., and Hjortdahl, P. 1995. Psykosocialt forebyggende arbeid blant krigsflyktninger. En opgave for primærhelsetjenesten? (*Psychosocial preventive work among war refugees: A task for the primary health service?*) *Tidskrift for Norsk Lægeforening* 115:23–26.

Bustos, E. 1990. Dealing with the unbearable: Reactions of therapists and therapeutic institutions to survivors of torture. In P. Suedfeld, ed., *Psychology and torture.* Hemisphere Publishing, New York.

———. 1992. Psychodynamic approaches in the treatment of torture survivors. In M. Basoglu, ed., *Torture and its consequences: Current treatment approaches.* Cambridge University Press, Cambridge, U.K.

Butchart, A., and Blanche, M. T. 1991. From discourses to narratives: Analysing talk about township violence. Health Psychology Unit, University of South Africa, Pretoria.

Carr, D. 1986. Narrative and the real world: An argument for continuity. *History and Theory* 25:117–31.

Cassel, E. J. 1982. The nature of suffering and the goals of medicine. *New England Journal of Medicine* 11:639–45.

Chagnon, N. A. 1977. *Yanomami: The fierce people*. Holt, Rinehart and Winston, New York.

Chemptob, C., Roiblat, H. L., Hamada, R. S., Carlson, J. G., and Twentyman, C. T. 1988. A cognitive action theory of post-traumatic stress disorder. *Journal of Anxiety Disorder* 2:253–75.

Chodoff, P. 1980. Psychotherapy with the survivor. In J. Dimsdale, ed., *Survivors, victims and perpetrators*. Hemisphere Publishing, Washington, D.C.

Cienfuegos, J., and Monelli, C. 1983. The testimony of political repression as a therapeutic instrument. *American Journal of Orthopsychiatry* 53:43–51.

Clifford, J., and Marcus, G., eds. 1986. *Writing culture*. University of California Press, Berkeley.

Comez-Diaz, L., and Padilla, A. M. 1990. Countertransference in working with victims of political repression. *American Journal of Orthopsychiatry* 60:125–34.

Corbin, J. 1987. Insurrections in Spain: Casas Viejas 1933 and Madrid 1981. In D. Riches, ed., *The anthropology of violence*. Basil Blackwell, London.

Cotler, I., ed. 1993. *Nuremberg forty years later: The struggle against injustice in our time*. McGill-Queen's University Press, Toronto.

Cox, M., and Theilgaard, A. 1987. *Mutative metaphors in psychotherapy: The Aeolian mode*. Tavistock, London.

Cozolino, L. J., Goldstein, M. J., Neuchterlein, K. H., West, K. L., and Snyder, K. S. 1988. The impact of education about schizofrenia on relatives varying in expressed emotion. *Schizofrenia Bulletin* 14:675–87.

Cullberg, J. 1983. *Krise og udvikling (Crisis and development)*. Hans Reitzels Forlag, Copenhagen.

Cunningham, M., and Silove, D. 1993. Principles of treatment and service development of torture and trauma survivors. In J. P. Wilson and B. Raphael, eds., *International handbook of traumatic stress syndromes*. Plenum Press, New York.

Dahl, C.-I. 1989. Some problems of cross-cultural psychotherapy with refugees seeking treatment. *American Journal of Psychoanalysis* 49:19–33.

Danieli, Y. 1980. Countertransference in the treatment and study of Nazi holocaust survivors and their children. *Victimology* 5:355–67.

———. 1988. Treating survivors and children of survivors of the Nazi holocaust. In F. Ochberg, ed., *Post-traumatic therapy and victims of violence*. Brunner/Mazel, New York.

Danieli, Y., Rodley, N. S., and Weisæth, L. 1996. *International responses to traumatic stress:*

Humanitarian, human rights, justice, peace and development contributions, collaborative actions and future initiatives. Baywood, New York.

Danish Medical Bulletin. 1987. Doctors, ethics, and torture. 34:185–216.

Davidsen-Nielsen, M., and Leick, N. 1987. *Den nødvendige smerte: Om sorg, sorgterapi og kriseintervention (Obligatory pain: Grief, grief therapy and crisis intervention).* Munksgaard, Copenhagen.

————. 1993. Om traumers natur: Nogle teoretiske overvejelser *(The nature of trauma: Theoretical considerations). Nordisk Psykologi* 1:55–61.

de Press, T. 1980. The survivor: An anatomy of life in the death camp. In J. E. Dimsdale, ed., *Survivors, victims and perpetrators: Essays on the Nazi Holocaust.* Hemisphere Publishing, New York.

Devereux, G. 1980. *Variations in psychotherapy procedures: Basic problems in ethnopsychiatry.* University of Chicago Press, Chicago.

Dobroszycki, L. ed. 1984. *The chronicle of the Lodz ghetto 1941–1944.* Yale University Press, New Haven.

Dohrenwend, B. 1966. Social status and psychological disorder. *American Sociological Review* 31:14–34.

Dreier, O. 1993. Psykosocial behandling: En teori om et praksisområde *(Psychosocial treatment: Theory and practice).* Dansk Psykologisk Forlag, Copenhagen.

Drozdek, B. 1996. The follow-up study of ex-concentration camp prisoners from Bosnia-Herzegovina: 3 years later. Proceedings from the Second World Conference of the International Society for Traumatic Stress Studies, Jerusalem, 9–13 June.

DSM-IV. 1994. American Psychiatric Association, Washington D.C.

DuBois, P. 1991. *Torture and truth.* Routledge, New York.

Dutton, D., and Painter, S. L. 1981. Traumatic bonding: The development of emotional attachments in battered women and other relationships of intermittent abuse. *Victimology* 6:139–55.

Eagle, M. N. 1987. *Recent developments in psychoanalysis: A critical evaluation.* Harvard University Press, Cambridge, Mass.

Eibl-Eibesfeldt, I. 1979. *The biology of peace and war.* Viking, New York.

Eitinger, L., and Weisæth, L. 1980. Stockholm-syndromet *(The Stockholm syndrome). Tidskrift for Norsk Lægeforening* 100:307–9.

Elklit, A. 1993. Offer for vold: En psykologisk analyse af sagesløse voldsofres situation, oplevelser og efterreaktioner *(Victim of violence: A psychological analysis of victims of unprovoked violence—Their situation, experiences and sequelae).* Aarhus Universitetsforlag, Aarhus.

Elsass, P. 1988. Depressionen som fattigdommens og underudviklingens symptom: Et case-studie af en colombiansk landsby *(Depression as a symptom of poverty and underdevelopment: A case study from a Colombian village). Nordisk Psykologi* 40:345–57.

————. 1991. Violencia: Et eksempel på en kulturpsykologisk synsmåde på vold *(Violencia: An example of a culture-psychological approach to violence).* In P. Berliner, B.

Karpatschof, and R. Kuschel, eds. *Vrede, konflikt, kultur (Anger, conflict, culture)*. Dansk psykologisk Forlag, Copenhagen.

————. 1992a. *Strategies for survival: The psychology of cultural resilience in ethnic minorities*. New York University Press, New York.

————. 1992b. The healing space in psychotherapy and theatre. *New Theatre Quarterly* 32:333–43.

————. 1993a. *Sundhedspsykologi: Et nyt fag mellem humaniora og naturvidenskab (Health psychology: A new subject between the humanities and natural science)*. Gyldendal, Copenhagen.

————. 1993b. Kriseindustrien: Om etisk kvalitetssikring af psykoterapi *(The crisis industry: Ethical quality control of psychotherapy)*. *Dansk Psykolog Nyt* 5:166–69.

————. 1993c. Qualitative methods in the evaluation of anxiety: Presentation of a research approach to torture survivors. *Torture* (suppl.) 1:8–12.

————. 1994a. Narratologi: Sundhedspsykologiens og den humanistiske forsknings bidrag til forståelsen af sygehistorien *(Narratology: The contribution of health psychology and humanistic research to the understanding of the illness story)*. *Månedsskrift for Praktisk Lægegerning* 4:515–29.

————. 1994b. Terapi er både neutralitet og engagement *(Therapy is both neutrality and engagement)*. *Social Kritik* 30:4–11.

————. 1995. Psykoterapien og det ydre rum: "Medforskerperspektiv" og "brugerindflydelse" som eksempler på psykologiens kontekstbegreber *(Psychotherapy and the external room: "Co-researcher perspective" and "user influence" as examples of psychological concepts of context)*. In H. P. Hansen and P. Ramhøj, eds., *Tværvidenskabeligt perspektiv på sundhed og sygdom (Cross-sectional scientific perspective of health and disease)*. Akademisk Forlag, Copenhagen.

Elsass, P., Rosenbaum, B., Kaasgaard, K., and Lauritsen, P. 1995. Klientoplevelsen af psykoterapi: En retrospektiv undersøgelse, hvor psykologer og lægers beskrivelse af samtaleforløb sammenlignes med deres patienter *(Psychotherapy as experienced by the client: A retrospective comparison of the therapeutic sessions by therapists and their patients)*. *Agrippa* 143–67.

Estroff, S. 1981. *Making it crazy*. University of California Press, Berkeley.

Fairbank, J. A., and Brown, T. A. 1988. Current behavioral approaches to the treatment of post-traumatic stress disorder. *Behavior Therapist* 10:57–64.

Federn, E. 1946. Essai sur la psychologie de la terreur *(Essay on the psychology of terror)*. *Syntåses* 1:79–96.

Festinger, L. 1957. *A theory of cognitive dissonance*. Stanford University Press, Stanford.

Figley, C. R. 1988. Post-traumatic family therapy. In F. M. Ochberg, ed., *Post-traumatic therapy and victims of violence*. Brunner/Mazel, New York.

Finn, M. G., and Sperling, M. B. 1993. Therapists' representations of psychotherapy: Special clients. *Contemporary Psychoanalysis* 29:343–51.

Fischman, Y. 1991. Interacting with trauma: Clinicians' responses to treating psychological aftereffects of political repression. *American Journal of Orthopsychiatry* 61:179–85.

Fischman, Y., and Ross, J. 1990. Group treatment of exiled survivors of torture. *American Journal of Orthopsychiatry* 60:135–42.

Flaherty, J. A., Gaviria, M., Pathak, D., Mitchell, T., Wintrop, R., Richman, J. A., and Birz, S. 1988. Developing instruments for cross-cultural psychiatric research. *Nervous and Mental Disease* 176:257–63.

Foa, E. B., Steketee, G., and Rothbaum, B. O. 1989. Behavioral/cognitive conceptualizations of post-traumatic stress disorder. *Behavior Therapy* 20:155–76.

Foucault, M. 1977. Overvågning og straf: Det moderne fængselsvæsens historie *(Discipline and punish: The birth of the prison)*. Rhodos, Copenhagen.

Frankl, V. E. 1967. *Psykologi og eksistens (Psychology and existence)*. Gyldendals Uglebøger, Copenhagen.

———. 1970. Psykiatri og sjælesorg: Grundlaget for logoterapi og eksistensanalyse *(Psychiatry and pastoral care: The basis of logo therapy and existential analysis)*. Gyldendal, Copenhagen.

Freud, A. 1942. The ego and the mechanisms of defence. Hogarth Press, London.

———. 1967. Comment on trauma. In E. E. Furst, ed., *Psychic trauma*. Basic Books, New York.

Freud, A., and Dann, S. 1951. An experiment in group upbringing. *Psychoanalytic Study of the Child* 6:127–68.

Freud, S. [1886] 1966. Report on my studies in Paris and Berlin. *Standard Edition* 1. Hogarth Press, London.

———. [1893] 1957. On the psychical mechanisms of hysterical phenomena. *Standard Edition* 3. Hogarth Press, London.

———. [1895] 1966. Melancholia. *Standard Edition* 1. Hogarth Press, London.

———. [1917] 1957. Mourning and melancholia. *Standard Edition* 14. Hogarth Press, London.

———. [1920] 1955. Beyond the pleasure principle. *Standard Edition* 18. Hogarth Press, London.

———. [1922] 1964. New introductory lectures on psychoanalysis. *Standard Edition* 22. Hogarth Press, London.

———. [1930] 1961. Civilization and its discontents. *Standard Edition* 21. Hogarth Press, London.

Friedman, P. 1948. The effects of imprisonment. *Acta Medica Orientalia* 7:163–67.

———. 1949. Some aspects of concentration camp psychology. *American Journal of Psychiatry* 105:601–5.

Fromm, E. 1973. *The anatomy of human destructiveness*. Holt, Rinehart and Winston, New York.

Frosch, J. 1983. *The psychotic process*. International Universities Press, New York.

Gammelgaard, J. 1993. *Katharsis: Sjælens renselse i psykoanalyse og tragedie (Catharsis in psychoanalysis and tragedy)*. Hans Reitzels Forlag, Copenhagen.

Geertz, C. 1973. *The interpretation of culture*. Basic Books, New York.

Genefke, I. 1992. Torture: A threat to democracy, a challenge to psychiatry. Introduction to the meeting of the American Psychiatric Association, May.

————. 1993a. Torture in the world today. Public hearing on the fight against torture and the role of rehabilitation centers, Brussels, December.

————. 1993b. Makthavernes tortur: Det mest effektive våben mod demokrati *(Torture by those in power: The most efficient weapon against democracy)*. In L. Weisæth and
L. Mehlum, eds., *Mennesker, traumer og kriser (People, traumas, and crises)*. Univer-
sitetsforlaget, Oslo.

————. 1994. Lyt til ondskabens ofre *(Listen to the victims of evil)*. *Weekendavisen*, 6
May.

Gent, E. M., and Zwart, F. M. 1991. Psychoeducation of partners of bipolar-manic
patients. *Journal of Affective Disorders* 21:15–18.

Gilligan, J. 1996. *Violence: Our deadly epidemic and its causes*. Putnam, New York.

Girard, R. 1977. *Violence and the sacred*. Johns Hopkins University Press, Baltimore.

Goldberger, L., and Breznitz, S., eds. 1993. *Handbook of stress: Theoretical and clinical aspects*. 2d ed. Free Press, New York.

Goldfeld, A. E., Mollica, R. F., and Pesavento, B. H. 1988. The physical and psychological sequelae of torture: Symptomatology and diagnosis. *Journal of the American
Medical Association* 259:2725–29.

Goldman, C. R. 1988. Toward a definition of psychoeducation. *Hospital and Community Psychiatry* 39:66–68.

Goldstein, M. J. 1992. Psychosocial strategies for maximizing the effects of psy-
chotropic medications for schizophrenia and mood disorder. *Psychopharmacology
Bulletin* 28:237–40.

Gonsalves, C. J. 1990. The psychological effects of political repression of Chilean exiles in the U.S. *American Journal of Orthopsychiatry* 60:143–54.

Good, B. J., Good, M. V., and Moradi, R. 1985. The interpretation of Iranian depressive illness and dysphoric affect. In A. Kleinman and B. Good, eds., *Culture and
depression: Studies in the anthropology and cross-cultural psychiatry of affect and disorder*.
University of California Press, Berkeley.

Grauer, N. 1969. Psychodynamics of the survivor's syndrome. *Canadian Psychiatric Association Journal* 14:617–22.

Grinker, R. R., and Spiegel, J. 1975. *Men under stress*. Blakeston, Philadelphia.

Grubrich-Simitis, I. 1981. Extreme traumatization as cumulative trauma: Psychoanalytic investigations of the effects of concentration camp experiences on survivors and their children. *Psychoanalytic Study of the Child* 36:415–50.

Haan, N. 1977. *Coping and defending*. Academic Press, New York.

————. 1985. Conceptualizations of ego: Processes, functions, regulations. In A.
Monat and R. S. Lazarus, *Stress and coping: An anthology*. Columbia University
Press, New York.

Hafkenscheid, A., and Lansen, J. 1992. Vicarious traumatization: Is het verschijnsel em-
pirish aantoonbaar? In A. J. de Jong, ed., *Therapeut en trauma*. Sinai Cahiers, Assen.

Harding, C. M. et al. 1987. The Vermont longitudinal study of patients with severe mental illness. *American Journal of Psychiatry* 144:718–35.

Hastrup, K. 1992. *Det antropologiske projekt: Om forbløffelse (The anthropological project: About astonishment).* Gyldendal, Copenhagen.

Hastrup, K., and Elsass, P. 1990. Anthropological advocacy: A contradiction in terms? *Current Anthropology* 3:301–11.

Hastrup, K., and Ramløv, K., eds. 1988. *Feltarbejde: Oplevelse og metode i etnografien (Field work: Experience and methods in ethnography).* Akademisk Forlag, Copenhagen.

———. 1989. *Kulturanalyse: Fortolkningens forløb i antropologien (Culture analysis: The course of anthropological interpretation).* Akademisk Forlag, Copenhagen.

Haynes, S. N., Lemsky, C., and Sexton-Radek, K. 1987. Why clinicians infrequently do research. *Professional Psychology: Research and Practice* 18:515–19.

Headley, L. A., ed. 1983. *Suicide in Asia and the Near East.* University of California Press, Berkeley.

Heelas, P. 1982. Anthropology, violence, and catharsis. In P. Marsh and A. Campbell, eds., *Aggression and violence.* Basil Blackwell, Oxford.

Helman, C. G. 1990. *Culture, health, and illness.* Wright, London.

Herman, J. L. 1992. *Trauma and recovery: The aftermath of violence—From domestic abuse to political terror.* Basic Books, New York.

Hilberg, R. 1980. The nature of the process. In J. E. Dimsdale, ed., *Survivors, victims, and perpetrators: Essays on the Nazi Holocaust.* Hemisphere Publishing, New York.

Hiok-Boon, E. 1983. Intraethnic characteristics and the patient-physician interaction: "Cultural blind spot syndrome." *Family Practice* 16:91–98.

Hjern, A., ed. 1995. *Diagnostik och behandling av traumatiserede flyktingar.* Studentlitteratur, Lund.

Høglund, S. 1988. Tolkning: Et instrument: Et interview med Enrique Bustos *(Interpretation: An instrument: An interview with Enrique Bustos).* Informationer fra Psykosocialt Team for Flyktninger i Norge, 1.

Højholt, C. 1992. Psykisk fattigdom eller fattig psykologi *(Psychological poverty or poor psychology). Udkast* 1:56–84.

———. 1994. *Perspektiver på psykosocialt arbejde (Perspectives of psychosocial work).* Dansk Psykologisk Forlag, Copenhagen.

Hoppe, K. D. 1971. The aftermath of Nazi persecutions reflected in recent psychiatric literature. In H. Krystal and W. G. Niederland, eds., *Psychic traumatization.* Little, Brown, Boston.

Horowitz, M. J. 1976. *Stress response syndromes.* Jason Aronson, New York.

———. 1986. Stress-response syndromes: A review of posttraumatic and adjustment disorders. *Hospital and Community Psychiatry* 37:241–49.

———. 1988. *Introduction of psychodynamics: A new synthesis.* Routledge, New York.

Horowitz, M. J., Marmar, C., Weiss, D. S., DeWitt, K. N., and Rosenbaum, R. 1984. Brief psychotherapy of bereavement reactions: The relationship of process to outcome. *Archives of General Psychiatry* 41:438–48.

Hougen, H. P. 1988. Physical and psychological sequelae to torture: A controlled clinical study of exiled asylum applicants. *Forensic Science International* 39:5–11.

Howell, S., and Willis, R., eds. 1989. *Society at peace: Anthropological perspectives.* Routledge, New York.

Huxley, A. 1967. *Tidens nar (Today's fool).* Aschehoug, Copenhagen.

ICD-10. 1992. World Health Organization, Geneva.

Igra, L. 1990. *Psykoterapi på liv og død: Om destruktivitet og livsvilje (Psychotherapy on life and death: On destructive or constructive approach to life).* Hans Reitzels Forlag, Copenhagen.

International Journal of Psychoanalysis. 1968. Vol. 49.

JAMA. 1996. Editorial. 276:416–17.

Janet, P. 1889. *L'automatisme psychologique: Essai de psychologie experimentale sur les formes inferieures de l'activité humaine.* Felic Alcan, Paris.

Janoff-Bulman, R. 1988. Victims of violence. In S. Fisher and J. Reason, eds., *Handbook of life stress, cognition, and health.* John Wiley, New York.

———. 1989. Assumptive worlds and the stress of traumatic events: Applications of the schema construct. *Social Cognition* 7:113–36.

Jensen, S. B. 1989. Magtcentre: Om overgreb og rehabilitering *(Power centers: Violations and rehabilitation). Information* 25 (July).

Jørgensen, M. 1991. Interview with Mozzafar Ghahreman. *Matrix* 2:3–12.

———. 1992. Anvendelsen af tolk i psykoterapi *(Use of the interpreter in psychotherapy). Matrix* 2:14–28.

Journal of Traumatic Stress. 1995. Special issue on traumatic memory research. Vol. 6.

Jung, C. G. 1963/1983. *Memories, dreams, reflections.* Flamingo, London.

Kalicanin, P., Lecic-Tosevski, D., Bukelic, J., and Ispanovic-Radojkovic, V. 1994. *The stresses of war and sanctions.* Institute for Mental Health, Belgrade.

Kardiner, A., and Spiegel, H. 1947. *War, stress and neurotic illness.* Hoeber, New York.

Kast, V. 1991. *Den største sorg i verden her: Drømme som vejvisere gennem sorgen (The worst grief of this world: Dreams as guides through grief).* Munksgaard, Copenhagen.

Keane, T. M., Albano, A. M., and Blake, D. D. 1992. Current trends in the treatment of post-traumatic stress symptoms. In M. Basoglu, ed., *Torture and its consequences: Current treatment approaches.* Cambridge University Press, Cambridge, U.K.

Keane, T. M., Fairbank, J. A., Caddell, J. M., and Zimmerling, R. T. 1989. Implosive therapy reduces symptoms of PTSD in Vietnam combat veterans. *Behavior Therapy* 20:245–60.

Kempe, R. S., and Kempe, C. H. 1978. *Child abuse.* Harvard University Press, Cambridge, Mass.

Kernberg, O. 1975. *Borderline conditions and pathological narcissism.* Jason Aronson, New York.

———. 1984. *Severe personality disorders: Psychotherapeutic strategies.* Yale University Press, New Haven.

Killingmo, B. 1989. Conflict and deficit: Implications for technique. *International Journal of Psychoanalysis* 70:65–79.

Kjersem, H. 1987. *Erfaringer fra arbejdet for asylsøgere (Experience with asylum seekers).* Dansk Røde Kors, Copenhagen.

Kleber, R. J., Figley, C. R., and Gersons, B. P. R., eds. 1995. *Beyond trauma: Cultural and societal dynamics.* Plenum Press, New York.

Kleinman, A. 1980. *Patients and healers in the context of culture.* University of California Press, Berkeley.

———. 1988a. *Rethinking psychiatry: From cultural category to personal experience.* Free Press, New York.

———. 1988b. *The illness narratives.* Basic Books, New York.

Kleinman, A., and Good, B., eds. 1985. *Culture and depression: Studies in the anthropology and cross-cultural psychiatry of affect and disorder.* University of California Press, Berkeley.

Kleinman, A., and Kleinman, J. 1985. Somatization: The interconnections in Chinese society among culture, depressive experiences and the meanings of pain. In A. Kleinman and B. Good, eds., *Culture and depression: Studies in the anthropology and cross-cultural psychiatry of affect and disorder.* University of California Press, Berkeley.

Klerman, G. L. 1987. Book review: Culture and depression. *Social Science and Medicine* 24:785–90.

Kordon, D., Edelman, L., Lagos, D., Nicoletti, E., Bozzola, R., Siaky, D., L'Hoste, M., and Kersner, D. 1986. *Efectos Psicologicos de la repression politica.* Editorial Sudamericana Planeta, Buenos Aires.

Kordon, D., Edelman, L., Lagos, D., Nicoletti, E., Kersner, D., and Groshaus, M. 1992. Torture in Argentina. In M. Basoglu, ed., *Torture and its consequences: Current treatment approaches.* Cambridge University Press, Cambridge, U.K.

Korsgaard, A. 1993. Post-traumatic stress disorder (PTSD), historical background. In A. Elklit, ed., *Psykologisk behandling af voldsofre: En symposierapport.* Dansk Psykologisk Forlag, Copenhagen.

Kosteljanetz, A., and Aalund, O. 1983. Torture: A challenge to medical science. *Interdisciplinary Science Reviews* 8:320–27.

Kren, G. M., and Rappaport, L. 1980. *The Holocaust and the crisis of human behaviour.* Holmes and Meier, New York.

Krystal, H. 1971. Trauma: Considerations of its intensity and chronicity. In H. Krystal and W. G. Niederland, eds., *Psychic traumatization.* Little, Brown, Boston.

———. 1978. Trauma and affects. *Psychoanalytic Study of the Child* 33:81–116.

———. 1982. Alexithymia and the effectiveness of psychoanalytic treatment. *International Journal of Psychoanalytical Psychotherapy* 9:353–88.

———. 1988. *Integration and self-healing: Affect, trauma, alexithymia.* Analytic Press, Hillsdale, N.J.

Kull, S. 1988. *Minds at war: Nuclear reality and the inner conflicts of denfense policymakers.* Basic Books, New York.

Kuschel, R. 1991. Psykologi, kultur og aggression: En introduktion *(Psychology, culture and aggression: An introduction)*. In P. Berliner, B. Karpatschof, and R. Kuschel, eds., *Vrede, konflikt, kultur (Anger, conflict, culture)*. Dansk psykologisk Forlag, Copenhagen.

Lacan, J. 1981. *Speech and language in psychoanalysis*. Johns Hopkins University Press, Baltimore.

Lakoff, G., and Johnson, M. 1980. *Metaphors we live by*. University of Chicago Press, Chicago.

Landrine, H. 1995. Clinical implications of cultural differences: The referential versus the indexical self. In N. R. Goldberger and J. B. Veroff, eds., *The culture and psychology reader*. New York University Press, New York.

Landry, C. 1989. Psychotherapy with victims of organized violence: An overview. *British Journal of Psychotherapy* 3:349–52.

Lansen, J. 1993. Vicarious traumatization in therapists treating victims of torture and persecution. *Torture* 3:138–40.

———. 1994. Treating victims of persecution and torture: The importance of supervision. Introduction to the RCT, Copenhagen, 19 January.

Lazarus, A. A. 1990. Can psychotherapists transcend the shackles of their training and superstitions? *Journal of Clinical Psychology* 46:351–58.

Lazarus, R. S., and Folkman, S. 1984. *Stress, appraisal, and coping*. Springer, New York.

Lederer, W. 1965. Persecution and compensation: Theoretical and practical implications of the "persecution syndrome." *Archives of General Psychiatry* 12:464–74.

Leff, J., Kuipers, L., Berkowitz, R., Eberlein-Vries, R., and Sturgeon, D. 1984. Psychosocial relevance and benefit of neuroleptic maintenance. *Journal of Clinical Psychology* 45:220–22.

Lévi-Strauss, C. 1967. *Structural anthropology: The sorcerer and his magic*. Doubleday, New York.

Lewis-Fernández, R., and Kleinman, A. 1994. Culture, personality and psychopathology. *Journal of Abnormal Psychology* 103:67–71.

Lifton, R. 1968. The survivors of the Hiroshima disaster and the survivors of Nazi persecution. In H. Krystal, ed., *Massive psychic trauma*. International Universities Press, New York.

Lifton, R. J., and Olson, E. 1976. The human meaning of total disaster: The Buffalo Creek experience. *Psychiatry* 39:1–18.

Lindy, J. D. 1986. An outline for the psychoanalytic psychotherapy of post-traumatic stress disorder. In C. R. Figley, ed., *Trauma and its wake: Traumatic stress theory, research, and intervention*, vol 2. Brunner/Mazel, New York.

———. 1987. *Vietnam: A case book*. Brunner/Mazel, New York.

Loganbill, C., Hardy, E., and Delworth, E. 1989. Supervision: A conceptional model. In P. Hawkins and R. Shohet, eds., *Supervision in the helping professions*. Open Universities Press, Philadelphia.

Lorenz, K. 1966. *On aggression*. Methuen, London.

Lotz, M. 1988. *Eventyrbroen (Fairytale bridge)*. Gyldendal, Copenhagen.

Lunde, I. 1982. Mental sequelae of torture. *Månedsskrift for Praktisk Lægegerning* 60:476–88.

Main, T. F. 1957. The ailment. *British Journal of Medical Psychology* 30:129–45.

Malan, D. H. 1976. *The frontier of brief psychotherapy*. Plenum Press, New York.

Malec, R., and Neimeyer, R. 1983. Psychological prediction of duration of inpatient spinal cord injury rehabilitation and performance of self-care. *Archives of Physical Medicine and Rehabilitation* 64:359–63.

Maluccio, A. 1979. *Learning from clients: Interpersonal helping as viewed by clients and social workers*. Free Press, New York.

Marsella, A. J., Friedman, M. J., Gerrity, E. T. Scurfield, R.M. (eds.) 1996: *Ethnocultural aspects of posttraumatic stress disorder*. American Psychological Association, Washington.

McCann, I. L., and Pearlman, L. A. 1990. *Psychological trauma and the adult survivor: Theory, therapy, and transformation*. Brunner/Mazel, New York.

McKeane, T. M., Zimmerling, R. T., and Caddell, J. M. 1985. A behavioral formulation of post-traumatic stress disorder in Vietnam veterans. *Behavior Therapy* 8:9–12.

McKegney, C. P. 1993. Surviving survivors: Coping with caring for patients who have been victimized. *Primary Care* 20:481–94.

McIvor, R. J., and Turner, S. W. 1995. Assessment and treatment approaches for survivors of torture. *British Journal of Psychiatry* 166:705–11.

Mead, G. H. 1932. *The philosophy of the present*. Open Court, Chicago.

Meerloo, J. A. M. 1969. Persecution trauma and the reconditioning of emotional life. *American Journal of Psychiatry* 125:1187–91.

Michelsen, K. 1989. *Synålejomfruen og lægevidenskabens menneskeopfattelse (The old maid's concept of man, and that of medical science)*. Munksgaard, Copenhagen.

Mirdal, G. 1987. *The interpreter in cross-cultural therapy*. Institute of Clinical Psychology, University of Copenhagen, Copenhagen.

Mishler, E. G. 1986. *Research interviewing: Context and narrative*. Harvard University Press, Cambridge, Mass.

Molin Jørgensen, K. 1992. En redegørelse for traumatisk stress og posttraumatisk adaptation eksemplificeret ved katastrofeoplevelsen *(An account of traumatic stress and post-traumatic adaptation exemplified by the disaster experience)*. Specialeafhandling. Psykologisk Institut, Aarhus Universitet.

Mollica, R. F. 1988. The trauma story: The psychiatric care of refugee survivors of violence and torture. In F. M. Ochberg, ed., *Post-traumatic therapy and victims of violence*. Brunner/Mazel, New York.

———. 1992. The prevention of torture and the clinical care of survivors: A field in need of a new science. In M. Basoglu, ed., *Torture and its consequences: Current treatment approaches*. Cambridge University Press, Cambridge, U.K.

Mollica, R. F., and Caspi-Yavin, Y. 1992. Overview: The assessment and diagnosis of torture events and symptoms. In M. Basoglu, ed., *Torture and its consequences: Current treatment approaches.* Cambridge University Press, Cambridge, U.K.

Mollica, R. F., Wyshak, G., and Lavelle, J. 1987. The psychosocial impact of war trauma and torture on Southeast Asian refugees. *American Journal of Psychiatry* 144:1567–72.

Montgomery, E. 1992. Co-creation of meaning therapy with torture survivors: A systemic/constructionist view. *Journal of Systemic Consultation and Management* 3:27–33.

Montgomery, E., and Foldspang, A. 1994. Criterion-related validity of screening for exposure to torture. *Danish Medical Bulletin* 41:588–91.

Mørch, M., Rosenberg, N., and Elsass, P., eds. 1995. *Kognitive behandlingsformer: Kognitiv terapi, psykoedukation og social færdighedstræning (Cognitive forms of treatment: Cognitive therapy, psychoeducation and training of social skills).* Hans Reitzels Forlag, Copenhagen.

Mørch, S. 1991. Hvad skal vi med kulturen: Kan kultur og handlingsteori forenes? *(What to do with culture: Can culture and action theory go together?)* Udkast 1.

Müller, O. 1990. Psykologisk behandling av torturofre: Noen kliniske erfaringer *(Psychologic treatment of torture victims: Some clinical experiences).* Tidskrift for Norsk Psykologforening 27:511–19.

Murphy, H. B. M. 1982. Cultural shaping and mental disorders. In W. R. Gove, ed., *Deviance and mental illness.* Sage Publications, Beverly Hills, Calif.

Neki, J. S., Joinet, B., Hogan, M., Hauli, J. G., and Kilonzo, G. 1985. The cultural perspective of therapeutic relationship: A viewpoint from Africa. *Acta Psychiatrica Scandinavica* 71:543–50.

Niederland, W. G. 1968a. An interpretation of the psychological stresses and defenses of concentration-camp life and the late aftereffects. In H. Krystal, ed., *Massive psychic trauma.* International Universities Press, New York.

Niederland, W. G. 1968b. Clinical observations on the "survivor syndrome." *International Journal of Psychoanalysis* 49:313–15.

Nissen, M. 1994. Brugerindflydelse og handlesammenhænge i psykosocialt arbejde *(Client influence and cooperation in psychosocial work).* Ph.D. diss., Psychology Laboratory, University of Copenhagen.

Obeyesekere, G. 1985. Depression, Buddhism, and the work of culture. In A. Kleinman and B. Good, eds., *Culture and depression: Studies in the anthropology and cross-cultural psychiatry of affect and disorder.* University of California Press, Berkeley.

Orhagen, T. 1992. *Working with families in schizophrenic disorders: The practice of psychoeducational intervention.* Linköping University Medical Dissertations, no. 363. Linköping, Sweden.

Osterweis, M., et al., eds. 1987. *Pain and disability.* National Academy Press, Washington, D.C.

Pachter, L. M. 1994. Culture and clinical care: Folk illness beliefs and behaviors and their implications for health care delivery. *JAMA* 9:690–94.

Parker, M., Parker, Å., and Yüksel, S. 1992. Psychological effects of torture: An empirical study of tortured and non-tortured non-political prisoners. In M. Basoglu, ed., *Torture and its consequences: Current treatment approaches*. Cambridge University Press, Cambridge, U.K.

Parkes, C. 1972. *Bereavement: Studies of grief in adult life*. Tavistock, London.

———. 1975. What becomes of redundant world models? A contribution to the study of change. *British Journal of Medical Psychology* 48:131–37.

Parnas, J. 1994. Det skizofrene spektrum *(The schizophrenic spectrum)*. In R. Hemmingsen, J. Parnas, T. Sørensen, A. Gjerris, T. Bolwig, and N. Reisby, eds., *Klinisk psykiatri*. Munksgaard, Copenhagen.

Paykel, E. 1978. Contribution of life events to causation of psychiatric illness. *Psychological Medicine* 8:245–54.

Peltzer, K. 1995. *Psychology and health in African cultures: Examples of ethnopsychotherapeutic practice*. IKO—Verlag für Interkulturelle Kommunikation, Frankfurt.

Pinto, P. A., and Gregory, R. J. 1995. Post-traumatic stress disorder with psychotic features. *American Journal of Psychiatry* 152:471–72.

Prince, R. 1980. Variations in psychotherapy procedures. In H. Triandis and J. Draguns, eds., *Handbook of crosscultural psychology*, vol. 6, 291–349. Allyn and Baker, Boston.

———. 1987. Alexithymia and verbal psychotherapies in cultural context. *Transcultural Psychiatric Research Review* 24:107–16.

Ramsay, R., Gorst-Unsworth, C., and Turner, S. W. 1993. Psychiatric morbidity in survivors of organized state violence including torture: A retrospective series. *British Journal of Psychiatry* 162:55–59.

Raphael, B. 1983. *The anatomy of bereavement*. Basic Books, New York.

Rasmussen, O.V. 1990. *Medical aspects of torture*. Lægeforeningens Forlag, Copenhagen.

Reeler, A. P. 1994. Is torture a post-traumatic stress disorder? *Torture* 4:59–63.

Reichelt, S., and Sveaass, N. 1994a. Når "glimrende" spørgsmål gir uforståelige svar: En utforskning av to familieterapeuters møte med flyktningefamilier i et socialkonstruksjonistisk perspektiv *(When "excellent" questions give incomprehensible answers: A study of the experience of two family therapists with refugee families in a social-reconstructive perspective)*, vols. 1 and 2. *Tidskrift for Norsk Psykologforening* 31:609–19, 663–70.

———. 1994b. Developing meaningful conversations with families in exile. *Journal of Refugee Studies* 7:39–57.

Reid, J., and Strong, T. 1987. Torture and trauma: The health care needs of refugee victims in New South Wales. Cumberland College of Health Sciences, Sydney, Australia.

———. 1988. Rehabilitation of refugee victims of torture and trauma. *Medical Journal of Australia* 148 (4 April).

Rhodes, L. 1984. "This will clear your mind": The use of metaphors for medication in psychiatric settings. *Culture, Medicine, and Psychiatry* 8:49–70.

Riches, D., ed. 1987. *The anthropology of violence*. Basil Blackwell, London.

Ricoeur, P. 1984. *Time and narrative*. University of Chicago Press, Chicago.

Rieker, P. P., and Carmen, E. H. 1986. The victim to patient process: The disconfirmation and transformation of abuse. *American Journal of Orthopsychiatry* 56:369–70.

Rockland, L. H. 1992. *Supportive therapy for borderline patients: A psychodynamic approach*. Guilford, New York.

———. 1994. Introduction to special section: Supportive psychotherapy. *American Journal of Psychotherapy* 48.

Roland, A. 1980. Psychoanalytic perspectives on personality development in India. *International Review of Psychoanalysis* 7:73–87.

Rosaldo, M. 1980. *Knowledge and passion: Ilongot notion of self and social life*. Cambridge University Press, Cambridge, U.K.

Rosenberg, N. K. 1987. Støttende psykoterapi ved sværere psykiatriske tilstande: Den forsømte gøgeunge *(Supportive psychotherapy in severe psychiatric conditions: The neglected cuckoo in the nest). Agrippa* 9:184–94.

Rycroft, C. 1986. *Psychoanalysis and beyond*. University of Chicago Press, Chicago.

Sachs, D. 1981. How to distinguish self-respect from self-esteem. *Philosophy and Public Affairs* 10:346–60.

Sachs, L. 1989. Hèlsa som kultur *(Health as culture)*. In S. M. Philipson and N. Uddenberg, eds., *Hèlsa som livsmening (Health as a meaning of life)*. Natur og Kultur, Stockholm.

Sande, H. 1991. Muslims under the midnight sun. *Nordisk psykiatrisk Tidskrift* 4:243–45.

Saporta, J. A., and van der Kolk, B. A. 1992. Psychobiological consequences of severe trauma. In M. Basoglu, ed., *Torture and its consequences: Current treatment approaches*. Cambridge University Press, Cambridge, U.K.

Sartorius, N., and Jablensky, A. 1976. Transcultural studies of schizophrenia. *WHO Chronicle* 30:481–85.

Sartorius, N., et al. 1983. *Depressive disorders in different cultures*. WHO, Geneva.

Scheper-Hughes, N. 1979. *Saints, Scholars, and Schizophrenics: Mental illness in rural Ireland*. University of California Press, Berkeley.

Schneider, J. 1980. Clinically significant differences between grief, pathological grief, and depression. *Patient Counselling and Health Education*, 19:161–69.

Schneidman, E. S. 1976. A psychologic theory of suicide. *Psychiatry Annuals* 6:76–89.

Schoeck, H. 1981. *The evil eye: A folklore casebook*. Garland, New York.

Schönpflug, W., and Battmann, W. 1988. The costs and benefits of coping. In S. Fisher and J. Reason, eds., *Handbook of life stress, cognition, and health*. John Wiley, New York.

Shehadeh, H. 1989. Skamfølelsen som opdragelsesinstrument *(The feeling of shame in child upbringing). Samspil* 8:16–18.

———. 1991. Skammens samfund *(The society of shame). Information*, 26–27 January.

Shweder, R. A. 1991. *Thinking through cultures: Expeditions in cultural psychology*. Harvard University Press, Cambridge, Mass.

Siegler, M., and Osmond, H. 1974. The sick role revisited. *Hastings Center Studies* 1:41–58.

Simpson, M. A. 1993. Traumatic stress and the bruising of the soul. In J. P. Wilson and B. Raphael, eds., *International handbook of traumatic stress syndromes*. Plenum Press, New York.

Solkoff, N. 1992. The Holocaust: Survivors and their children. In M. Basoglu, ed., *Torture and its consequences: Current treatment approaches*. Cambridge University Press, Cambridge, U.K.

Solnit, A. J., and Kris, M. 1967. Trauma and infantile experiences. In S. S. Furst, ed., *Psychic trauma*. Basic Books, New York.

Solomon, S. D., Gerrity, E. T., and Muff, A. M. 1992. Efficacy of treatments for post-traumatic stress disorder: An empirical review. *Journal of the American Medical Association* 268:633–38.

Somasundaram, D. J., and Sivayokan, S. 1994. War trauma in a civilian population. *British Journal of Psychiatry* 165:524–27.

Somnier, F., and Genefke, I. 1986. Psychotherapy for victims of torture. *British Journal of Psychiatry* 149:323–29.

Somnier, F., Vesti, P., Kastrup, M., and Genefke, I. K. 1992. Psychosocial consequences of torture: Current knowledge and evidence. In M. Basoglu, ed., *Torture and its consequences: Current treatment approaches*. Cambridge University Press, Cambridge, U.K.

Spitzer, R. L., and Williams, J. B. 1988. Revised diagnostic criteria and a new structured interview for diagnosing anxiety disorder. *Journal of Psychiatry Research* 22:55–86.

Stæhr, A., Stæhr, M., Behbehani, J., and Bøjholm, S. 1993. *Treatment of war victims in the Middle East*. International Rehabilitation Council for Torture Victims, IRCT, Copenhagen.

Stone, D. 1984. *The disabled state*. Temple University Press, Philadelphia.

Straker, G. 1987. The continuous traumatic stress syndrome: The single therapeutic interview. *Psychology in Society* 8:48–78.

Strauss, A., and Corbin, J. 1990. *Basics of qualitative research: Grounded theory, procedures and techniques*. Sage Publications, Beverly Hills, Calif.

Strupp, H. H. 1981. Clinical research, practice and the crisis of confidence. *Journal of Consulting and Clinical Psychology* 49:216–20.

Stuker, P. B., Winstead, D. K., Galina, Z. H., and Allain, A. N. 1991. Cognitive deficits and psychopathology among former POWs and combat veterans of the Korean conflict. *American Journal of Psychiatry* 148:67–72.

Stuker, P. B., Winstead, D. K., Goist, K. C., Malow, R. M., and Allain, A. N. 1986. Psychopathology subtypes and symptom correlates among former prisoners of war. *Journal of Psychopathology and Behavioral Assessment* 8:89–101.

Sue, D. W. 1981. *Counseling the culturally different: Theory and practice*. John Wiley, New York.

Sue, S., and Zane, N. 1995. The role of culture and cultural techniques in psychotherapy: A critique and reformulation. In N. R. Goldberger and J. B. Veroff, eds., *The culture and psychology reader.* New York University Press, New York.

Sue, S., Zane, N., and Young, K. 1994. Research on psychotherapy with culturally diverse populations. In A. E. Bergin and S. L. Garfield, eds., *Handbook of psychotherapy and behavioral change.* John Wiley, New York.

Suedfeld, P., ed., 1990. *Psychology and torture.* Hemisphere Publishing, New York.

Sveaass, N. 1994. The organized destruction of meaning. In N. J. Lavik, M. Nygård, N. Sveaass, and E. Fannemel, *Pain and survival: Human rights violations and mental health.* Scandinavian University Press, Oslo.

Taussig, M. 1987. *Shamanism, colonialism, and the wild man: A study in terror and healing.* University of Chicago Press, Chicago.

Teodoro, L. V., and Sicam, P. P. 1995. Torture survivors and caregivers. Proceedings of the international workshop on therapy and research issues, University of the Philippines, Quezon City.

Terr, L. C. 1979. Children of Chowchilla. *Psychoanalytic Study of the Child* 34:552–623.

Timerman, J. 1981. *Prisoner without a name, cell without a number.* Knopf, New York.

Torture. 1993. Suppl. 1, 8–12.

Torture: The annual report, 1994, 1995. 1.

Turner, B. 1985. *The body and society.* Basil Blackwell, Oxford.

Turner, S. W., and Gorst-Unsworth, C. 1990. Psychological sequelae of torture: A descriptive model. *British Journal of Psychiatry* 157:475–80.

———. 1993. Psychological sequelae of torture. In J. P. Wilson and B. Raphael, eds., *International handbook of traumatic stress syndromes.* Plenum Press, New York.

Tyler, J. D., and Clark, J. A. 1987. Clinical psychologists reflect on the usefulness of various components of graduate training. *Professional Psychology* 18:381–84.

van der Dennen, J. M. G. 1980. *Problems in the concepts of definitions of aggression, violence and some related terms.* Polomologisch Instituut, Rijksuniversiteit Groningen, Groningen.

van der Kolk, B. A. 1987. *Psychological trauma.* American Psychiatric Press, Washington, D.C.

van der Kolk, B. A., Boyd, C., Krystal, J. H., and Greenberg, M. 1984. Post-traumatic stress disorder: Psychological and biological sequence. In B. A. van der Kolk, ed., *Post-traumatic disorders, clinical insight series.* American Psychiatric Association, Washington, D.C.

van der Veer, G. 1992. *Counselling and therapy with refugees: Psychological problems of victims of war, torture and repression.* John Wiley, New York.

Vanggaard, T. 1991. Skam og skyld *(Shame and guilt). Bibliotek for Læger* 1:161–74.

van Willigen, L. 1992. Organization of care and rehabilitation services for victims of torture and other forms of organized violence: A review of current issues. In M. Basoglu, ed., *Torture and its consequences: Current treatment approaches.* Cambridge University Press, Cambridge, U.K.

von Franz, M. L. 1989. *Eventyrfortolkningen (The interpretation of fairy tales)*. Gyldendal, Copenhagen.

Wallerstein, R. S. 1986. *Forty-two lives in treatment: A study of psychoanalysis and psychotherapy*. Guilford, New York.

Weine, S., and Laub, D. 1995. Narrative constructions of historical realities in testimony with Bosnian survivors of "ethnic cleansing." *Psychiatry* 58:246–60.

Werbert, A., and Lindbom-Jakobson, M. 1993. The "living dead": Survivors of torture and psychosis. *Psychoanalytic Psychotherapy* 2:163–79.

Werman, D. S. 1981. Technical aspects of supportive psychotherapy. *Psychiatric Journal of the University of Ottawa* 6:153–60.

———. 1992. *The practice of supportive psychotherapy*. Brunner/Mazel, New York.

Westermeyer, J. 1990. Working with an interpreter in psychiatric assessment and treatment. *Journal of Nervous and Mental Disease* 12:745–49.

WHO. 1996. *Mental health of refugees*. World Health Organization, Geneva.

WHO ICD-10. 1994. *Psychiatric conditions and behavior disorders: Classification and diagnostic criteria*. Munksgaard, Copenhagen.

Wiesel, E. 1961. *Dawn*. Bantam Books, New York.

Williams, C. L. 1994. Facilitating the process of healing and coping in refugees. 8. Nordiske konference for psykoterapeuter, der arbejder med traumatiserede flygtninge *(Nordic conference for psychotherapists working with traumatized refugees)*, Bergen.

Willingen, L. H. M., ed. 1993. *Care and rehabilitation of victims of rape, torture, and other severe traumas of war in the republics of ex-Yugoslavia*. UNHCR. Pharos Foundation, Utrecht.

Wilson, J. P., and Jacob, L. D., eds. 1994. *Countertransference in the treatment of PTSD*. Guilford, New York.

Winnicott, D. W. 1975. Aggression in relation to emotional development. In M. Masuds and R. Khan, eds., *Through paediatrics to psycho-analysis*. Hogarth Press, London.

Wolfenstein, M. 1957. *Disaster*. Free Press, Illinois.

Wortman, S. B., and Silver, R. C. 1991. The myths of coping with loss. In A. Monat and R. S. Lazarus, eds., *Stress and coping: An anthology*. Columbia University Press, New York.

Yalom, I. D. 1980. *Existential psychotherapy*. Basic Books, New York.

Zubin, J., and Spring, B. 1977. Vulnerability: A new view of schizophrenia. *Journal of Abnormal Psychology* 86:103–26.

Index

About the Author

Peter Elsass is Professor of Clinical Psychology at the University of Copenhagen and the author of *Strategies for Survival: The Psychology of Cultural Resilience in Ethnic Minorities*, also available from NYU Press.

For ten years he has been affiliated with the Rehabilitation Center for Torture Survivors in Copenhagen, which is the first center of its kind in the world. He is a member of the center's scientific staff and has done research there concerning the process and outcome of psychotherapeutic treatment.